THE OLD TESTAMENT OF THE OLD TESTAMENT

Patriarchal Narratives and Mosiac Yahwism

THE OLD TESTAMENT OF THE OLD TESTAMENT

R. W. L. MOBERLY

Wipf and Stock Publishers
EUGENE, OREGON

Wipf and Stock Publishers
199 West 8th Avenue, Suite 3
Eugene, Oregon 97401

The Old Testament of the Old Testament
Patriarchal Narratives and Mosaic Yahwism
By Moberly, R.W.L.

ISBN: 1-57910-731-1
Publication date: 2001, .
Previously published by Augsburg Fortress Press, 1992.

For Meredith
with much love

Contents

Editor's Foreword	ix
Preface	xiii
Abbreviations	xv
Introduction	1
1. God's Self-Disclosure as YHWH	5
2. Why Is the Name YHWH Used in Genesis?	36
3. The Religion of the Patriarchs	79
4. The Old Testament of the Old Testament	105
5. The Old Testament and Jewish-Christian Dialogue	147
6. Paradigms for Pentateuchal Criticism	176
Epilogue	203
Bibliography	206
Index of Authors	218
Index of Biblical Passages	220

Editor's Foreword

In its classic expression, pentateuchal criticism reached a variety of theological conclusions about the various sources and about their relationships one to another. The best known one—and the one that also helped underscore the rightness of source criticism as a literary science—had to do with the relationship between the oldest source, J, and the youngest source, P. The Jahwist believed that the divine name Yahweh had been revealed quite early on in God's dealings with humanity. As Gen. 4:26 puts it: "At that time people began to invoke the name of the LORD [YHWH]." The Priestly writer (and his Elohist forebears), on the other hand, gave prominence to the Mosaic period as the time when the personal name of God was revealed, and therefore before this time the generic name for God (Elohim) was the name of choice. It was argued that the P-text at Exod. 6:1-9 raised this observation to the level of status confessionis and put beyond doubt the correctness of literary critical source divisions prior to this juncture. As Exod. 6:3 puts it: "I appeared to Abraham, Isaac, and Jacob as God Almighty [El Shaddai], but by my name The LORD [YHWH] I did not make myself known to them."

In a brilliant and penetrating way, Moberly has called this conclusion into question. He argues that all the sources, including J, agree that an important cleavage between the patriarchal and Mosaic periods is to be acknowledged. But then he pushes beyond this literary and exegetically grounded observation to press home key theological questions. While the reader may take exception to Moberly's literary and exegetical judgments at this or that point, it will be impossible to ignore the sheer energy of his analysis and the probing way he pushes on to raise fundamental theological questions which are a consequence of the source-critical method itself. The practitioners of source criticism have at times understood the directly theological implications of the method itself and have frequently given prominence to theological issues and theological inquiry in assessing biblical texts from a source-critical perspective. But Moberly wants to lodge an objection at this point and make a critical distinction between theological judgments that follow from historical and sociological reconstructions and a "truly theological approach" which is "theological from the outset."

At several junctures Moberly acknowledges his indebtedness to Brevard Childs and Childs's recent call for a canonical approach to exegesis and interpretation. One will see in Moberly's analysis an assessment of the field (and its frequently all too narrow historical interests) that is at points reminiscent of the work of Childs. It would be fair to say they share similar enemies. But there is another way in which Moberly stands closer to the more traditional approach of Gerhard von Rad, especially as he acknowledges the rightness of critical method or makes his own adjustments but then pushes beyond matters of method and history to raise theological concerns inherent in the method itself. In that sense Moberly's approach might be termed "theological-critical" rather than canonical- or form-critical. In my judgment Moberly has spotted terrain that stretches out beyond von Rad and Childs both, and yet he also points up areas of similarity and common concern that link them up in exciting and provocative ways.

But the proof of the pudding is in the eating. Moberly advances a rich and stimulating collection of observations concerning source criticism, both in its more traditional forms as well as in the more modern work of Van Seters, Thompson, Blum, Rendtorff, and others. Yet he does not stop here. He proceeds to press on to a modern theological issue, Jewish-Christian dialogue, and to offer his own fresh proposals in a manner that flows directly from his exegetical work and his theological inquiry into source-critical division of the Pentateuch. The relationship between patriarchal religion and Mosaic Yahwism is set forth as a helpful analogy and paradigm for understanding the relationship between Old and New Testaments and between Jews and Christians anxious to relate to one another in theologically responsible ways. The same rigor that marks his analysis of source criticism is carried over into his proposal for Jewish-Christian dialogue. Just as theological appropriation ought never to be an add-on that follows from the "more serious" historical work of exegesis, as Moberly argues with such precision and conviction, so, too, Moberly's concrete theological application of his critical findings exhibits the same thoroughness and final concern for careful analysis that marks his evaluation of pentateuchal method, with its blind spots and occasional achievements.

In *The Old Testament of the Old Testament* Moberly has looked at pentateuchal criticism from an altogether fresh angle and has registered far too many stimulating and provocative items for discussion than could or should be catalogued here. He has asked important new questions, not just provided an array of footnotes to a method received without further ado. Anyone who has bothered to keep up with recent moves in pentateuchal study knows that certain fundamental conclusions are being called into question, from a variety of different angles. Moberly's angle is theological, and his overture is bold and thought provoking.

Christopher R. Seitz

Preface

This book began as a lecture, the Tyndale Old Testament Lecture for 1988, which was delivered at Tyndale House, Cambridge, on July 14, 1988. I am deeply grateful to the committee of the Tyndale Fellowship for their invitation to deliver the lecture, not least because without it my occasional musings on the divine name might never have developed in the way they have.

In the course of expanding my lecture into a book, numerous people have helped by reading portions of the text and offering their criticisms. In particular I would like to mention my Durham Old Testament colleagues Tony Gelston and Robert Hayward, both of whom read and commented on the complete draft. In chapter 5 some confusion in my thought was pointed out by John Sawyer and Rabbi Michael Hilton, which has enabled me at least to be clearer even if not to secure their agreement. I am grateful to Walter Brueggemann for accepting the work for publication on the basis of the original lecture and for suggesting directions in which the argument might develop and also to Christopher Seitz for reading the whole draft and helping me sharpen my argument in places.

Finally, I would like to express my indebtedness to someone who has not read any of the text at all—Brevard Childs. I have learned much from many, but in recent years I have learned most from Childs. His willingness to ask difficult and sometimes unwelcome questions as part of an attempt to reconceptualize the nature of biblical theology has been for me a liberation and an inspiration. I still do not understand all the issues clearly. But I think I have at least begun to see what the task of modern biblical theology might involve.

Abbey House
Palace Green
Durham, England

Walter Moberly

Abbreviations

AB	Anchor Bible
ASTI	*Annual of the Swedish Theological Institute*
ATD	Das Alte Testament Deutsch
BHS	*Biblia hebraica stuttgartensia*
BKAT	Biblischer Kommentar: Altes Testament
BTB	*Biblical Theology Bulletin*
BWANT	Beiträge zur Wissenschaft vom Alten und Neuen Testament
BZ	*Biblische Zeitschrift*
BZAW	Beihefte zur *ZAW*
ExpTim	*Expository Times*
FRLANT	Forschungen zur Religion und Literatur des Alten und Neuen Testaments
HBT	*Horizons in Biblical Theology*
HTR	*Harvard Theological Review*
HUCA	*Hebrew Union College Annual*
JBL	*Journal of Biblical Literature*
JSOT	*Journal for the Study of the Old Testament*
JSOTS	Journal for the Study of the Old Testament: Supplement Series
JTS	*Journal of Theological Studies*
MT	Masoretic Text
NIV	New International Version
OBO	Orbis biblicus et orientalis
OTL	Old Testament Library
REB	Revised English Bible

RSV	Revised Standard Version
SBLMS	SBL Monograph Series
TZ	*Theologische Zeitschrift*
VT	*Vetus Testamentum*
WBC	Word Biblical Commentary
WMANT	Wissenschaftliche Monographien zum Alten und Neuen Testament
WTJ	Westminster Theological Journal
ZAW	Zeitschrift für die alttestamentliche Wissenschaft

Introduction

Reading the Bible well is no easy matter.

No book in human history has been read and studied more than the Bible, and one might expect that such a long history of reading would have produced a store of accumulated wisdom that would make the modern reader's task relatively straightforward. In one sense, this is indeed so. The wealth of factual information and interpretative insight that is available in commentaries, studies, and expositions can enable any readers who use these resources to sharpen and deepen the quality of their reading in a wide variety of ways. In another sense, however, reading the Bible remains problematic. Not only in the sphere in which most people encounter the Bible (that is, the preaching, teaching, and worship of the Christian church) is there an amazing diversity of practical usage on the part of preachers and teachers. But also in the scholarly realm, where one might expect that academic study could objectively establish "the meaning of the text," there is at present little consensus as to what constitutes a good reading of the biblical text. When confronted by the often competing claims of, say, historical, canonical, sociological, feminist, and new literary critical readings—not to mention the complications introduced by various fundamentalist stances of greater or lesser sophistication—many readers of the Bible may well feel somewhat bewildered as to how they should read the text.

The issues at stake are enormous and represent a major debate to which we obviously cannot do justice in the present study. In fact, a little reflection will rapidly make clear that the problems are not of a kind that ever could be resolved in such a way as to preclude continuing debate and disagreement, although that does not mean that degrees of clarification and consensus cannot be obtained. Anyway, given the importance of the issue of how to read the Bible well and the hope that this short book might in some way help clear rather than muddy the waters, it will be appropriate to preface the reading of the text offered in the next few chapters with a brief statement of precisely what we are, and are not, trying to do.

Debates about the Bible often focus on questions of method—the relative merits of, say, either form criticism and redaction criticism or else structuralism or deconstructionism. All such debates have their place, but they do not go to the heart of the matter. Rather, the crucial question, which is prior to questions of method and sets the context for them, is that of purpose and goal. To put it simply, *how we use the Bible depends on why we use the Bible.* In practice, many of the disagreements about how are, in effect, disagreements about why, and failure to recognize this leads to endless confusion.

To say that the basic determinant for what counts as reading the Bible well depends on why we want to read it has the merit of bringing three crucial factors to the fore. First, it directs our attention to the fact that the meaning of the Bible cannot be separated from the questions and concerns of its interpreters. This interrelatedness (in one way or another) of text and interpreter is the crucial insight of modern hermeneutical debate and was, indeed, in certain forms, conventional wisdom within traditional Christian theology prior to the epistemological revolution that began with Descartes. Although to some it may sound puzzling or threatening, as if the implication were that people can make what they like of the text, this is not the case. There remain all sorts of criteria and constraints that distinguish better readings from worse readings (though the specification of criteria lies at the heart of the problem). Nonetheless the basic point is that there is no such thing as *the* meaning of the biblical text, as if that could be established without reference to the use made of it by the interpreter.

Second, it directs us to reflect upon the function that the Bible predominantly has for most of those who read it. The Bible functions as holy scripture for the Christian church, and the main reason people read it is because they are seeking understanding and guidance on basic questions about God and humanity, life and death. The assumption that the Bible has something vitally important to say about the fundamental needs and concerns of human beings draws people to the Bible and underlies the greater part of biblical study, both professional and amateur. A good proportion of the debates about appropriate methods of biblical study is at heart an expression of uncertainty as to precisely how the study in question may illuminate, rather than leave untouched or perhaps even obscure, the desire of Christians to understand God and humanity better as a result of the study.

Third, we have to bear in mind that the Bible is read for purposes other than those of Christian faith. On the one hand, the bulk of it, the Hebrew scriptures, may be read as scripture from the perspective of Jewish faith (an important issue in this study, to which we will return later). On the other hand, the Bible may also be read from the perspective of no faith at all. Insofar as the Bible is unarguably a major source of ancient history, it may legitimately be studied by the ancient historian without prejudice as to its continuing religious significance. Likewise, the Bible may be studied as a work of literature. Or the Bible may be studied as a major contributory factor to the culture of Western civilization, out of a desire to understand that culture better. It may be the case that approaches to the Bible in historical, literary, or cultural ways are often corollaries of a recognition of its religious significance. But they are certainly not always so, and they are valid in their own right.

The purpose of this study is to offer a reading of the text that will explore certain aspects of the relationship between the above points. In particular, a major concern will be the relationship between the authoritative status of the Bible and the ways believers read and interpret it. The dynamics inherent in this interrelationship are more subtle than sometimes supposed and deserve careful investigation. Essentially I see it as a question of what it means to do biblical theology, and biblical theology is what I wish to do. Nonetheless the third point (in conjunction with the first) must serve as a reminder that the whole exercise is an attempt to show *one* way of reading the Bible, not *the* way. Too much ink has been spilt in arguing the merits of approaches to the Bible that, rightly or wrongly, have been advocated or perceived as *the* way. Since such debates are ultimately futile, I have no desire to add to them here.

CHAPTER 1

God's Self-Disclosure as YHWH

Our starting point will be an issue that has been basic to much pentateuchal study: the use within pentateuchal narratives, especially Genesis 12–50, Exodus 3 and 6, of the name of God, YHWH.[1] This is an obvious starting point, for it is a commonplace of Hebrew thought that a name may say something about the character of its bearer (e.g. Gen. 32:28; Ruth 1:20; 1 Sam. 25:25). It is therefore inherently likely that the use of the name of God was, at least sometimes, a significant theological issue for the writers of the Pentateuch. It is also unsurprising that a study of the name of God, together with various other designations and titles, has been much used down the centuries by Jew and Christian alike as a traditional method of considering theological questions about the character and nature of God.

Modern scholarship has not dissented from this biblical and traditional understanding, for modern studies often have statements such as "The name of the deity reveals the deity's true nature" or "The nature of God is thus compressed in the name of

1. Throughout this work I will avoid the conventional modern vocalization of the divine name (i.e., Yahweh) largely out of deference to the Jewish reverential tradition of nonuse of the name. I do not think, however, that it is necessarily improper for Christians to use the name in its vocalized form, and I find it puzzling that Paul van Buren, who criticizes Christian use of Yahweh, seems to regard such use as inherently disrespectful and implicitly sneering (*Discerning the Way: A Theology of the Jewish Christian Reality* [New York: Seabury Press, 1980], 32–33). I cannot see that a Christian use of Yahweh need be any less reverential than a Christian use of Jesus. Both names may be misused, but neither need be.

God."[2] Note, however, that although theological interest has not been lacking in modern study, modern study has nonetheless differed from its antecedents in the predominantly historical way in which the phenomenon of the divine name has often been approached. The use or nonuse of the name YHWH has been central to attempts to recognize and reconstruct the literary sources of Genesis, while the use of other appellations, such as El Shaddai or "God of your father," has featured prominently in historical reconstructions of the religion of the patriarchs. Our own study will itself not be concerned primarily with the meaning of the divine name as such, at least in the way that this is usually conceived, either in terms of the etymology and history of the tetragrammaton or the precise sense of Exod. 3:14.[3] Rather, our concern will be to set the use of the name against the wider pentateuchal context and to argue that only when name and context are held together can we perceive the significance that the divine name held for the writers of the Pentateuch.

Our approach to this question will follow the most explicit lead that the Old Testament itself gives. This means that we must start not in Genesis but rather at the beginning of Exodus. For the narratives that tell of the call of Moses to be God's chosen agent for bringing Israel out of Egypt (Exod. 2:23—7:7)[4] raise the question of the name of God and the relationship between the way in which God is to be known to Moses and Israel and the way by which God was known to Israel's ancestors, the patriarchs.

Within these narratives are two explicit statements about the name of God (Exod. 3:13-15, 6:2-3), both of which have gener-

2. W. H. Schmidt, *The Faith of the Old Testament* (Oxford: Blackwell, 1983; German, 1968, 1972), 13; G. Quell, "Kurios," in G. Kittel, ed., *Theological Dictionary of the New Testament,* vol. 3, trans. G. W. Bromiley (Grand Rapids: Eerdmans, 1965), 1070.

3. For a survey of modern discussion of these issues, see G. H. Parke-Taylor, *Yahweh: The Divine Name in the Bible* (Waterloo, Ontario: Wilfred Laurier Univ. Press, 1975).

4. The precise delimitation of the call of Moses is not immediately obvious from the text, both because of the repetitive nature of the text (the content of two sections relates to Moses' commissioning, one in Exodus 3–4 and the other in Exodus 6) and because the material relating to Moses' call anticipates and merges with the wider narrative context. The issue is not crucial to our thesis, however. The most controversial issue, the relationship of Exodus 6 to Exodus 3–4, will be dealt with at the end of the chapter.

ated an enormous discussion.[5] Since the significance of these passages is both crucial and controversial, it is important that their exegesis and interpretation should both be related to their immediate and wider context and be seen to cohere with a general understanding of pentateuchal criticism and interpretation. Therefore the reading of the text that is offered in the rest of this chapter must be taken as one part of a cumulative argument that is developed throughout the book.

THE STRUCTURE AND CONTENT OF THE CALL OF MOSES

The narratives telling of the call of Moses are lengthy and incorporate a wide range of concerns, many of which must be passed over at present. Generally speaking, the two major concerns are (1) God's self-disclosure to Moses and commissioning of him to bring Israel out of Egypt and (2) the various difficulties that Moses has in responding to his commission. If one considers an outline of Moses' call as a whole, both these concerns can clearly be seen:

Exod.	2:23-25	God's response to Israel's slavery in Egypt, which sets the context for the story that follows.
	3:1-6	God appears to Moses at the mountain of God (Horeb/Sinai).
	3:7-10	God announces the coming deliverance of Israel from Egypt and commissions Moses to act as God's agent.
	3:11—4:12	Moses raises four objections to his commission; each objection is met by an appropriate reassurance from God: (a) 3:11-12; (b) 3:13-22; (c) 4:1-9; (d) 4:10-12.
	4:13-17	Moses tries to decline his commission, God is angry, and the problem is resolved by the appointment of Aaron.
	4:18-31	Moses returns to Egypt.

5. Sufficient guides to the extensive debates and bibliography on these passages can be found in recent Exodus commentaries: B. S. Childs, *Exodus* (London: SCM, 1974); W. H. Schmidt, *Exodus,* BKAT 2 (pts. 2 and 4) (Neukirchen-Vluyn: Neukirchener Verlag, 1977, 1988); C. Houtman, *Exodus,* Commentaar op het Oude Testament (Kampen: J. H. Kok, 1986); J. I. Durham, *Exodus,* WBC 3 (Waco, Texas: Word, 1987). See also P. Weimar, *Die Berufung des Mose,* OBO 32 (Göttingen: Vandenhoeck & Ruprecht, 1980).

5:1-21	Moses confronts the pharaoh and achieves nothing except an exacerbation of Israel's hardship.
5:22-23	Moses laments to YHWH.
6:1-8	God reassures Moses about Israel's deliverance, and reaffirms the earlier self-revelation as YHWH.
6:9-12	Despite God's reassurance, Israel does not listen to Moses, and Moses fears similar rejection by the pharaoh.
6:13-27	Writer's note about God's commission of Moses and Aaron and their position within Israel's genealogy.
6:28—7:7	Resumptive and anticipatory summary statement of God's commissioning of Moses and Aaron.

Within the overall sequence of Moses' call, the second of Moses' objections to his commission (Exod. 3:13) explicitly raises the issue of the name of God that is our present concern. Before we can look at the interpretation of Exod. 3:13-15 in detail, however, we must first set it in its narrative context and consider a number of preliminary issues.

The Context Provided by Exodus 3:1-12

The location for God's call of Moses is specified at the outset— "the mountain of God" (*har ha'elohim,* Exod. 3:1b). In terms of the story it is striking that the place is already so designated, since it appears to presuppose some existing tradition of divine presence at the mountain, despite the lack of previous reference in the pentateuchal narrative to the presence of God in this location. It is not uncommon, therefore, for this and other reasons, to historicize the text and argue that there was a pre-Moses tradition of divine presence at that place (a suggestion commonly connected with the Kenite hypothesis, that Moses learned of the worship of YHWH from the Kenite/Midianite tribes among whom he stayed and into whose priestly family he married). So, for example, M. Weinfeld observes, "Sinai/Horeb is named *hr h'lhym* ("the mountain of God") even before the divine call to Moses at the burning bush (Exod. 3:1) and prior to the revelation to the people of Israel (Exod. 4:27; 18:5). It has therefore been rightly observed that this mountain was venerated long before Moses, as may be learned also from the fact that Jethro, the Midianite/Qenite priest, comes to the "mountain of God" (Exod.

18:5) in order to sacrifice and partake of the holy meal "in the presence of God" (v. 12).[6]

Far more likely, however, the writer chooses the phrase because he is writing from within a Yahwistic context where the notion of God's mountain is a well-established concept. That is to say, the tradition of divine presence implied in Exod. 3:1 is to be related, not to the context of the story, but to the context of the storyteller. The fact that, in terms of the telling of Israel's story (starting with the call of Abraham, Israel's ancestor, in Genesis 12), it is the first time that this phrase is used suggests that the writer is depicting an important new beginning. But he does so from a perspective in which what began in Exodus 3 has long since been taken as established. So he uses language that is naturally redolent with presupposition and overtone.

Taken on its own, the phrase "the mountain of God" might most naturally refer to Jerusalem, since the similar phrases "mountain of YHWH" or "my holy mountain" (cf. "holy ground," Exod. 3:5) elsewhere in the Old Testament consistently refer to Mount Zion.[7] In the context of Exodus, however, where

6. M. Weinfeld, "The Tribal League at Sinai," in P. D. Miller, P. D. Hanson, and S. D. McBride, eds., *Ancient Israelite Religion: Essays in Honor of Frank Moore Cross* (Philadelphia: Fortress, 1987), 303. Cf. the passing comment by J. J. M. Roberts, when discussing Yahwism's openness to external influences, that "the revelation of the divine name takes place at a mountain site that had apparently long been sacred to tribes in the area (Exod 3:1)" ("In Defense of the Monarchy," in *Ancient Israelite Religion,* 379). For a classic statement of this approach, see S. R. Driver, *Exodus* (Cambridge: Cambridge Univ. Press, 1911), 18–19.

A commonly suggested alternative explanation is that the reference to the mountain of God anticipates its significance later in the story. For example, S. R. Driver mentions this in passing as a possibility (*Exodus,* 18), and most recently it is advocated by N. M. Sarna (*Exodus,* JPS Torah Commentary [Philadelphia and New York: Jewish Publication Society, 5751/1991], 14). But this still fails to do justice to the problem posed by the text, a problem which cannot be solved simply within the parameters of the text as narrative. The text has been written by a narrator who stands at some remove from the context of the story he tells. The narrator takes for granted, and incorporates in the story, things that could not be taken for granted in the story's own context.

7. For "mountain of YHWH" *(har yhwh),* see Gen. 22:14; Isa. 2:3//Mic. 4:2; Zech. 8:3; Ps. 24:3. The sole exception is Num. 10:33, where the reference is clearly to Sinai.

For "my holy mountain" *(har qodšî),* see Isa. 11:9; 56:7; 57:13; 65:11, 25; 66:20; Ezek. 20:40; Joel 2:1; 3:17 (Heb. 4:17), Obadiah 16; Zeph. 3:11; Ps. 2:6. Cf. also "your holy mountain" (Ps. 15:1; 43:3; Dan. 9:16 [cf. 9:20]); "his holy mountain" (Ps. 3:5; 48:1 [Heb. 2], 99:9); "the holy mountain" (Isa. 27:13; Jer. 31:23); "glorious holy mountain" (Dan. 11:45).

Moses is staying in Midian (Exod. 2:15, 21-22), any direct reference to Zion is clearly inappropriate, and so the mountain in question must be the other great mountain in Israelite tradition (that is, Sinai/Horeb) as a clarificatory note at the end of Exod. 3:1 makes explicit. Indeed the precise phrase "the mountain of God" *(har ha'elohim)* is only used in the Old Testament with reference to Sinai/Horeb (Exod. 4:27; 18:5; 24:13; 1 Kings 19:8).

Despite the fact that in the context of the story the mountain is Sinai/Horeb rather than Zion, one probably should not draw the contrast between them too strongly, for the kind of thing that is said about Sinai as "the mountain of God" in Exodus 3 and 19ff. is said elsewhere in the Old Testament about Zion, and there is a typological similarity between the two mountains.[8] The mountain of God is a holy place, a sanctuary, where YHWH is specially present; there YHWH's chosen people gather to worship YHWH, and to do this they must live in accordance with the requirements of holiness. When, therefore, the writer says that Moses came to the mountain of God, the reader who, like the writer, is familiar with Israel's traditions is encouraged to see this episode within the context of both the Sinai and the Zion traditions of which this is the initial episode.

Such initial expectations with regard to the mountain of God are rapidly developed by two other features in the text. First, the symbol of God's presence is fire, as subsequently in the great encounter with Israel at Sinai (Exod. 19:18), an aspect given particular prominence in Deuteronomy (Deut. 4:11, 12, 15, 33, 36; 5:4, 22-26). Indeed, the Deuteronomic account of the Sinai theophany when YHWH appears to Israel naturally resonates with the narrative of Exodus 3 when YHWH appears to Moses—"Then the Lord spoke to you out of the midst of the fire; you

In Ezek. 28:14, 16 the references to "holy mountain of God" and "mountain of God" unusually refer primarily to Eden (28:13). Given, however, the predominant idiomatic use of such language with reference to Jerusalem, an imaginative typological linkage of Eden with Zion is likely here.

For a historical introduction to the issue, see R. Clifford, *The Cosmic Mountain in Canaan and the Old Testament* (Cambridge, Mass.: Harvard Univ. Press, 1972).

8. See, for example, the references to God's holy mountain in Exod. 15:13, 17, where the language could refer equally to either Sinai or Zion.

heard the sound of words, but saw no form; there was only a voice" (Deut. 4:12, RSV). Elsewhere, it is likely that the fire of God's presence in the holy place is represented ritually and symbolically; the burning of lamps on the lampstand in tabernacle and temple probably symbolized God's presence, while the lampstand itself was possibly a stylized representation of the burning bush.[9]

Second, when after the initial summons (3:4b) God first speaks to Moses (3:5-6), God's first words are words of warning and restriction, based on the fact that the ground where God is present in the bush is holy ground *('admat-qodeš hu').* This is the first significant use of the Hebrew root *qdš* (holiness) in the story of Israel that begins with Abraham,[10] and it is consistent with the related first use of "mountain of God." The Yahwistic writer knows that it is fundamental to Israel's traditions that YHWH is holy, and because YHWH is holy Moses and Israel must accept the regulations of holiness (restrictions on approach in the area of the sanctuary and on normal dress and behavior). Thus the opening words of Moses' call alert the reader to implications characteristic of YHWH and YHWH's sanctuary.

The writer is telling his story from the perspective of Mosaic Yahwism in which certain things about YHWH are presupposed. Thus he feels free to use the familiar divine name sometimes within the story (3:2, 4a), since he knows that it is YHWH who is calling Moses. Within the context of the story, however, it does not follow that Moses knows that it is YHWH who is calling him, and this now becomes the crucial issue.

After the initial warning God makes a self-announcement to Moses with the words "I am the God of your father *('anoki 'elohe 'abika),*[11] the God of Abraham, the God of Isaac, and the God of

9. See C. L. Meyers, *The Tabernacle Menorah* (Missoula, Mont.: Scholars, 1976).

10. The significance of the previous nonuse of the root *qdš* will be discussed in chap. 3.

11. The surprising use of the singular *father,* despite three fathers being named, is probably to recall the characteristic Genesis wording where, despite other variations in the formula, the word *father* is always in the singular. From the perspective of Exodus, which looks back on the patriarchal period as a whole, it is natural to use the plural *fathers,* as in Exod. 3:13, 15, 16. Thus the

Jacob." One might have expected God to announce "I am YHWH" *('ani yhwh),* as indeed happens later (Exod. 6:2). The fact that God, in God's first recorded address to Moses, makes self-reference not with the familiar Israelite name but with a descriptive title as God of the patriarchs allows, and indeed suggests, the possibility that Moses is not yet supposed to know God by the name YHWH but rather simply as God of the patriarchs. Israel's story so far has been the story of the patriarchs, and the title "God of your father" (if it really is a title and not simply a descriptive epithet) is certainly descriptive of God's involvement with Israel's ancestors, as recorded in Genesis 12–50. The actual wording, in a variety of forms, is not uncommon within Genesis 12–50, occurring some fifteen times. Moses' response of hiding his face is an action of appropriate reverence that certainly shows no hesitation that this is indeed God. But it still leaves open whether or not Moses knows this God as YHWH.

God then speaks again (the writer again using the name YHWH, as familiar to himself and the reader) and first announces the divine intention to bring Israel out of oppression in Egypt (3:7-8). Then God repeats the basic motive of concern for Israel in its oppression and introduces a crucial new element—Moses is to be the agent through whom YHWH brings about the deliverance of Israel (3:9-10). This introduces a theological dynamic that is fundamental to Yahwism. Although YHWH can manage without human mediation and can both act directly (as at the Red Sea, Exodus 14, though Moses does play a limited role) and speak directly (as in the Ten Words/Commandments, Exodus 20), the normal pattern for life is that YHWH both acts and speaks through the agency of human beings (especially prophets, priests, and kings)[12] who are called by YHWH for that purpose. Since Moses is presented as the archetypal agent of YHWH's will (the language and concepts of prophet, priest, and king are all used of him in the pentateuchal traditions), it is

formula in 3:6 is transitional between the usage of Genesis and that of Exodus. The variant reading *fathers* conforms 3:6 to the regular Exodus usage.

12. Wise men are different, because the basic presupposition of the wisdom tradition is a theology of creation whose theological mode of discourse is characteristically "from below" (i.e., "Go to the ant, O sluggard; consider her ways, and be wise") rather than "from above" (i.e., "Thus says YHWH . . .").

appropriate that in the initial encounter between YHWH and Moses the basic pattern of divine and human action should be spelled out. Again, it should be noted that this is the first time in Israel's story that this theological dynamic appears. Although the patriarchs live life under God, there is hardly any sense of their being agents through whom YHWH acts or speaks to others.[13] Only when Moses is called by YHWH at YHWH's holy mountain does this new pattern for life become apparent.

Moses, however, is less than overjoyed at the prospect of being YHWH's agent to deliver Israel from Egypt. He does not refuse the responsibility of his commissioning, but he is reluctant to undertake it and so produces a series of objections, relating mostly to his sense of personal inadequacy. After the initial objection and divine reassurance (3:11-12), the second objection (3:13) raises the issue of the name of God.

The Interpretation of Exodus 3:13-15: Preliminary Issues

Before we consider 3:13-15 in detail, six issues will best be dealt with separately in advance, in order to clear the ground.

First is the question of the significance that should be attributed to the fact that the issue of God's name—both Moses' question and God's answer—arises only within the context of Moses' objections to his commissioning. In terms of the story, one could easily imagine that, had Moses directly assented to God's charge, no statement about God's name might have been needed or given. Does this mean that what is said about God's name is not of fundamental importance but is only incidental to the story?[14]

The assessment of this issue depends on the degree of legitimacy to be attributed to Moses' objections. Is Moses simply being feeble and evasive,[15] or is he a man of genuine, albeit

13. Joseph may be a partial exception, when he refers to himself as sent *(šalaḥ)* by God to Egypt to preserve Israel alive during the famine (Gen. 45:5-8). Yet this awareness of being sent by God is retrospective, and Joseph was never formally sent *(šalaḥ)* in the manner of a prophet. Consistent with this, Joseph is not aware of himself speaking and acting on God's behalf in the manner of a prophet. Cf. below, chap. 3, 94.

14. This issue is often overlooked but is brought to the fore by Childs, *Exodus,* 74–76. My understanding of it differs somewhat from that of Childs.

15. S. Bigger, for example, comments on the story in Exodus 3–4 that "the narrator heavily underscores Moses' ineptitude. . . . This downrating of Moses

hesitant and immature, faith? Although there may be some element of the former, there are two good reasons for seeing the latter aspect as predominant.

In terms of a wider Old Testament context, a characteristic of call narratives, in which a person is called either to speak or to act on YHWH's behalf (e.g., Isaiah 6, Jeremiah 1, Judges 6), is that those called express some kind of reluctance and question YHWH about what they are called to say or do. This questioning of God, similar in important ways to the lament psalms, is never portrayed as improper but is always taken seriously by God as a legitimate (even if incomplete) response to God's call. Since Moses is presented as the archetypal example of the person who both acts (Exod. 3:7-10) and speaks (Exod. 3:13-15) on YHWH's behalf, it is intrinsically likely that the Exodus writer considered the call of Moses an appropriate place to explore a fundamental issue that the call of YHWH generally poses.

This intrinsic likelihood is supported by the development of the story in context, where both the fact that the Exodus writer develops Moses' four objections at such length and the fact that God takes all the objections with the utmost seriousness (only becoming angry when Moses' questions become a refusal) suggest that the narrator indeed viewed the whole story as paradigmatic of a fundamental problem in the life of faith. This problem is the potentially demanding nature of God's call, which is such that human nature may shrink back and need reassurance. This means, therefore, that Moses' questions are as basic to the narrative as God's commissioning, and material introduced in the context of Moses' questions need not be of incidental or secondary significance within the context depicted.

A second issue is the fact that what is said to Moses about the name of God is said to Moses alone. The basic point is that the encounter between Moses and YHWH envisages nobody else present. Moreover, it should be noted that the crucial words about the name and nature of God (*'ehyeh 'ašer 'ehyeh,* 3:14a) are not, as such, part of what Moses is told to say to the Israelites

contrasts starkly with the powerful man who stands before Pharaoh" ("Moses," in S. Bigger, ed., *Creating the Old Testament: The Emergence of the Hebrew Bible* [Oxford: Blackwell, 1989], 123).

(although the play on *'ehyeh* (v. 14b) and *yhwh* (v. 15a) is part of his announcement) nor, apparently, is the statement underlining the definitive nature of knowing God in this way (v. 15b). This seems to represent an understanding of God initially given to Moses alone.

This initial restriction of God's self-revelation to Moses needs to be related to a wider feature of the Exodus (and pentateuchal) traditions, that is, the unique access of Moses to the mind of God. Elsewhere in Exodus, apart from the Ten Commandments, which God speaks directly to the people of Israel and which they find so overwhelming that they beg Moses to act as mediator (Exod. 20:1-21; cf. the elaboration of this in Deut. 5:22-33), it is only to Moses (and sometimes Aaron) that God speaks. In particular, there are three other passages in Exodus in which God says something about the divine name, Exod. 33:19; 34:5-7, 34:14 (of which 34:5-7 is the most extensive and the most important), and each is in a context where Moses is the sole recipient of God's words. These, together with Exod. 3:14-15, are the only passages in the whole Bible in which the name of God is spoken about by God. Israel's knowledge of God as YHWH, crucially set in the context of the fundamental traditions of Exodus and Sinai, is given by God to Moses.

This dimension of Israel's tradition—that whatever Israel knows about the name of God, it knows only through the mediation of Moses to whom alone a direct self-revelation of God has been given—should be taken seriously by the interpreter. Yet all too often the theological significance of Moses' access to the mind of God has become skewed by other interests.

On the one hand, it has often been assumed that the tradition must be translatable into straightforward historical categories ("Did it happen like that, or not?") if its significance is to be maintained ("If it didn't happen like that, we can't trust the text"), often as a corollary of Mosaic authorship ("Moses must have written it, since he was the only one in a position to know"). Such historicizing begs the question of the nature of the text and the appropriate categories for understanding it, for the text is anonymous and embodies some of the perspectives of developed Mosaic Yahwism. Nonetheless it usually represents a concern to do justice to the implications of Moses' role, implications that tend to receive little attention in many conventional documentary and traditiohistorical analyses.[16]

On the other hand, insofar as the question of the origins of Israel's knowledge of God as YHWH has been addressed, it has usually been in historical terms whose concerns, while legitimate, have been largely oblique to the concerns of the Exodus text. Probably the most famous example is the Kenite hypothesis. Whatever the merits of this as a historical hypothesis, its merits as a heuristic tool for interpreting the story of Exodus 3 are almost nonexistent. Its effect is mainly negative, since it introduces concerns alien to the story.

The present study will not explore the significance of the role of Moses as such. The point here is simply that, unless the role Moses has in the text is given full imaginative significance by the interpreter, without being too quickly pressed into historical categories of one kind or other, the nature and concerns of the Exodus 3 tradition will not be accurately appreciated.

A third issue is the extent of text relevant to our enquiry. Of the four divine responses to Moses' four objections, the second response, in 3:13-22, is much the longest. It is also the least straightforward in terms of its inner logic and continuity. That is, while initially (3:14-15) the divine speech is clearly answering the question posed, it moves on to Moses gathering the elders of Israel, the stubbornness of the pharaoh, YHWH's overwhelming deliverance of Israel, and Israel despoiling the Egyptians, in such a way that by the end the speech is hardly any longer answering the question of 3:13.

Within 3:13-22 as a whole, a marked shift comes at 3:16. First, there is a command to "Go," which serves to move the focus of attention away from Moses' present dialogue with God toward the future encounter with Israel. Second, Moses is to gather the elders of Israel *(ziqne yisra'el),* whereas in 3:13, 14, and 15 the reference is consistently to the Israelites *(bene yisra'el)* as a whole. Third, the elders are not imagined as raising any objec-

16. For a recent attempt to take seriously the narrative portrayal of Moses, see G. W. Coats, *Moses: Heroic Man, Man of God,* JSOTS 57 (Sheffield: JSOT, 1988).

tions to Moses when he speaks to them (3:18a), despite Moses' concern (3:13). Fourth, all the opposition to Moses will come from the pharaoh, whose refusal to let Israel go is a different kind of problem to that raised by Moses in 3:13. If 3:16ff. is read on its own, it looks more like a straightforward commissioning charge (not dissimilar to 4:21-23) than part of an answer to an objection. Within the immediate context of 3:13-22 one may best make sense of this by supposing that 3:16-22 envisages developments subsequent to Moses' initial encounter with Israel as a whole, which is envisaged in 3:13-15. God's words in 3:16-22 seek to terminate the objections of Moses by returning to the development of his commission and also foreshadowing later developments in the story. This means that 3:13-15 functions as a relatively self-contained unit within the divine speech and so constitutes the appropriate focus of attention.

Fourth is the question of the internal coherence of 3:13-15. As the text stands, it has a cumulative and repetitive nature which emphasizes the momentous importance of what is being said. This aspect of the text, however, has been almost universally interpreted by modern commentators as evidential of the stages of its composition in terms of both sources and redaction. Two features in particular have been appealed to. First is the fact that verse 15 appears to provide the answer to the question of verse 13, which raises doubts about the status of verse 14. Second is the fact that there are three speech introductions (vv. 14a, 14b, 15a) within the one speech by God. But no consensus has been reached about which parts of the text are source and which are redaction and how many redactors may have been involved.[17]

Any discussion of the coherence of 3:13-15 must give due weight to the question of what is and is not appropriate to coherent Hebrew literary style. Unfortunately, given the relative paucity of narrative material extant from ancient Israel and given our distance from and consequent difficulty in discerning its

17. P. Weimar offers a convenient synoptic analysis (*Die Berufung des Mose,* 367ff.); cf. also M. Saebø, "Offenbarung oder Verhüllung? Bemerkungen zum Charakter des Gottesnamens in Ex 3,13–15," in J. Jeremias and L. Perlitt, eds., *Die Botschaft und die Boten* (Neukirchen-Vluyn: Neukirchener Verlag, 1981), 43–55.

various literary conventions, this kind of issue is extremely difficult to resolve. In any event, it would probably be helpful to cease asking the unanswerable question as to whether the text was originally composed as a unity and to ask instead whether the text as it now stands is a unified and coherent composition. If the question is posed in this way, an affirmative answer is entirely reasonable.[18] On the one hand, the explicatory wordplay about the divine name in verse 14 prior to its announcement in verse 15 is perfectly intelligible, especially since it is presupposed that the reader is, in fact, already familiar with what the answer will be. The Hebrew predilection for wordplay makes verse 14 an enhancement to, rather than a distraction from, this crucial moment in Israel's story. On the other hand, speech introductions are commonly used within a speech to distinguish different elements within it, in a way analogous to modern use of punctuation and paragraphs.[19] The three speech introductions each introduce distinct yet related content that can without difficulty be interpreted in sequential manner as a coherent address—as will be seen below.[20]

Fifth, it should be noted that something is peculiar and exceptional about both the form and the content of the second of Moses' objections to his commissioning. The other three objections are all in one way or other straightforward expressions of personal inability and inadequacy, each of which is met by appropriate words of reassurance. The difficulty Moses raises in 3:13 is of an entirely different kind, a point usually obscured by a conventional source-critical and form-critical analysis which fo-

18. Despite, for example, M. Fishbane's assertion, characteristic of many commentators, that "the sequence and meaning of the ensuing passage (vv. 14-15) is, in the preserved tradition, somewhat garbled" (*Text and Texture: Close Readings of Selected Biblical Texts* [New York: Schocken, 1979], 67).

19. See, e.g., Gen. 17:3, 9, 15; 20:9, 10; 21:6, 7; 41:39, 41; 47:3, 4; Ruth 2:20; 1 Sam. 17:8, 10, 34, 37; 26:9, 10, 17, 18. For an interesting discussion of the phenomenon, see S. Bar-Efrat, *Narrative Art in the Bible,* JSOTS 70 (Sheffield: Almend, 1989; Hebrew, 1979), 43–45. Bar-Efrat suggests that speech introductions within a speech indicate a pause which invites some kind of response from the listener, either a reply or some kind of action. In the context of Exod. 3:13-15 this would suggest a pause for Moses to reflect on the weighty implications of the two pronouncements in 3:14. See also the discussion in G. Fischer, *Jahwe Unser Gott: Sprache, Aufbau und Erzähltechnik in der Berufung des Mose (Ex 3–4),* OBO 91 (Freiburg Schweiz, Universitätsverlag/Göttingen: Vandenhoeck & Ruprecht, 1989), 41–45.

20. See below, pp. 21ff.

cuses on similarities of vocabulary and question form in 3:11 and 3:13. The convention is to see 3:9-15 as original to E and its two objections as analogous to the questions raised in prophetic call narratives elsewhere in the Old Testament and to see the other two objections in 4:1, 10 as secondary expansions of the tradition.[21] In 3:13, however, Moses' difficulty is not one of personal inadequacy (as in 3:11, 4:10) or of how he can overcome reluctance to take him seriously (as in 4:1) but of potential ignorance should the Israelites ask about the name of God, a question that on the face of it seems somewhat surprising, particularly when compared with the more practical and personal nature of the other difficulties Moses envisages. In context, the question and answer of 3:13-15 both have an unusually abstract theological character.

The distinctive nature of 3:13-15 may be further appreciated through reflection on its similarity to the common formula of a child's question (Exod. 12:26-27, 13:14-15; Deut. 6:20-25; Josh. 4:6-7, 21-33). This formula, perhaps originating in a liturgical and catechetical context,[22] functions in the text as a rhetorical device for didactic purposes. The similarity between Exod. 3:13-15 and this formula can be seen in several respects.

First, the question asked is always envisaged as hypothetical, at a time subsequent to that of the story. Second, the imagined question is always based on the key word *mah* ("What is the meaning of . . .?"). Third, the context is always the story of the origin or basis of something fundamental in Israel's religious traditions (Exodus 3, Divine Name; Exodus 12 and 13, Passover; Deuteronomy 6, Shema; Joshua 4, Entry into Promised Land). Fourth, either the explicit terminology or the implicit concept of perpetual remembrance *(zkr lĕʿolam/ʿad ʿolam)* is present (explicitly, Exod. 3:15b, 12:24; Josh. 4:7b), since the fundamental traditions are to have permanent vitality within Israel's life.[23]

21. See, e.g., Schmidt, *Exodus,* 124, 131; A. W. Jenks, *The Elohist and North Israelite Traditions,* SBLMS 22 (Missoula, Mont.: Scholars Press, 1977), 41.

22. See J. A. Soggin, "Kultätiologische Sagen und Katechese im Hexateuch," *VT* 10 (1960): 341–47.

23. Perhaps even the terminological similarity of the son(s) *(ben, banim)* asking a father and the children of Israel *(bene yisra'el)* asking Moses is not entirely fortuitous.

Of course, distinctive features about Exod. 3:13 make it other than a simple variant on the child's question formula. Instead of children asking their fathers, it is the people of Israel as a whole asking Moses; 3:13 envisages a unique rather than a recurrent situation (though the paradigmatic nature of the story qualifies this point); and 3:13 has neither a religious ritual to provoke the question nor a short account of YHWH's action on behalf of Israel in response. Nonetheless, these differences are not incompatible with 3:13-15 functioning in a way similar to the child's question. Thus the literary form of 3:13-15 suggests its possible indebtedness to usage in didactic contexts in Israel's life. As it stands, it functions as a paradigmatic didactic text, giving Israel's account of how Israel knows the name of God.

This recognition both of the unusual character of 3:13-15 and of its separateness from 3:16-22 brings us to a point recognized by virtually all modern commentators, that the text of 3:13-22 gives every impression of having a complex prehistory. Precisely what this might have involved is unclear, and there is no consensus. There is no obvious resolution of what might be original and what might be later development.

For present purposes the important point is that 3:13-15 looks to be a distinct and coherent unit that represents a mature theological presentation of the tradition that the name YHWH was first revealed to Moses at Sinai. Although the writer has imaginatively expressed the material in terms of the context of Moses' initial encounter with God and his objections to his commissioning and it is possible to interpret the material in terms of that context, the material retains a somewhat artificial feel, since its genre sets it apart from the rest of the dialogue between Moses and God. In modern critical terms, 3:13-15 appears to represent a kind of narrative theology, that is, the expression of a theological proposition in story form rather than in an abstract or analytical mode of discourse.

Sixth and finally, it is worth noting that, despite the intense debate and extensive disagreement surrounding the interpretation of 3:13-15, the biblical text itself is, in a sense, remarkably straightforward. From a text-critical point of view there are no problems, there is no difficult grammar or syntax (except in the precise interpretation of 3:14a), and no rare or difficult words are used. In fact, the text is expressed with a brevity and simplicity that might well suggest that the writer considered the meaning of the text to be self-evident. Perhaps, therefore, if we can accurately discern the assumptions and perspectives of the writer, a straightforward and satisfactory interpretation will be entirely possible. This is our thesis.

The Interpretation of Exodus 3:13-15: Textual Analysis

> Then Moses said to God, "I am about to encounter the people of Israel.[24] When I say to them, 'The God of your fathers has sent me to you,' and they say to me, 'What is his name?' what shall I say to them?" God said to Moses, "I AM WHO I AM" *('ehyeh 'ašer 'ehyeh)*. And he said, "Say this to the people of Israel, 'I AM *('ehyeh)* has sent me to you.'" God also said to Moses, "Say this to the people of Israel, 'YHWH *(yhwh)*, the God of your fathers, the God of Abraham, the God of Isaac, and the God of Jacob, has sent me to you': this is my name for ever, this is how I am to be remembered in all generations." (My translation)

To begin with, it will be appropriate to outline the structure and flow of the verses. First, because verse 15 appears to constitute the specific answer to the question of verse 13, since it resumes the title originally used ("The God of your fathers") and adds to it the requested name YHWH, verse 14 is given a distinctive function as an introduction and an explication, in some way, of the divine name YHWH given in verse 15. The answer to Moses' question is not given immediately. Rather, God first makes a general point about himself, "*'ehyeh 'ašer 'ehyeh*" (I AM WHO I AM). This general point is then compressed into the single Hebrew word *'ehyeh* (I AM), and used as though it were the name of God, "*'ehyeh* has sent me to you" (v. 14b). Thus the general point about God is tantamount to God's actual name.

24. Moses' opening words are commonly rendered as a conditional: "If I come . . ." (e.g., RSV, NIV, REB, Childs, Durham). But this obscures the fact that the same idiom—*hinneh 'anoki ba' 'el*— is used in a nonconditional sense in Exod. 19:9 and 18:6 (where the introductory *hinneh* is lacking in the MT but attested in the versions). In these other two passages the words are used to introduce an important formal encounter and so should have the same sense in 3:13.

Only then is the name of God—YHWH—given (v. 15a). The effect of this play on words *('ehyeh/yhwh)* is to draw attention to the perceived implications of the name YHWH, implications related to what God will be or do, understood in terms of the Hebrew verb *hayah* (to be).

Second, the divine answer of 3:14-15 is rounded off by verse 15b. This directly follows the use of the name YHWH as the answer to the question of verse 13 and is emphatic about the importance of the name as the way in which God is always to be known. Indeed, verse 15b is expressed in a parallelism that gives the language a close affinity to poetry. The Hebrew words *šem* (name) and *zeker* (lit. memorial, remembrance) are commonly used in poetic parallelism elsewhere in the Old Testament.[25] This gives a heightened sense of the significance of the statement and also makes a fitting conclusion to this part of the divine pronouncement.

Thus the flow of 3:13-15 is (1) imagined question from Israel about God's name, when Moses is sent to Israel (v. 13); (2) statement by God about God in language that anticipates what follows (v. 14a); (3) anticipatory explication of God's name through a play on the verb *hayah* (v. 14b); (4) the giving of God's name (v. 15a); (5) concluding emphasis on the significance of the name.

What then is the meaning and significance of the question and answer? When it is set in context, we have already noted that when God first speaks to Moses the divine self-announcement does not use the divine name YHWH but instead has the words "I am the God of your father" (3:6), which presumably represents the way by which Moses is supposed to know God. Moses picks up this divine title in his second objection when he imagines himself going to the people of Israel and saying to them, "The God of your fathers has sent me to you" (3:13). That is, Moses imagines himself speaking to Israel about his mission and referring to the God who has sent him with a title that is presumably as familiar to them as to him—for there is no reason to suppose

25. See, e.g., Isa. 26:8; Ps. 135:13; cf. Hos. 12:5 (Heb 6) where *zeker* is used as a synonym for *šem*.

that the narrator thought the people of Israel, as the descendants of the patriarchs, would be unfamiliar with the patriarchal relationship of their God. Thus the text appears to assume that both Moses and Israel know God as the "God of their father(s)."

The difficulty that Moses envisages, however, is that, when he mentions this "God of the fathers" who has sent him, he might be asked, "What is his name?" *(mah šemo),* and he wants to know how to answer. The nature of the assumptions embodied in this question and in Moses' not knowing how to answer constitute the interpretative crux. It should be noted, therefore, that the primary concern of the text is not solely with the name of God as an issue in its own right, crucial though that is, for the words "has sent me [i.e., Moses] to you [i.e., Israel]" *(šelaḥani 'alekem)* recur three times, each time immediately preceded by a designation or name of God:

v. 13 (Moses speaking):	When I say to them, "The God of your fathers *has sent me to you,"* and they ask me, "What is his name?" what shall I say to them?
v. 14 (God speaking):	Say this to the people of Israel, "I AM *has sent me to you."*
v. 15 (God speaking):	Say this to the people of Israel, "YHWH the God of your fathers, the God of Abraham, the God of Isaac, and the God of Jacob, *has sent me to you."*

Thus the concern of the text is with the relationship between the name of God and the sending of Moses to Israel. All three elements (YHWH, Moses, and Israel) need to be held together if the text is to be understood. The general point is that what is said about the name of God is only meaningful in the context of Israel's awareness of itself as addressed by God through the mediation of Moses. Generally speaking, only as the human community of Israel knows itself to live in relationship to God does it make sense to talk about the name and nature of God. Specifically, it is only in and through Moses being sent to Israel that Israel knows God as YHWH; the revelation of God to Israel is linked to a particular human figure who is the agent and mediator of that revelation.

We have already noted that Moses is portrayed as the archetypal agent of God's will. Indeed, it seems clear that Moses is being portrayed specifically as a prophet. Although the actual word *nabi'* is not used, the concept—a person called by God and sent to speak on God's behalf to Israel—is present. Moreover, vocabulary other than *nabi'* that is strongly characteristic of prophetic texts is used. On the one hand, the verb *send (šalaḥ)* is commonly used in the Old Testament to designate a prophet's commission from God (e.g., Isa. 6:8; Jer. 1:7; Ezek. 2:3). On the other hand, the prophet speaks in YHWH's name (e.g., Jer. 14:14-15), characteristically prefacing his message with the formula "Thus says YHWH" (e.g., Amos 1:3, 6, 9), which is precisely the formula used by Moses and Aaron when first they address the pharaoh (Exod. 5:1). So when Exod. 3:13-15 is concerned with the *name* of the deity who has *sent* Moses, the passage is linked both conceptually and terminologically to the concerns of prophecy. This means that Moses is being portrayed as the archetypal Hebrew prophet—the one who is sent to speak to Israel in YHWH's name. The text's concern with the disclosure of the name of God is in no sense an abstract concern raised for its own sake but is integrally related to Moses' role as the classic example of that phenomenon of prophecy by which historic Israel in practice encountered their God.

Within this context we still must explain the emphasis given to the name YHWH, and the most natural explanation is that the writer is depicting the first revelation of the name to Moses and through him to Israel. Both Moses and Israel start by knowing God as "God of your father(s)" (3:6, 13), and the name YHWH is then given and added to the designation "God of your fathers" in a way that makes clear the identity and continuity of YHWH as Israel's God with the God known to the patriarchs. They still have the same God, but now God is to be known in perpetuity by the new name YHWH.

The text of Exod. 3:13-15 thus portrays how and why Moses spoke in YHWH's name in a way suggestive of wider concerns about the nature of God's relationship with Israel as mediated through human agency, especially that of the prophet. That is, if Moses was able to speak to Israel in YHWH's name because YHWH, when asked, disclosed that name to him and told him to use it when speaking to Israel, then in principle that is the case with other prophets also. It is through the word of the prophet like Moses that Israel is addressed by YHWH (a point given classic exposition in Deut. 5:22-33; 18:9-22). The name YHWH has been given by God through Moses to Israel as a whole, and the name carries unique significance and authority for Israel.

To sum up, the natural and consistent implication of the text is that it is depicting the name YHWH being given for the first time to Moses and through him to Israel. As such the story depicts a new beginning within the story of Israel, distinct from what preceded in the time of the patriarchs. The cumulative factors in context that support this interpretation are numerous. It is the story of Moses' first encounter with God, an encounter in which God initially speaks as "God of your father(s)." Only when a specific question about God's name is put does God disclose the name YHWH. It is an encounter in which Moses is given unique access to the mind of God and is sent by God to speak to Israel in God's name, an encounter that is naturally foundational for all that follows. There is the first reference to "mountain of God," which gives a setting for the story at Sinai/Horeb and which creates the nexus YHWH-Sinai-Moses-Israel, a nexus foundational to Israel's traditions yet unprecedented in the story of Israel previously (Genesis 12–Exodus 2). There is the first use of the language of holiness in conjunction with God and the first depiction of the commissioning of a prophet, both major characteristics of Yahwism, which extend the nexus of Exodus 3 to YHWH-Sinai-holiness-Moses-prophecy-Israel. There is the imagined first formal encounter of Moses with Israel as a whole *(bene yisra'el)* in which the people of Israel ask about the name of their God. There is the use of the name YHWH in response to this request, the emphasis on the implications of the name together with the emphasis that this is God's name in perpetuity. And there is the didactic nature of that portion of the text that conveys God's name. All these together make best sense if the point of the text is a new beginning, a new beginning focused in the new name YHWH yet represented by a nexus of interrelated elements.

Admittedly, there is still more to be said. We have not yet fully explored the exegesis of Israel's imagined question *mah šemo.* Moreover, objections may be raised against our interpretation, either objections that may relate to the kind of difficulties one could easily imagine if one pictures Moses trying to persuade Israel to listen to him by using a name of God that was hitherto unknown to them or objections relating to the extensive use of the name YHWH in Genesis prior to the time of Moses. These issues, however, may be postponed until the next chapter.[26] The point essential to our thesis, that the story of Exodus 3 is meant to depict God's initial self-revelation as YHWH, should be clear.

The Context of Exodus 6:2-3

The second explicit statement about the name of God is Exod. 6:2-3. The context of this is set by Moses' failure to achieve anything when he first confronts the pharaoh on behalf of YHWH, as YHWH has commanded him. After the return to Egypt, Moses and Aaron initially address the pharaoh with a confident use of a normal prophetic formula, "Thus says YHWH, the God of Israel . . ." (Exod. 5:1). Unfortunately, the pharaoh responds by saying that he's never heard of YHWH and so has no intention of doing what he says. The pharaoh's point is primarily one of precedent—the gods whom he is prepared to recognize do not include one called YHWH; though there is also a matter of will—the pharaoh is only prepared to do what he wants to do. Moses and Aaron then instantly climb down and refer to God as "the God of the Hebrews," which is presumably a designation already familiar to the pharaoh, as the people of Israel in Egypt are consistently called Hebrews in Exodus 1 and 2. They also make a lesser request, couched in rather more supplicatory tones than their initial peremptory demand, depicting God in a way that might be supposed to appeal to an Egyptian and only using the new name YHWH in an incidental way (5:3).[27] The outcome is no different, however. The pharaoh is still unimpressed and will concede nothing. Rather, he decides to make life worse for Israel, and the rest of the episode tells of a growing spiral of

26. See below, pp. 59ff.

27. It is interesting to compare what Moses and Aaron say in 5:1, 3 with what Moses is told to say in 3:18. Their initial command is considerably stronger than 3:18, their climb-down request weaker. Is the reader to suppose that adherence to the wording of 3:18 might have produced a slightly less hostile response from the pharaoh?

cynical oppression, violence, and despair (5:4-21). Moreover, there is no sense of YHWH's presence or action in all this. If the name YHWH is meant to indicate God's dynamic presence with Israel, active on its behalf, the initial encounter with the pharaoh is where one would expect this to become apparent. Instead, just when things start to get difficult, YHWH makes no difference at all and appears to be absent.

Moses then responds to this turn of events by returning to YHWH with a lament (5:22-23), since things had not happened as he had expected—although, as the narrator tells the story, YHWH had already indicated that the problem of the pharaoh's opposition would not be easily resolved (3:19; 4:21). YHWH does not explain the disappointment but responds to Moses with words of emphatic reassurance; YHWH will so act that the pharaoh will be compelled to send Israel out of Egypt (6:1). As with the account of Moses' objections to his call in Exodus 3 and 4, it seems likely that the narrator sees the specific episode related as paradigmatic of a widespread phenomenon in the life of faith—opposition, disappointment, the apparent absence of God and God's failure to be and do what God's people had been led to expect, the kind of situation frequently depicted in the psalms of lament. But although life under YHWH does not necessarily turn out in the way one might have expected, and indeed YHWH does not explain or justify why this should be so, Moses demonstrates the appropriate response by turning to YHWH, and YHWH does not disappoint in the ensuing words of reassurance.

Within this context of reassurance to Moses God speaks further (6:2-8). Presumably, the general tenor of the address in 6:2-8 should be understood as similar to that of 6:1, that is, a reaffirmation of what had already been said to Moses but had apparently been called into question by YHWH's failure to act and Moses' consequent disappointment.

The Interpretation of Exodus 6:2-3

Since the crucial words in 6:2-3 are part of a longer speech, here is a translation of the speech as a whole.

> And God spoke to Moses and said to him, "I am YHWH. I appeared to Abraham, to Isaac, and to Jacob, as El Shaddai (and by my name YHWH I did not make myself known to them), and what

> is more *(wĕgam)* I established my covenant with them, to give them the land of Canaan, the land they sojourned in, and what is more *(wĕgam)* I have heard the groaning of the people of Israel whom the Egyptians are enslaving, and I have remembered my covenant. Therefore say to the people of Israel, 'I am YHWH. So I will bring you out from under the burdens of the Egyptians, and I will deliver you from your slavery to them, and I will rescue you with an outstretched arm and with great acts of judgment. And I will take you to be my people, and I will be your God. Then you will know that I am YHWH your God, who brings you out from under the burdens of the Egyptians. And I will bring you to the land that I swore with uplifted hand to give to Abraham, to Isaac, and to Jacob, and I will give it to you as your possession. I am YHWH.'" (Exod. 6:2-8, my translation)

Generally speaking, the address meets Moses' disappointment by drawing attention to the name of God and to God's commitment to Israel. These two are presumably interconnected, the latter in some way explicating the former. The fact that God's name is YHWH says something fundamental about God in terms of the divine commitment to the people of Israel as their God who will deliver them (esp. 6:6-7). As Childs puts it, "The content of the message which is bracketed by this self-identification formula [I am YHWH] is actually only an explication of the name itself and contains the essence of God's purpose with Israel. First, there is the promise to deliver: 'I will redeem you with an outstretched arm.' Secondly, there is their adoption into the covenant as the people of God: 'I will take you for my people, and I will be your God.' Thirdly, there is the gift of the land which had been promised to the Fathers: 'I will give it to you for an inheritance.' The name of Yahweh functions as a guarantee that the reality of God stands behind the promise and will execute its fulfillment."[28] Within this general context, certain specific points may be noted.

First, as in Exod. 3:13-15, a distinction is made between what God says to Moses and what Moses is to say to the people of Israel. The section of God's address that includes reference to the different ways in which God is known, and which is theologically

28. B. S. Childs, *Exodus,* 115.

most demanding, is said to Moses alone as part of his reassurance (6:2-5) and does not function as part of his message to the people of Israel (6:6-8). In what Moses is to say to them, he is to speak in YHWH's name and use language that, in the light of the rest of the Old Testament (esp. Ezekiel), might well be called conventional; that is, there is no contrast between God as El Shaddai to the patriarchs and God as YHWH to Israel. Rather, that distinction is ignored, as God is YHWH, and it is YHWH who promised the land to the patriarchs. This means that the point about the different ways in which God is known functions as part of Moses' unique access to the mind of God and part of God's reassurance to Moses in his distress but is not seen as central to the needs of Israel in their distress.

Second, the thrust of God's reassurance to Moses is to give him reasons from the past to trust in God in the present. The translation of the repeated *wegam* attempts to bring out the cumulative effect of God's appeal to what God has done in the past, that is, the continuity of the making and remembering of the covenant (6:4-5) with the divine self-revelation as El Shaddai (6:3a).[29] Specifically, reference is made to the tradition of Genesis 17 in which God makes a self-disclosure to Abraham as El Shaddai and makes a covenant with him. It may be that Moses is supposed to be either unaware or forgetful of this. For although God's concern for the covenant is something the reader already knows about as a presupposition for the call of Moses (Exod. 2:24), nothing was said about this to Moses in his original commission; in that context, although God is the God of the patriarchs (3:6, 13), there is no reference to the covenant with the patriarchs. The reference to the patriarchal covenant tells Moses something that was already operative but of which he was apparently unaware and which provides a reason for him to continue to trust God

29. For this rendering of *wegam,* see C. J. Labuschagne, "The emphasizing particle *gam* and its connotations," in W. C. van Unnik and A. S. van der Woude, eds., *Studia Biblica et Semitica (T. C. Vriezen Festschrift)* (Wageningen: Weenman, 1966), 197. The proposal sometimes made to render *wegam* differently in v. 4 and v. 5 seems to me to obscure the cumulative flow of God's discourse and the parenthetical nature of v. 3b (e.g., P. Auffret, "The Literary Structure of Exodus 6.2-8," *JSOT* 27 [1983]: 47; Schmidt, *Exodus,* 268).

despite his initial disappointment; the covenant represents a commitment on God's part which will not be nullified by Egyptian opposition. If, therefore, God is to act powerfully as YHWH and deliver Israel from oppression in Egypt, this is something entirely consistent which is only to be expected in the light of how God has already acted in the past.

Third, although the predominant emphasis is on continuity between what God has done in the past and what God is going to do now, there is nonetheless a note of discontinuity—God's name YHWH was not known before. The actual reference to this in 6:3b is clearly parenthetical, since it interrupts the flow of God's account of the divine revelation to the patriarchs (Genesis 17) in 6:3a, 4. Why should this parenthetical reference be necessary at all?

Initially, it would seem that the reference functions as a comment on the content of the tradition of Genesis 17. That is, although God is now known as YHWH, God did not make the covenant with the patriarchs under this name but rather as El Shaddai. Since, however, God is referred to by a number of different titles and epithets in pentateuchal tradition (and throughout the Old Testament) and this is usually seen as natural and unremarkable, some special reason would be needed for drawing attention to the nomenclature at this point, a reason presumably connected with the emphasis on the name YHWH in the address—it prefaces the whole address and prefaces and concludes the message Moses is to deliver to the people of Israel.

The insistence on God's name as YHWH is, in fact, remarkable. Nowhere else in pentateuchal narrative or indeed in any narrative of the Old Testament is such stress laid upon the divine name. In terms of the immediate context this is most naturally understood as meeting the uncertainty that Moses and Israel might be presumed to feel about this new name in the light of their disappointment in chapter 5. Indeed, the fact that God has already become known to Moses by a name that was not given to the patriarchs and that God has also made known what this name means puts Moses in an especially privileged position. Moses' privilege of knowing God as YHWH makes it all the more incumbent upon him to respond faithfully to God's charge laid upon him. Despite Moses' disappointment and quick abandonment of speaking prophetically in the name of YHWH, this is the name that is to be used and which will be honored by God in acts of power.

Moreover, the expression "I am YHWH" has a resonance that suggests a further significance beyond that of the immediate narrative context. From the likely perspective of the narrator, the expression is well known and rich in association from its use in the regular worship of Israel.[30] This means that the familiar language of Israel's worship is related to Moses and the Exodus. The reader is encouraged to see Moses as archetypal priest as well as archetypal prophet, the model of all who speak in YHWH's name within Israel's worship. These authoritative pronouncements in YHWH's name are rooted in YHWH's authoritative reassurance to Moses and Israel when in doubt whether YHWH really was a God who would deliver them from slavery in Egypt.

Thus the purpose of Exod. 6:2-3 is related to the purpose of the divine speech as a whole—a reassurance to Moses rooted in God's covenant with the patriarchs, a reaffirmation of his commission, a reminder of the privileged knowledge of God he was given at the burning bush and of what this will mean for him and for Israel. Although we will return to the exegesis and interpretation of Exod. 6:2-3 in the next chapter to amplify and defend the interpretation offered here,[31] enough has been said to make clear the sense of the passage in relation to our argument.

The Interpretation of Exodus 6:2-3 in Relation to the Priestly Document

At this point it will be appropriate briefly to relate our interpretation to the conventional understanding of the passage as a parallel, not a sequence, to the account of Moses' call in Exodus 3. As Noth put it, "There can be no doubt that in 6.2ff. we have the P version of the same incident as appeared in the JE version in 3.1ff."[32]

30. See esp. W. Zimmerli, "I am Yahweh," in his *I am Yahweh* (Atlanta: John Knox, 1982), 1–28.

31. See below, pp. 55ff.

32. M. Noth, *Exodus* (London: SCM, 1962; German, 1959), 58.

Our interpretation has concentrated on reading the text as it stands, where Exod. 6:2ff. is clearly a reassurance and reaffirmation of Moses' call in Exodus 3, but this is not necessarily incompatible with the text having once functioned in a different way. Again, as Noth put it, "The result [of the work of the pentateuchal redactor] is that within the sequence of events in the Pentateuch as a whole [Exod. 6:2ff.] now appears in connection with the promise of 6.1 as a confirmation of the commission given to Moses and an invitation to make new demands of Pharaoh. The wording, however, shows that originally this was an independent treatment of the theme of the one call and commissioning of Moses."[33]

The crucial issue to decide is not the distinctiveness of much of the P material in the Pentateuch, about which there remains a strong consensus even amidst the current uncertainties about pentateuchal criticism. The question is rather whether P was in origin an independent account of Israel's history and traditions, parallel to the JE account as in conventional pentateuchal criticism, or whether it was from the outset dependent on the JE account as an interpretative development of it. This latter position has been advocated on a number of occasions, in a well-known essay by F. M. Cross,[34] and also by J. Van Seters, R. Rendtorff, and E. Blum in their proposals for a new approach to pentateuchal criticism.[35] The proposal, however, has remained a minority option that has not yet found favor, either among Exodus commentators,[36] or among pentateuchal critics more gener-

33. Ibid.

34. F. M. Cross, "The Priestly Work," in his *Canaanite Myth and Hebrew Epic* (Cambridge, Mass.: Harvard Univ. Press, 1973), 293–325.

35. J. Van Seters, *Abraham in History and Tradition* (New Haven and London: Yale Univ. Press, 1975), 285; R. Rendtorff, *The Problem of the Process of Transmission in the Pentateuch,* JSOTS 89 (Sheffield: JSOT, 1990; German, 1977), 136–70, esp. 169–70; E. Blum, *Die Komposition der Vätergeschichte,* WMANT 57 (Neukirchen-Vluyn: Neukirchener Verlag, 1984), 420–58. Blum has a useful survey and bibliography of other scholars who have proposed understanding P in this way (pp. 425–26). See also Blum's important *Studien zur Komposition des Pentateuch,* BZAW 189 (Berlin: de Gruyter, 1990). Another interesting study is J.-L. Ska, "La Place d' Ex 6.2-8 dans la narration de l'exode," *ZAW* 94 (1982): 530–48.

36. See, e.g., Childs, *Exodus,* 111, 114; Durham, *Exodus,* 73–4, 77; Schmidt, *Exodus,* 270–72.

ally.[37] This is not the place to try to engage with the issue as a whole, but it is appropriate to indicate how our understanding of Exodus 6 relates to the debate.

Our reading of the text has shown the extent to which the function of Exod. 6:2-3 is complementary to that of Exod. 3:13-15. Each passage is appropriate to its context. Generally speaking, we can fairly say that the consensus view of 6:2-3 as an independent account of the revelation of the name YHWH has always been weak in terms of exegesis in context. There have always been objections, which are well set out by B. Jacob,[38] to the effect that the phrase "I am YHWH" does not function to introduce a new name and that the point of the passage is the reassurance to Moses about the character of God. The force of these objections is recognized by Childs.[39] Admittedly, these objections have usually been advanced with regard to the problem posed by the usage of YHWH in Genesis (which we will consider in the next chapter), but they remain cogent within the context of the book of Exodus itself where Exodus 6 does not portray the revelation of the name YHWH simply because the name has already been revealed in Exodus 3.

The strength of the consensus view has rested on three considerations: the repetitive nature of Exod. 6:2—7:13 when set alongside Exodus 3–4; the terminology characteristic of P that is not present in Exodus 3–4; and the plain sense of Exod. 6:3b as indicating that the name YHWH is newly given to Moses.

The repetitive nature of the text is perhaps the least weighty consideration. As the story of Exod. 2:23—7:7 stands, Moses' response to the call of God is a gradual process of reluctance, obstacles, and disappointment being met by repeated reassur-

37. See, e.g., J. A. Emerton, "The Priestly Writer in Genesis," *JTS* 39 (1988): 381–400; K. Koch, "P—Kein Redaktor! Erinnerung an zwei Eckdaten der Quellenscheidung," *VT* 37 (1987): 446–67. Interestingly, Koch discusses Exod. 6:2-8 as a test case (pp. 462–66) and sees the fundamental argument for the original independence of P to be the extensive use of the name YHWH in Genesis. This is the issue we discuss in the next chapter. Koch nowhere engages with the kind of considerations we propose here and in the next chapter.

38. B. Jacob, *The Second Book of the Bible: Exodus* (New Jersey: Ktav, 1991), ad loc.

39. Childs, *Exodus,* 113.

ances from God; the process is not straightforward but uneven and full of surprises, as, for example, a high point (4:31) is followed by a low point (5:21-23), and Moses continues to be hesitant (6:12) even after YHWH's reassurance (6:2-8). Finally, however, Moses reaches a point where he can speak and act confidently and consistently in YHWH's name. Once one has felt the force of this portrayal, it is difficult not to feel that it is an intentional and integral part of the tradition. It could simply mean that a redactor of parallel traditions did the job well, but equally it could remove the need to hypothesize the redactor in the first place. As for the distinctive P terminology of the passage, that in no way requires only one way of envisaging the Priestly process within the Pentateuch and is perfectly compatible with P as a development of an existing narrative tradition. With regard to Exod. 6:3b, it is indeed the case that the name YHWH is newly given to Moses—but it is in Exodus 3 that the disclosure is made (and the usage in Genesis will be considered in the next chapter).

In addition to these considerations, a number of other considerations must be taken into account which support the view that Exodus 6 is inherently a sequel, not a parallel, to Exodus 3. First and foremost, in Exodus 3 the revelation of the divine name is at the holy sanctuary of the mountain of God, forming the nexus YHWH-Sinai-Moses-Israel. In Exodus 6 the context is Egypt, which would seem an intrinsically odd place for any Israelite tradition to have envisaged the revelation of the divine name taking place, least of all P given P's customary association of YHWH with holiness and YHWH's sanctuary, especially when precisely such an association is already present in the tradition of Exodus 3.[40] Second, it is only in Exodus 3 that Israel is depicted as wanting to know about the name of their ancestral God and that Moses is instructed to tell Israel that YHWH is God's name. In Exodus 6, the passing reference to the newness of the divine

40. The reference in Ezek. 20:5 to God making a self-revelation to Israel in the land of Egypt and saying to them, "I am YHWH your God," does not tell against this. For the Ezekiel passage does not mention the role of Moses and is not concerned with the distinctions present within the Exodus text. Rather it is making the general point that God's dealings with Israel as YHWH go back to the time of Israel's captivity in Egypt.

name is addressed to Moses alone and is not part of his message to Israel.

Certain lesser features of the text also support this understanding. Exodus 3 contains a theophany, an appropriate context for the revelation of God's name; Exodus 6 contains no theophany. Exodus 3 includes an explicit revelation of the divine name; Exodus 6 includes no explicit revelation of the name but rather a passing reference to its newness. In Exodus 3, the concern is with the name of God in relation to the mission of Moses; in Exodus 6, after Moses' initial disappointment, the question is whether God really will deliver Israel, and so the focus is on God's character in relation to God's commitment to Israel. In Exodus 3, God's commitment to Israel on account of their ancestors is only implicit in the title "God of your fathers"; in Exodus 6, when Moses needs reassurance, this commitment is made explicit in terms of a covenant.

In the light of all these considerations together, I find it highly improbable that Exod. 6:2-8 was ever intended to function as an independent account parallel to Exodus 3. Rather, it seems far more likely that it was composed for the context within which it now stands.

Finally, despite their differences, we must emphasize that on three crucial points Exodus 3 and Exodus 6 are identical. The first is that God was revealed to Moses, on behalf of Israel, as having the name YHWH. The second is that Moses and Israel did not previously know this name. The third is that it is the God of the patriarchs, Israel's ancestral God, who is revealed as YHWH. Both passages thus make the assumption that although it is one and the same God who was God of the patriarchs and is God of Israel, something is novel and discontinuous in this God's self-revelation to Moses as YHWH. The possible theological significance of this combination of continuity and discontinuity within God and the divine dealings with the people of God is the crucial issue that is in due course to be explored.

CHAPTER 2

Why Is the Name YHWH Used in Genesis?

In our exposition of Exod. 3:13-15 and 6:2-3 we have argued that the text portrays the name YHWH as newly revealed to Moses and hitherto unknown. Before going any further we must consider the one obvious objection to this scheme of things. This is the simple fact that the name YHWH is not first used in Exodus, as the preceding exposition might perhaps have led one to expect, but rather is used and used extensively within Genesis. How is this to be explained?

Our own answer to this, which forms an essential part of our thesis, can be stated briefly. The use of the name YHWH in Genesis conveys the perspective of the storytellers who tell the originally non-Yahwistic patriarchal stories from within the context of Mosaic Yahwism. As the storytellers take for granted that YHWH the God of Israel is also the God of Abraham, Isaac, and Jacob, they feel free to use the familiar divine name when telling the stories of their ancestors, even though they are aware that the name was first disclosed to Moses. It is our thesis that all the pentateuchal writers share a common tradition that the divine name was first revealed by God to Moses, and yet all feel free to use the divine name where they consider appropriate in the patriarchal stories. Like most traditional storytellers, the pentateuchal narrators to some extent merge their own perspective with that of the stories they tell—and no doubt would not have been greatly moved by the criticism that from a strictly historical perspective such a practice entails anachronism. This answer will be elaborated a little more later on, but a brief statement is sufficient at present, since the essential point is easy to grasp.

It must be admitted that this proposal is, in a sense, nothing new. In general terms it has not infrequently been suggested as a possible explanation for the use of the divine name in Genesis. John Bright, for example, comments that "all the patriarchal narratives were written from the point of view of Yahwistic theology by men who were worshipers of Yahweh; whether they used the name or not, they had no doubt that the God of the patriarchs was actually Yahweh, God of Israel, whom the patriarchs, whether consciously or unconsciously, worshiped." (He goes on, appropriately to his own concerns, to reassert his historian's agenda: "Nevertheless, we cannot impose the faith of later Israel on the patriarchs. Theologically legitimate though it may be to do so, it is not historically accurate to say that the God of the patriarchs was Yahweh.")[1] Even with regard to the issue of the processes of composition embodied in the pentateuchal narratives of Genesis and Exodus, the proposal is not without precedent. As long ago as the twelfth century, in the course of his commentary on Exod. 6:3, Ibn Ezra mentioned (though only to rebut) a Rabbi Joshua, who had suggested that all the occurrences of YHWH in Genesis were additions to the stories made by Moses himself,[2] and this same proposal has also been made in more recent times.[3] What is entirely lacking, however, is any

1. J. Bright, *A History of Israel,* 3d ed. (London: SCM, 1981), 97. Cf. the passing mention of this as a possible explanation of the use of the divine name in Genesis in H. J. Flanders, R. W. Crapps, and D. A. Smith, *People of the Covenant: An Introduction to the Old Testament,* 3d ed. (New York and Oxford: Oxford Univ. Press, 1988), 166.

2. See Ibn Ezra on Exod. 6:3 in the *Mikra'ot Gedolot: Shemot* (p. 76 in my Jerusalem edition of 1971).

3. It is a remarkable fact that not only the problem we are concerned with but also the solution we advocate were both clearly enunciated in Spinoza's *Tractatus Theologico-Politicus,* a book which could reasonably be claimed to be the first work of modern biblical criticism. Spinoza writes:

"Before I proceed I ought to explain how it comes that we are often told in Genesis that the patriarchs preached in the name of Jehovah, this being in plain contradiction to the text above quoted [Exod. 6:2-3]. . . . The writer of the Pentateuch did not always speak of things and places by the names they bore in the times of which he was writing, but by the names best known to his contemporaries. God is thus said in the Pentateuch to have been preached by

attempt to develop the possible implications of this proposal in any thorough or systematic way within the context of modern pentateuchal criticism. We undertake to do this here, and it will necessitate a lengthy and detailed discussion.

In some ways, much of the rest of this chapter does not so much take the thesis forward as broaden and consolidate the basic point about the novelty of God's self-revelation to Moses as YHWH. This is made necessary by the fact that my proposal, at least in the way I envisage it, runs counter to a widespread consensus within Old Testament study. Nonetheless, this discussion will enable us to justify and to amplify our interpretation of Exodus 3 and 6 by relating it to contemporary pentateuchal criticism, and will thereby provide a firmer foundation for the superstructure we wish to build upon it.

SETTING THE CONTEXT: A FAMILIAR PUZZLE

The problem of the relationship between Exodus 3 and 6 and the uses of the name YHWH in Genesis is familiar to all Old Testament scholars. Indeed it could not unreasonably be said that the consensus resolution of it provides *the* foundation stone for modern pentateuchal criticism with regard to pentateuchal narrative, comparable to the role that a seventh-century date and a connection with Josiah's reform plays for Deuteronomy in an analysis of pentateuchal law. We will therefore first set out what are the essential factors in the problem and then look at the way modern study has generally sought to resolve it.

The problem has three essential ingredients. First are passages that seem to suggest that God was revealed to the patriarchs explicitly as YHWH—i.e., God says to them, "I am YHWH"—in a way that is incompatible with Exodus 3 and 6. H. H. Rowley, for example, commented that "to find a flat contradiction between Ex. vi.2f, which states that God was not known to the

the patriarchs under the name of Jehovah, not because such was the name by which the patriarchs knew Him, but because this name was the one most reverenced by the Jews" (*A Theologico-Political Treatise* [New York: Dover, 1951. ET from Latin by R. Elwes], 178–79).

For a more recent suggestion of this approach, see F. G. Smith, "Observations on the Use of the Names and Titles of God in Genesis," *Evangelical Quarterly* 40 (1968): 103–9, esp. 105.

patriarchs by the name Yahweh, and passages in Genesis (xv.7, xxviii.13) which represent Him as saying to the patriarchs 'I am Yahweh' is easy."[4]

Second is the explicit statement of Gen. 4:26 that in the primeval period "people began to call upon the name of YHWH." This explicit statement of Gen. 4:26 has been given great weight by modern scholars as crystalizing a tradition to the effect that the name YHWH was known before the time of Moses.

Third are stories in Genesis that are consistently told in terms of YHWH with no apparent evidence of this being a redactional alteration or qualification of an originally different name or title of God. For example, several stories in the Abraham cycle (Genesis 12, 13, 15, 18, 24) display such consistent usage of the name YHWH. Although this factor is less often appealed to than the previous two, it constitutes a consistent corollary and so must equally be taken into account.

There is thus an apparent contradiction between Exodus 3 and 6, which appear to say that the name of YHWH was not known till the time of Moses, and the text of Genesis, focused in Gen. 4:26 (for convenience, we shall refer to Gen. 4:26 in its role of focusing a wider Genesis tradition as Gen. 4:26, etc.), which appears to say that the name of YHWH was known from earliest times, long before Moses. This is the puzzle that has stood at the heart of much modern pentateuchal criticism. How should it be resolved?

THE MODERN CONSENSUS SOLUTION: THE DOCUMENTARY HYPOTHESIS

The consensus of modern scholars has insisted that both the Exodus and the Genesis texts should be taken at their apparent face value: The plain sense of the text reveals two divergent traditions within Israel as to the origin of the name YHWH. These two divergent traditions have been identified with distinct literary sources. On the one hand, Gen. 4:26 and the material in

4. H. H. Rowley, *From Joseph to Joshua* (London: Oxford Univ. Press, 1950), 149; cf. W. H. Schmidt, *Exodus,* BKAT 2 (Neukirchen-Vluyn: Neukirchener Verlag, 1977, 1988) 271. Interestingly, these same passages were appealed to by Ibn Ezra in the context of his rebuttal of Rabbi Joshua (cf. n. 2).

Genesis that uses the name YHWH prominently have led to their source being named the Yahwist/Jahwist (J). On the other hand, Exod. 3:13-15 and 6:2-3, together with various Genesis passages that do not use the name YHWH, have been attributed to the Elohist (E) and the Priestly writer (P) respectively. This has become such a commonplace of modern scholarship that it is routinely mentioned without need for justification in most standard works on the Old Testament.

For example, W. Zimmerli begins his Old Testament theology with a discussion of the divine name and says at the outset, "How does the faith of the Old Testament come by its knowledge of the name of its God? The Old Testament can be heard to give various answers: a) J uses the name 'Yahweh' without hesitation even in the primal history and the patriarchal narratives. In the context of J, the statement in Genesis 4:26 stands out. . . . b) E and P take a different approach. Each in its own way represents a specific view of how the name of Yahweh was revealed. According to both, this takes place in the time of Moses. . . ."[5] In a recent Old Testament introduction A. Ohler says with regard to the origins of Israel's knowledge of the name YHWH that "the witness of the Bible is not quite clear upon this point." After outlining the supposedly differing viewpoints she sums up, "Did Israel learn through Moses the name of Yahweh and its interpretation [i.e., Exod. 3:10-15, ascribed to E], or only the name [i.e., Exod. 6:2-8, ascribed to P], or was the name known very much earlier [i.e., Gen. 4:26, ascribed to J]?"[6] J. M. Miller and J. H. Hayes in their recent textbook history of Israel say, "The origins of Yahwism are hidden in mystery. Even the final edited form of Genesis–II Kings presents diverse views on the matter. Thus Gen. 4:26, attributed by literary critics to the so-called 'Yahwistic' source, traces the worship of Yahweh back to the earliest days of the human race, while other passages trace the revelation and worship of Yahweh back to Moses (Ex. 6:3)."[7]

5. W. Zimmerli, *Old Testament Theology in Outline* (Edinburgh: T. & T. Clark, 1978; German, 1972, 1975), 18.

6. A. Ohler, *Studying the Old Testament: From Tradition to Canon* (Edinburgh: T. & T. Clark, 1985; German, 1972–73), 22.

7. J. M. Miller and J. H. Hayes, *A History of Ancient Israel and Judah* (London: SCM, 1986), 111. One may also note the unargued presentation of this view in works that seek to popularize the findings of modern biblical

The contradiction between these sources has been variously interpreted. Generally speaking, the most common approach has been to suggest that J and E/P represent the historical traditions of separate groups within the nation of Israel. Thus, for example, T. W. Mann comments concerning Exod. 6:2-3 that it "clearly contradicts much of the book of Genesis, but it may accurately reflect the background of some groups within 'Israel' who had never heard of Yahweh until they encountered the God of the Exodus story."[8] A classic exposition of this approach was offered by H. H. Rowley in his *From Joseph to Joshua.* According to Rowley, the introduction of the worship of YHWH under Moses, as in E and P, represents the historical tradition of those tribes who were led by Moses and subsequently became the northern tribes of Israel. The pre-Mosaic worship of YHWH, as in J, was confined to that group of southern tribes which became part of historical Israel but had not, in fact, come under the leadership of Moses. That is, different tribes first came to worship God as YHWH at different times. Thus the differing statements as to the origins of the worship of YHWH can both be seen to be rooted in historical tradition, and their difference serves to reveal something of the diversity of the groups that were incorporated within historical Israel.[9]

In fact, one may easily get the impression from reading the numerous expositions of this general approach that it may be considered something of a model of how historically oriented criticism can satisfactorily explain, and in one way resolve, contradictions in the biblical text without recourse to the special pleading or strained exegesis that brings biblical study into scholarly disrepute. As long as the modern reader has an appropriate historical awareness then there is actually no real contradiction in the text.[10]

scholarship for a wide audience; see, e.g., R. E. Brown, J. A. Fitzmyer, and R. E. Murphy, eds., *The New Jerome Biblical Commentary,* 2d ed. (London: Chapman, 1990), 47.

8. T. W. Mann, *The Book of the Torah: The Narrative Integrity of the Pentateuch* (Atlanta: John Knox, 1988), 170 n. 3.

9. Rowley, *From Joseph to Joshua,* 149, 153–55.

10. A good example of the kind of confidence felt by early popularizers of modern historically oriented biblical criticism can be found in A. H. McNeile, *The Book of Exodus* (London: Methuen, 1908, 1917, 1931), 34. It is the more

The way in which this approach attempts to do justice to the plain meaning of the text, combined with the way in which (in conventional pentateuchal criticism) it neatly dovetails with a range of other literary and historical considerations, makes it unsurprising that it should have commanded a wide scholarly consensus. Admittedly, recent debate has made it no longer possible to take for granted a consensus on pentateuchal criticism. Nonetheless, it is remarkable that, to the best of my knowledge, not one of the recent critiques of conventional pentateuchal criticism has offered or even attempted to offer a convincing alternative explanation of the puzzle of the divine name.[11] It is not difficult to point to inadequacies in conventional source criticism based (in part, as the case was always cumulative) on alternation in the use of YHWH and Elohim. But to do so without offering a preferable alternative explanation of Exodus 3 and 6 and the usage of YHWH within Genesis is of only limited value.[12] I do

telling both because of its ignorance of Jewish biblical scholarship and because it is so at variance with contemporary critical moods. Commenting on Exod. 6:3 McNeile writes, "A signal instance of the gradual way in which God leads his people into a fuller understanding of His word is afforded by the fact that it is only in the last 150 years that the attention of students has been arrested by these verses. How is it that though God here says that up to this point His name Yahweh has not been known, yet in the book of Genesis the patriarchs appear to know it well and use it freely? The question cannot be answered except by the recognition that varying traditions have been incorporated from different sources."

11. The following critiques of the consensus have no discussion of this issue and offer at best a passing reference to it: J. Van Seters, *Abraham in History and Tradition* (New Haven and London: Yale Univ. Press, 1975); H. H. Schmid, *Der Sogenannte Jahwist* (Zurich: Theologischer Verlag, 1976); R. Rendtorff, *The Problem of the Process of Transmission in the Pentateuch,* JSOTS 89 (Sheffield: JSOT, 1990); E. Blum, *Die Komposition der Vätergeschichte,* WMANT 57 (Neukirchen-Vluyn: Neukirchener Verlag, 1984); T. L. Thompson, *The Historicity of the Patriarchal Narratives,* BZAW 133 (Berlin and New York: de Gruyter, 1974), and *The Origin Tradition of Ancient Israel: I. The Literary Formation of Genesis and Exodus 1–23,* JSOTS 55 (Sheffield: JSOT, 1987).

12. The nearest approach to a fresh engagement with this issue is R. N. Whybray, *The Making of the Pentateuch: A Methodological Study,* JSOTS 53 (Sheffield: JSOT, 1987), 63–72. Whybray convincingly shows the inadequacy of conventional arguments for distinct sources and authors on the basis of varying divine nomenclature. He does not, however, make clear how the tension between Gen. 4:26 and Exod. 3:13-15; 6:2-3 should be explained, even though he appears to favor the sort of solution advocated here.

E. Blum briefly discusses the problem in his most recent book, *Studien zur Komposition des Pentateuch,* BZAW 189 (Berlin and New York: de Gruyter,

not think that any of the recent "new looks" at pentateuchal criticism have yet given reason to abandon the statement of Noth that "regardless of scholarly ingenuity, no one has offered a more plausible explanation of the usage of the divine names than the view that these were two originally independent narrative works, the 'Yahwist' and the 'Elohist,' which were later combined,"[13] and the statement of Weiser that "Exod. 3 and 6 enables us to see that the use of different names for God is based on quite definite theories which point to different trends in the separate sources."[14] An engagement with the consensus view, therefore, must still be the starting point for any would-be alternative view.

Apart from advancing my own positive alternative to the consensus view, we must engage the consensus view on its own terms. It has at least four difficulties even on its own premises, and I will mention them in ascending order of seriousness.

First is the fact that the name YHWH is occasionally used in Genesis in material generally attributed to E and P (e.g., Gen. 20:18; 22:11, 14 [E]; 17:1; 21:1b [P]), which is surprising if E and P strictly maintained, in opposition to J, that the name YHWH was unknown before Moses. If these references were held genuinely to belong to E and P, one would presumably need to argue that E and P were not trying to show that the name YHWH was known but were simply using the familiar name to make a point about the identity of the God of the patriarchs with the God of Moses. But if this be allowed in these passages, it could follow that many other usages of YHWH in Genesis might be so explained, and a major criterion for distinguishing J from E and P would thereby be seriously undermined.

1990), 234–35. He accepts the basic (and questionable) premise that the Genesis passages which use the divine name reveal a tradition at odds with Exod. 6:3. Consequently, he sees Exod. 6:3 as a striking example of Priestly interpretation of an older tradition, a new way of understanding it. Whether, however, the discrepant traditions would have been left juxtaposed in this way, with considerable ingenuity needed on the part of the reader to comprehend them, seems to me highly doubtful.

13. M. Noth, *A History of Pentateuchal Traditions* (Chico: Scholars Press, 1981; German, 1948), 23. Cf. the comments on the criterion of the divine name in C. Westermann, *Genesis 1–11* (Minneapolis: Augsburg; London: SPCK, 1984; German, 1974), 578–80.

14. A. Weiser, *Introduction to the Old Testament* (London: DLT, 1961; German 4th ed., 1957), 74.

Thus the more natural move is to question whether these passages genuinely belong to E and P, and indeed doubts have been expressed about all of them. One can without difficulty explain some of the passages as editorial, arising either from the problems of combining traditions (e.g., Gen. 17:1) or from independent comment on a particular tradition (e.g., Gen. 20:18) or from secondary harmonization with usage elsewhere (e.g., Gen. 22:11). It remains unclear, however, whether all the anomalous references to YHWH (esp. Gen. 22:14a) can be satisfactorily explained in this way, and there is always a danger of the argument becoming circular when it can too easily incorporate contrary evidence by appeal to an editor. These passages, therefore, are not necessarily incompatible with the consensus view, but they do sit a little uneasily within it.

Second, the consensus view does not really explain all that it purports to explain. This is well illustrated by the supposition that in the patriarchal stories (and to a considerable extent elsewhere, too) the Elohist always refers to God by the nonspecific generic term *'elohim,* i.e., "God." It is all very well for Weiser to talk of "quite definite theories" underlying nonusage of the divine name in E and P. But at least with regard to E, nobody has been able to offer a plausible account of what the theory is, especially when the Elohist is set in his generally supposed historical context. This is well put by W. H. Schmidt (a defender of the consensus view) as follows: "How could E have regularly used not the proper name 'Yahweh' but the generic concept 'Elohim' (and this without adding any recognizable distinguishing sign and even without using the article)? This, in the northern kingdom of about 800 B.C., and thus in a situation in which as the Elijah stories and the preaching of Hosea tell us, Yahweh and Baal stood in harsh opposition! No really satisfactory explanation has been found of the fact that this documentary source avoids the name for God that was specific to Israel."[15] Schmidt goes on to suggest that perhaps the usage represents the "author's intention of emphasizing God's transcendence and thus indi-

15. W. H. Schmidt, *Introduction to the Old Testament* (London: SCM, 1984; German, 1979, 1982), 89–90.

rectly a certain universalism about his own faith,"[16] but he clearly realizes that this does not solve the problem.

Not only so, but a documentary analysis tends to obscure possibly significant distinctions within the text, in particular the fact that the distribution of usage of YHWH and Elohim varies considerably. Despite the supposed predominance of the Yahwist in the patriarchal stories as a whole, in fact only in the Abraham cycle does the usage of YHWH predominate. By contrast, in the Jacob cycle, the use of Elohim is considerably more frequent than that of YHWH. And in the Joseph cycle, YHWH is used hardly at all, and the stories use Elohim consistently throughout.[17]

In our proposal, as it will be developed, all these factors can be explained. The regular usage of Elohim is because the writers take seriously the pre-Yahwistic context of the patriarchal stories, a context in which God was naturally referred to by a generic term, since God's name had not yet been revealed. It is consistency with the world of the patriarchs—the issue to be examined in the next chapter—that gives a convincing reason for the usage of Elohim. Yet the usage of YHWH is equally explicable because of the retelling of the patriarchal stories from a Yahwistic perspective and their partial accommodation to that perspective. And in particular, the predominance of YHWH in the Abraham cycle is consistent with the fact that, as we shall see, the Abraham stories have been most accommodated in their retelling to the patterns of Yahwism.[18]

Third is the long-recognized problem of whether conventional documentary analysis may not do violence to the integrity of particular stories. It will be appropriate to consider Exodus 3 in this light, since this story is central to our thesis, and it is a narrative customarily divided into J and E strands. Although some disagreement exists over precise detail and possible editorial glosses, the consensus is that the main narrative is J and that it tells only of a theophany and commissioning (since according to J the divine name is already known) and that all interest in the

16. Ibid., 90.
17. See below, pp. 178f.
18. See below, pp. 135f., 140ff.

divine name in 3:13-15 belongs to E. Thus a common source-critical analysis divides the text as follows: J, 3:1abα (i.e., to "wilderness"), 2-4a, 5, 7-8, 16-22 (and 4:1-16); E, 3:1bβ, 4b, 6, 9-15.[19] Several difficulties with this may be noted.

An old point, given fresh force by recent attention to Hebrew narrative method, is that such an analysis fragments the text in an implausible way. In general terms, the E version is so thin that it lacks all narrative interest yet this minimal narrative setting is considered appropriate for the all-important content of 3:9-15.[20] The J narrative, as the bulk of the text, is more coherent. Yet even here it is unclear how far the commissioning of Moses can stand in this form; according to 3:7-8, 16-17, Moses has to do no more than announce that YHWH will deliver Israel; yet Moses' reluctance to speak and act (4:1, 10, 13) would seem to presuppose precisely the fuller commitment to be God's agent that is only spelled out in the text in 3:9-10.

More specifically, it is unclear how much basis there is in the text for a division into J and E. Although conventionally much has been made of the alternation of divine appellations *('elohim* and *yhwh),* certainly no real difficulty exists with the narrative flow in the opening section, 3:1-6.[21] Thus commentators tend to emphasize the apparent doublet in 3:7-8 and 3:9-10 as the clearest indicator of different literary sources, in the light of which one may look for overlapping sources elsewhere in the narrative also.[22] Yet, as was seen in the previous chapter, 3:9-10 is a

19. For conventional source analysis of Exodus 3 see B. S. Childs, *Exodus,* OTL (London: SCM, 1974), 52. Schmidt (*Exodus,* 109) develops the analysis in comprehensive detail.

20. Noth comments, "In the E version of course the former narrative element [i.e., the encounter with God] has faded away completely; God just suddenly calls Moses by name (v. 4b) and no descriptive details are given either of the surroundings or of how this calling takes place" (*Exodus* [London: SCM, 1962; German, 1959], 38). I find it puzzling that Noth does not appear to regard this "fading away" as in any way problematic.

21. The alternation between YHWH and Elohim in v. 4 may perhaps represent differences of perspective. Thus from the narrator's perspective God is known to be YHWH (v. 4a), while Moses perceives the deity who addresses him as Elohim (v. 4b). Cf. J. Magonet, "The Bush That Never Burnt (Narrative Techniques in Exodus 3 and 6)," *Heythrop Journal* 16 (1975), 304–11; G. Fischer, *Jahwe Unser Gott,* OBO 91 (Freiburg Schweiz: Universitätsverlag/ Göttingen: Vandenhoeck & Ruprecht, 1989), 115–19.

22. See, e.g., Childs, *Exodus,* 53; Schmidt, *Exodus,* 107, 109.

complement, not a parallel, to 3:7-8 because it makes clear that the action of YHWH is to be carried out through the human agency of Moses. Admittedly, the similarity of content in 3:7 and 3:9 makes the narrative style somewhat pleonastic, but that is neither inappropriate in context (given that YHWH's concern for Israel's plight is fundamental to the story and each time does not stand on its own but is linked to the complementary words of deliverance) nor uncharacteristic of Hebrew narrative elsewhere in the Old Testament.[23]

Further, from a form-critical perspective, we also noted in the previous chapter that the customary linkage of 3:13-15 with the first of Moses' objections in 3:11-12 as part of an Elohistic prophetic call narrative runs counter to the fact that, in the sequence of Moses' objections, 3:11 belongs with 4:1 and 4:10 but 3:13-15 stands out as distinctive in both form and content.[24] The conventional attribution of 3:9-15 to E cuts across the most significant distinction present within the text.

Finally, with regard to Exodus 3, conventional analyses have tended to obliterate and have been impervious to dimensions of the text that have become apparent in our interpretation. That is, a division of the text into J and E does no justice to the closely interrelated cluster of "firsts" in Israel's story.[25] The revelation of the divine name is part of a nexus: YHWH-Sinai-holiness-Moses-prophecy-Israel. This nexus is lost in a division of the story into J and E. For example, a reconstructed J version still has reference to holy ground. Yet without reference to the mountain of God,[26] and with no particular significance attaching to the

23. For a discussion of the repeated "and now" *(we'attah)* in 3:9, 10, see Fischer, *Jahwe Unser Gott,* 73. Fischer examines the phenomenon of repeated "and now" throughout the Old Testament and shows that it usually ends a speech in which a person seeks something from someone else. The first "and now" sums up what has already been said, the second continues or draws a consequence from the first and usually introduces a request or task for the other person; see, e.g., 1 Sam. 24:21-2, 25:26-7, 26:19-20.

24. Above, pp. 18f.

25. Above, p. 25.

26. There may still be a hint as to the location if the word for bush, *seneh* (3:2), is meant to evoke the name Sinai. The wordplay, however, is only effective if one already has reason on other grounds to suppose that the place of the theophany may be Israel's known place of encounter with YHWH.

usage of the divine name in this context, the holy ground loses much of its significance. Conversely, a reconstructed E version has the mountain of God and a first use of YHWH but no initial usage of the language of holiness. To observe that the nexus of interrelated significance is lost is not an unanswerable objection, for the concerns of the story as it now stands could always be ascribed to the creative insight of a redactor. Nonetheless the difficulties that are raised by a conventional J and E analysis must at least make one ask again whether this is the most appropriate way of analyzing and understanding the text. The issue is not whether there is traditiohistorical depth within the Exodus 3 tradition, for such depth was basic to our interpretation. The issue is whether an analysis in terms of J and E illuminates rather than obscures the significant processes embodied within the text.

Fourth, the most serious difficulty for the consensus view is posed by the supposed historical persistence of the tradition of YHWH's initial self-disclosure to Moses in the face of the Yahwistic tradition that denied it. While from a modern historical perspective the supposition of different groups with different traditions as a reconstruction of the early history of Israel has an obvious general plausibility, one can hardly ascribe a modern historical perspective on Israel's early traditions to the writers of the Old Testament, not least because the general tenor of pentateuchal traditions with its unified and genealogical understanding of Israel hardly supports most modern historical theories (however much one may argue for evidence for such theories as preserved within the text).

This means that P, conventionally dated the latest of pentateuchal sources, poses a particular difficulty with its tradition of Exod. 6:2-3. It is hardly sufficient to say that P followed the tradition in E (Exod. 3:13-15) and did so because this was a strong and persistent, indeed historically authentic, tradition.[27]

27. F. M. Cross, for example, says, "It is no longer possible to doubt that the Priestly tradition [Exod. 6:2f.] rests ultimately on historical memories preserved in conservative cultic materials" ("Yahweh and the God of the Patriarchs," *HTR* 55 [1962]: 244). Cf. his *Canaanite Myth and Hebrew Epic* (Cambridge, Mass.: Harvard Univ. Press, 1973), 47 and n. 15. Such is the consensus about this point that, strikingly, it is retained in the otherwise arbitrary and speculative account of Israel's origins by J. Dus, "Moses or Joshua? On the Problem of the Founder of the Israelite Religion," *Radical Religion* 2 (1975): 26–41, esp. 27.

For, by conventional reckoning, by the time P was written E had already long since been redactionally combined with J in a narrative sequence in which the editors had used J to provide the structure and most of the content. That is, the tradition that would have been prevalent in the time of P would be one dominated by the Yahwistic tradition of apparent knowledge of YHWH from primeval times with its extensive usage of the divine name in both primeval and patriarchal traditions.

The problem of how P could have come by his tradition is compounded if one asks the related question as to how the pentateuchal traditions about the divine name were understood by the pentateuchal redactors—both those who combined J with E and those who combined JE with P. Each time they would have been faced with the discrepancy between the use of YHWH in Genesis and the Exodus tradition of its disclosure to Moses, and they would have had to make some decision about how to integrate their material. Essentially, three possible stances can be ascribed to the editors, which I give in ascending order of likelihood: ignorance, reverent tolerance, desire to harmonize.

Given the crucial importance of the issue at stake—the name of Israel's God—the supposition that pentateuchal redactors might have been unaware of the discrepancy in their material is in my judgment incredible and may be dismissed without more ado.

A more serious possibility is the supposition that the editors showed such reverence for their material that they wished to preserve each tradition in its own integrity despite the discrepancy between them; piety can tolerate inconsistency. In general historical terms this is entirely plausible. In a common understanding of the redaction of pentateuchal narratives, however, the editors displayed a considerable freedom and range of interpretative moves in their integration of traditions. For example, duplicate or parallel accounts could be handled in at least three different ways: (1) they could be made distinct and sequential (e.g., the wife of the patriarch endangered, Gen. 12:10-20; 20:1-18; 26:6-11; the call of Moses, Exod. 3:1—6:1; 6:1—7:13); (2) they could be merged with each other (e.g., the flood, Gen. 6:5—9:17; the rebellion of Korah, Numbers 16); or (3) one account could be preserved while the other was suppressed (e.g., the P account of the ark, Exod. 25:10-22, with no remaining JE account). If such suppositions are at all justified, it does seem unlikely that in the case of the name of God no serious integrative attempt should have been made.

A fresh attempt to suggest the possibility of reverential preservation of discrepancy was made by S. Sandmel in a stimulating article that was one of the earliest contributions to the current rethinking on pentateuchal criticism. On the basis of the high level of tolerance of formal contradiction in postbiblical Haggadah Sandmel argued that the presence of contradictions within the biblical text simply would not have bothered an ancient editor.[28] But, although some of the latest parts of the Old Testament do begin to exhibit interpretative tendencies of the sort that flourished later, it is simply anachronistic to retroject in any general way the interpretative tendencies of early rabbinic Judaism into the formative period of Israel's literary traditions.

Likewise unconvincing is J. I. Durham's attempt to solve the problem by making Sandmel's point about postbiblical Haggadah into a general principle of theological method. Durham supposes that the different pentateuchal writers each "follow their own and different emphasis" without undue concern for what others have said. He concludes, "Not the least of the merits of such a view is the elimination of the supposed 'conflicts' of Gen 4:26 and Exod 3:13-14 with the present passage [Exod. 6:3] (Sandmel, *HUCA* 32 [1961]: 19–29). Each facet of the account of God's revelation of himself may thus be permitted to reflect the light of man's perception of his Presence in its own distinct way. We should always keep in mind the diversity of our own perceptions of God and not demand of the biblical thinkers a unanimity of experience and a logicality of expression we ourselves cannot demonstrate."[29] It may well be that diversity of viewpoint is a general and indeed necessary aspect of theological insight, and it is certainly true of the Bible taken as a whole. But this in no way

28. S. Sandmel, "The Haggadah within Scripture," *JBL* 80 (1961): 105–22.

29. J. I. Durham, *Exodus*, WBC 3 (Waco, Tex.: Word, 1987), 77. Durham's reference to Sandmel's article, "Genesis 4:26" (*HUCA* 32 [1961]: 19–29), is a little puzzling, for it was Sandmel's article in *JBL* of the same year ("The Haggadah within Scripture," *JBL* 80 [1961]: 105–22) that more fully addressed the issue that concerns Durham.

begins to address the problem of viewpoints that are not simply differing but are in outright contradiction, especially when such viewpoints are juxtaposed in a sequential narrative that is recognized to have been extensively reflected upon and molded accordingly.

This leaves harmonization as the most likely option. In the light of the prominence given to the Yahwistic narrative by the editors the natural harmonizing option would be to suppose that the name YHWH had indeed been revealed in primeval times and that what was new in the call of Moses was not the name as such but rather the giving of a new meaning and significance to an already familiar name. This is clearly a realistic possibility, and, as we shall see, this stance has been adopted by numerous commentators both medieval and modern in their attempts to understand the puzzle in the pentateuchal text.

If harmonization be assumed, however, it does raise its own potential difficulties, especially of method and procedure on the part of the interpreter. It is, of course, perfectly intelligible to surmise that traditions telling of an original disclosure of the name YHWH should have been subsequently reinterpreted to mean the disclosure of the meaning of an already-known name and that the alert historian should be able to discern this shift of meaning within the textual tradition. But what if the editors who made this reinterpretation also modified the text itself so that it should make their meaning clear, with the result that the text as it now stands genuinely bears the harmonistic meaning? It could mean that, even if a reinterpretation had taken place, we might no longer be in a position to know about it. Or one could come full circle and argue that no reinterpretation ever took place because it was not, in fact, needed—the assumption that the developments took place could originate in modern scholarly ingenuity and not in any genuine historical developments in Israel's traditions. The point is that it is not difficult to hypothesize in such a way as to undermine the original premise of the argument that a contradiction exists between Exodus 3 and 6 and the text of Genesis, such that an appeal to diverse traditions is necessary. It is all too easy to saw off the branch one is sitting on.

The recognition of these differing hypothetical possibilities does not, of course, determine which is likely to have been the case. The issue can only be resolved, if at all, by a careful exegesis of the texts in question in conjunction with a persuasive overall model of the development of tradition. It should have become clear, however, that the consensus understanding of diverse historical traditions in the text does create difficulties in relation to Israel's own understanding and molding of its authoritative traditions; in the light of Israel's own extensive interpretative activity on its foundational texts, it is highly questionable whether the pentateuchal text could genuinely bear the kind of meaning that the documentary hypothesis has ascribed to it.

There are, therefore, major difficulties for the consensus resolution of the problem of the divine name, difficulties which in my judgment amount to a virtual refutation. Admittedly, none of the difficulties raised are novel, and responsible scholars have continued to maintain the consensus view even in an awareness of its difficulties. But one may surmise that this is largely because of the absence of a persuasive alternative, which is what any genuine refutation must also be able to offer. Because of this need to find some alternative an increasing number of scholars have begun to abandon the documentary hypothesis and strike out in new directions. Our own positive alternative, the nature of which we have already begun to indicate, will continue to emerge throughout the argument of this book.

Before we continue to develop our own proposal, however, we must look first at an alternative resolution of the apparent contradiction between Gen. 4:26, etc., and Exodus 3 and 6. For, given the apparent contradiction, there is another obvious approach to that already examined. That is, one can look again at each of the crucial passages and check that they have, in fact, been rightly understood. The apparent contradiction may be the result of misunderstanding.

THE TRADITIONAL AND CONSERVATIVE APPROACH: A REAPPRAISAL OF EXODUS 3 AND 6

The view that the contradiction between Gen. 4:26, etc., and Exodus 3 and 6 rests on a misunderstanding of the latter passages has commonly been adopted. In modern study it has been something like a persistent minority report alongside the consensus view already outlined. What was said above about the problem facing the pentateuchal redactors and the way they are likely to have resolved it applies equally to numerous commentators down the ages. As already noted, this is essentially a harmonizing position whose strength lies in the obvious seriousness with which it takes the need to understand the text as meaningful in its own right. The essence of the approach is to argue that what is new in Exodus 3 and 6 is not the name YHWH as such but rather the meaning of the name. If it is the giving of a new and distinctive content to an already familiar name that is the meaning of Exodus 3 and 6, then the apparent contradiction with Gen. 4:26, etc., is resolved. This approach has been particularly favored by traditional and conservative scholars who have felt, rightly or wrongly, that the documentary hypothesis impugned the integrity of the biblical text,[30] though the approach has had a variety of advocates.[31]

Although this approach has been a minority option in modern Old Testament study associated particularly with traditional and conservative scholarship, it is important to emphasize that it represents the most obvious way of reading the text and would most likely be adopted by anyone to whom the puzzle of the

30. See, e.g., Christian scholars such as C. F. Keil and F. Delitzsch, *Commentary on the Old Testament, I: The Pentateuch* (reprint, Grand Rapids: Eerdmans, 1980), 467–68; J. A. Motyer, *The Revelation of the Divine Name* (London: Tyndale Press, 1959); E. A. Martens, *Plot and Purpose in the Old Testament* (Leicester: IVP, 1981), 13 n. 6; W. C. Kaiser, Jr., "Exodus," in F. E. Gaebelein, ed., *The Expositor's Bible Commentary,* vol. 2 (Grand Rapids: Zondervan, 1990), 339–42. This approach is popularized in the *New International Version Study Bible* (London: Hodder & Stoughton, 1985, 1987), 94.

Alternatively one may note the work of Jewish scholars such as B. Jacob, *Exodus,* (New Jersey: Ktav, 1991) ad loc; U. Cassuto, *A Commentary on the Book of Exodus* (Jerusalem: Magnes, 1967; Hebrew, 1951), 77–79; M. H. Segal, *The Pentateuch—Its Composition and Its Authorship, and Other Biblical Studies* (Jerusalem: Magnes, 1967), 5–7; N. Leibowitz, *Studies in Shemot: Exodus,* vol. 1 (Jerusalem: World Zionist Organization, 1976), 132–40.

31. See, e.g., M. Buber, *Moses* (Oxford and London: Phaidon, 1946), 48–55; E. Jacob, *Theology of the Old Testament* (London: Hodder & Stoughton, 1958; French, 1955), 49–50; S. Mowinckel, "The Name of the God of Moses," *HUCA* 32 (1961): 121–33; R. Abba, "The Divine Name Yahweh," *JBL* 80 (1961): 320–38; J. Magonet, "The Rhetoric of God: Exodus 6.2-8," *JSOT* 27 (1983): 65–66; Y. T. Radday, "'Wie ist sein Name?' (Ex 3:13)," *Linguistica Biblica* 58 (1986): 87–104.

divine name was pointed out and who was not aware of the documentary hypothesis as a possible explanation. As a way of trying to understand the text, it appears to be at least as old as Targum Ps-Jonathan.[32] And even when one is prepared to accept the documentary hypothesis, the attractions of this alternative approach remain. This emerges clearly in an interesting recent discussion by W. G. Plaut. When commenting on Exodus 6 Plaut first notes the familiar problem: "This statement [Exod. 6:3] contradicts the frequent occurrence of the name YHVH in Genesis." Second, he outlines the predominant scholarly interpretation in terms of distinct P and J traditions. Third, he alludes in a footnote to what is in essence the position we are advocating—Rabbi Joshua as cited by Ibn Ezra—only to dismiss it as "equally radical [as P and J]." Fourth, he says of the P and J analysis that, "while this explanation overcomes the apparent contradictions, it does not deal with the text as it now is. For we may assume that these problems were as clear to the redactor of the Torah as they are to us."[33] Plaut thus finds himself virtually forced to adopt the traditional position that a new insight into an already familiar

32. Ps.-Jonathan's rendering of Exod. 6:2-3 is as follows: *wmlyl yyy 'm msh w'mr lyh 'n' yyy hw' d'tglyty 'lk bgw snyy' w'mryt lk 'n' yyy: w'ytglyty l'brhm l'yzhq wly'qb b'l sdy wsmy yyy brm b'py skynty l' 'yt'yd't lhwm:* "YHWH spoke with Moses and said to him, 'I am YHWH who was revealed to you in the midst of the bush, and I said to you, I am YHWH. And I was revealed to Abraham, to Isaac, and to Jacob as El Shaddai, and my name YHWH I did not make known to them except in the face of my Shekinah.'" The point of this appears to be that the patriarchs knew God as Israel does, through God's Shekinah, but they did not know the meaning of the divine name as expounded by God to Moses at the burning bush. In its own way, therefore, the Targum would appear to be making the point of Moses being given a new insight into the meaning of an already familiar name.

It is not clear how far there is any attempt to engage with this issue in the earlier versions and Targums. The LXX and Vulgate have "I did not show (οὐκ ἐδήλωσα, non indicavi) my name to them," which probably just represents an attempt to resolve the syntax of the sentence (see further below). Since the relationship of the noun "(my) name" to the verb is unclear, the translators take it as an object and so treat *noda'ti* as equivalent to the Hiphil *hoda'ti.* A simple syntactical resolution is probably more likely than seeing the wording as an attempt to make a point about a mode of disclosure as opposed to simple familiarity with the name (though the latter is not impossible). Similarly, Targums Onkelos and Neofiti more or less follow the Hebrew except that they, too, take "my name" as the object of the verb, which they have in a causative form (Onkelos: *hwd'yt;* Neofiti: *'wd'yt*).

33. W. G. Plaut, ed., *The Torah: A Modern Commentary* (New York: Union of American Hebrew Congregations, 1981), 424–25.

name must be the meaning of the text as it now stands. It must be said, however, that most advocates of this approach regard it as an alternative to the documentary hypothesis, not as a redactional modification developing from it.

With regard to both Exod. 3:13-15 and Exod. 6:2-3 advocates of this approach have put forward numerous arguments, both exegetical and contextual. A brief consideration of them will be useful for testing our own reading of these passages offered in the previous chapter. As the arguments are more straightforward with regard to Exod. 6:2-3, we will consider this second passage first.

A Reappraisal of Exodus 6:2-3

The explicit statement of 6:3b, "and by my name YHWH I did not make myself known to them [i.e., Abraham, Isaac, and Jacob]," is the most serious obstacle to this whole approach. Even if this is only a parenthetical note, if it means what it says—or appears to say—the harmonizing approach is doomed.[34] The

34. It has been not uncommon for conservative scholars to see Exod. 6:3 as the lynchpin of the whole documentary hypothesis, such that if once the harmonizing interpretation can be established over against the consensus interpretation, then the whole documentary hypothesis is, in principle, thereby undermined. See, e.g., R. D. Wilson, "Yahweh (Jehovah) and Exodus 6:3," *Princeton Theological Review* 22 (1924): 108–19, esp. 116 (reprinted in W. C. Kaiser, ed., *Classical Evangelical Essays in Old Testament Interpretation* [Grand Rapids: Baker, 1972], 29–39); W. J. Martin, *Stylistic Criteria and the Analysis of the Pentateuch* (London: Tyndale Press, 1955); S. D. Glisson, "Exodus 6:3 in Pentateuchal Criticism," *Restoration Quarterly* 28 (1985–86): 135–43; G. E. Whitney, "Alternative Interpretations of *lōʾ* in Exodus 6:3 and Jeremiah 7:22," *WTJ* 48 (1986): 151–59.

The claims of W. J. Martin are particularly extravagant: "It is on the basis of the accepted translation of this verse [Exod. 6:3], that the theory of the composite character of the Pentateuch has been most confidently defended. On examination, it becomes apparent that the argument depends . . . on a single word and that a mere particle, the negative *lo*. Probably never in the whole history of exegesis, whether classical or biblical, has so much been made to depend on a single word. . . . The removal of this verse would deprive Pentateuchal criticism of its one piece of indisputably objective evidence, for varieties in style can be classed only as subjective. . . . It may seem strange that a superstructure of the intricacy and dimensions of Pentateuchal criticism should have for its first and main foundation a single passage, or to be exact, actually only a particle in the passage" (pp. 16–17, 19). Although Martin's thesis is unwarranted, given the cumulative nature of arguments for the documentary hypothesis, it is clear that for the conservative position everything does indeed stand or fall by the interpretation of this one verse.

necessary strategy, therefore, is to retranslate and/or reinterpret the Hebrew so that it says something else. The difficulty, however, is that the Hebrew presents no serious difficulty. This has meant that, although several ingenious retranslations have been offered, there is no unanimity that any particular rendering has pinpointed *the* matter of grammar, syntax, or vocabulary that has been supposedly misconstrued in the conventional rendering, though one approach does command a reasonable consensus. We will start by considering a couple of minority options.

First, one can recast the clause as a whole, turning the apparently negative statement into a rhetorical question expecting a positive answer. Thus G. R. Driver translates, "I am Jehovah; and I appeared to Abraham, Isaac, and Jacob as God Almighty; and did I not (or, of course I did) let myself be known to them as to my name Jehovah (?)."[35] Interestingly, the only justification Driver offers for this is contextual, in terms of the familiar puzzle, especially how P would have understood existing tradition. He says of the conventional translation that it "is scarcely credible when the reader had been told that 'then men began to call upon the name of Jehovah' (Genesis 4:26, J); the substance if not the actual circumstance of the first passage must have been known to the author of the second passage (cf. Genesis 28:13, J)."[36] Of course, this could be right; but in terms of the problem of the apparent contradiction, it tends to beg the question. What is really needed is evidence within Exod. 6:3 itself that it means something other than the conventional rendering, and there is nothing in the text, such as an interrogative particle, to indicate that the clause is a question. Admittedly, in terms of Hebrew idiom, it is possible to ask a question without an interrogative particle; but the problem is whether there is any justification in terms of the immediate context for finding such a question in 6:3—an issue Driver ignores. W. J. Martin (whose work is referred to by Driver) does offer an argument from the immediate context when he points to the fact that the following words in 6:4 begin with "and also" *(wegam)* and thus imply a positive, not a

35. G. R. Driver, "Affirmation by Exclamatory Negation," *Journal of the Ancient Near Eastern Society of Columbia University* 5 (1973): 109.
36. Ibid.

negative, statement preceding them.[37] We have already seen, however, that the point of 6:3-4, with its appeal back to Genesis 17, is indeed positive but that 6:3b is parenthetical, with 6:4 continuing the positive point of 6:3a.

A different attempt to make 6:3b into a positive statement is offered by F. I. Andersen, who boldly argues that the common Hebrew negative, *lo',* can, in fact, have a positive meaning. He argues that there is a poetic parallelism in 6:2-3. Given the parallelism between "I am YHWH" *('ani yhwh)* and "and my name YHWH" *(ušemi yhwh),* there should also be a parallelism between "I showed myself to Abraham . . ." and "I made myself known to them"; if the former words are positive, then the latter must be also; this parallelism "compels recognition of *lo'* as assertative."[38] Whether, in fact, this parallelism is "compelling" is doubtful to say the least. And how on earth would any reader of biblical Hebrew be expected to recognize that *lo'* here does not have its familiar negative meaning—except, of course, by appeal to the conundrum of the apparent contradiction with Gen. 4:26, etc.? It would appear that for Andersen, as for Driver, arguments about the Hebrew of Exod. 6:3b are only introduced to buttress a conviction about what the text must mean when read against the context of Genesis. The suggestion that *lo'* in 6:3b does not mean "not" needs a far better argument to become remotely plausible.[39]

Probably the most serious option for reinterpreting 6:3b is to build upon a combined grammatical and syntactical point relating to the verb in the clause *noda'ti.* This was the approach adopted by traditional Jewish commentators and is well expressed by Rashi. Rashi argued that, if the Hebrew meant "but I did not make my name YHWH known to them," the verb would need to be Hiphil with a causative sense, i.e., *ušemi yhwh*

37. Martin, *Stylistic Criteria,* 18.

38. F. I. Andersen, *The Sentence in Biblical Hebrew* (The Hague: Mouton, 1974), 102.

39. G. E. Whitney ("Alternative Interpretations") gives examples of passages where *lo'* has the meaning of "not only" (e.g., Exod. 16:8, 1 Sam. 8:7) and argues that it has this meaning in Exod. 6:3. In the context of Exod. 6:3, however, such a rendering makes little sense and depends entirely on the conflict with the usage of the divine name in Genesis.

lo' hoda'ti lahem.[40] The form *noda'ti* is Niphal, which must have a reflexive or passive sense with God as the subject; when this is construed with the negative it must mean "I did not make myself known" or "I was not known." This means that the syntax of "my name YHWH" is not entirely clear, but it cannot be either the subject ("my name YHWH was not known") or the direct object ("I did not make my name YHWH known") of the clause. Syntactically, it may either be construed with the preposition *be,* that is, "by," which could be carried over from *be'el šadday* in 6:3a, or else be a double subject or an internal accusative (in terms of translation it probably makes little difference),[41] that is, "by/as to my name YHWH, I did not make myself known to them." The point of all this is that the emphasis on what was not known is on *God as YHWH;* that is, the text is clearly making a point primarily about the character of God as revealed differently to the patriarchs and to Moses, not about the patriarchs' ignorance of a particular word. This then opens the possibility that what was denied to the patriarchs was solely knowledge of the meaning of the name, rather than the name as such. Thus J. A. Motyer, who carefully develops this line of argument, translates 6:2-3, "And God spoke to Moses, and said to him: I am Yahweh. And I showed myself to Abraham, to Isaac, and to Jacob in the character of El Shaddai, but in the character expressed by my name Yahweh I did not make myself known to them."[42]

It should be noted, however, that at most this argument shows the possibility of drawing a distinction in 6:3b between knowledge of the name (which the patriarchs had) and knowledge of its meaning (which is given to Moses), not that such a distinction is necessary. Given the fact that the text is indeed drawing attention to the meaning implied by the name YHWH by way of contrast to El Shaddai, the text may just as well mean that both the name and its meaning were not given to the patriarchs but are given to Moses. Indeed, this latter sense is much more likely (in

40. M. Rosenbaum and A. M. Silbermann, eds., *The Pentateuch with the Commentary of Rashi: Exodus* (Jerusalem: Silbermann, 1972), 24.

41. See, e.g., Schmidt, *Exodus,* 268; Houtman, *Exodus I (1:1—7:13)* (Kampen: J. H. Kok, 1986), 470.

42. Motyer, *Revelation,* 11–17, esp. 12.

the light of our interpretation in the previous chapter), unless one already has good reason to suppose that the name YHWH could not now be revealed for the first time—which simply brings one back to the wider contextual issue about the use of the divine name in Genesis.

A Reappraisal of Exodus 3:13-15

With regard to Exod. 3:13-15, the exegetical issue is similar to 6:2-3. Apart from appeal to the wider context, attention has focused on the precise meaning of the imagined question "What is his name?" *(mah šemo).* Some argue that the meaning of the question is effectively "What is the meaning of his name?" and that therefore the question would not be a request for a new and hitherto unknown name but rather for elucidation of the implications of an already familiar name.[43]

The justification for this is twofold. First, *mah* can undoubtedly have the sense of "what is the meaning of?" as, for example, in the phrase *mah ha'edoth* (Deut. 6:20), which RSV renders "What is the meaning of the testimonies?" Indeed *mah* has this sense in all the examples of the child's question already noted previously (Exod. 12:26; 13:14; Josh. 4:6, 21). Second, Judg. 13:17 gives one unambiguous instance in the Hebrew Bible when an unknown name is asked for and the wording of the question is *mi šemeka* (lit., "Who is your name?") rather than *mah šemeka* (lit., "What is your name?"). If Exod. 3:13 were a request for an unknown name, would not therefore the Hebrew use *mi* rather than *mah?*[44]

It is indeed a valuable insight that the Hebrew *mah šemo* is concerned with the meaning of the name. Again, however, the crucial issue is whether a concern with the meaning of the name entails that the name itself must already be known and excludes the possibility that the name as well as its meaning is given.

43. See, e.g., Motyer (*Revelation,* 17–24), developing the suggestion of Buber (*Moses,* 48), which was itself the representation of a classic Jewish understanding.

44. Interpreters of Exod. 3:13 have also commonly appealed to the similar question in Gen. 32:27. But since the precise meaning of Gen. 32:27 is itself a matter of debate, it is unclear how far the verse can assist in the elucidation of Exod. 3:13.

Although one may maintain the former as a theoretical possibility, it in no way follows that it should be preferred to the view that both a name hitherto unknown and an indication of its meaning is being given. Indeed, rather than being a case of either/or it is more likely a case of both/and.[45] This decision is not arbitrary, for we have already seen that the newness of the divine name in Exodus 3 is part of a whole interrelated nexus of "firsts" in Israel's story in Exodus 3, and we can still offer an explanation for the use of the divine name in Genesis. Moreover, it should be noted that despite the usage of *mi šemeka* in Judg. 13:17, it does not follow that *mah* as well as *mi* would not be an acceptable way in biblical Hebrew of asking what someone's name is.[46] There is no compelling idiomatic reason, therefore, why the question should not be understood as asking both for a name that is not known and for the meaning of that name.

Contextually, two arguments with regard to 3:13-15 are advanced. One has to do with the familiar wider context—the use of the name already in Genesis. We need not go further into that here.

The second argument concerns the specific context of Exodus 3 and the likely problems posed by Moses' imagined initial public encounter with Israel (3:13). Although the interpretation we offered in the previous chapter is perfectly coherent and meaningful in terms of the story on one level, on another level it does not resolve questions that may naturally be asked, questions about the implications of Israel's and Moses' supposed ignorance of the name YHWH prior to its disclosure to Moses. For as soon as one tries to imagine a plausible scenario for the announcement of a new divine name, the whole thing becomes peculiarly problematic.

In the first place, if Israel already knew and worshiped the God who had sent Moses as "God of their fathers," why should they want to ask for God's name rather than simply respond to what Moses said? Their question seems unnecessary. This would appear to mean that their question could only be a genuine one

45. Cf. Childs, *Exodus,* 74–77. Childs also comments similarly on Exod. 6:2-3 (*Exodus,* 113).

46. *BHS* notes this reading in some Hebrew MSS at Judg. 13:17.

either if they themselves were uncertain about the identity of this deity (presumably because of their living in a polytheistic culture) or if they knew about their God but wished to test Moses to see if he also knew. In the former case, if Israel were in fact uncertain about the identity of the deity sending Moses, how on earth would their question achieve the purpose of establishing the divine identity to their own satisfaction if in answer they were given a new and hitherto unknown name? It would seem, therefore, that if Moses' answer with the name YHWH were to resolve any difficulty then that name must already be known to Israel in some way. The question would only seem to be realistic if it were some kind of test of Moses—for example, asking him to validate himself by showing knowledge of the name of God which every true Israelite (or at least every aspiring leader within Israel) was supposed to know but which Moses, coming as he did from Midian, might not know (such a test would be more rigorous if knowledge of the name YHWH was not widespread within Israel but was a secret cult name).[47]

In short, the problem may be expressed this way: In real life, if

47. The following are two typical expressions of this approach. F. I. Andersen comments, "There is no hint in Exodus that YHWH was a new name revealed first to Moses. On the contrary, the success of his mission depended on the use of the familiar name for validation by the Israelites. Moses interrogated the Revealer precisely to convince himself that it really was the god of the ancestors who had called him . . . the secret name was certainly known to the Israelites and to God himself *[sic]*" (*Sentence,* 102).

N. M. Sarna comments, "The present text of Exodus 3:14-15 implies a new departure, for Moses himself does not know this Name. But he assumes that the people do; otherwise, why should they find Moses' reply either meaningful or acceptable? How would it authenticate him in their eyes if they were ignorant of it?" (*Exploring Exodus: The Heritage of Biblical Israel* [New York: Schocken, 1987], 51).

Rather more imaginatively, though at the same time more questionably, S. Mowinckel offers a possible reconstruction of the scenario envisaged in Exod. 3:13. When Moses would say, "God has sent me," the people would answer, as in Exod. 5:2, "Which God?" to which Moses would respond, "The God of our Fathers." But then the people would say, "The god of our fathers, you say! But do you not know his name? Otherwise how can we believe that it is He who has spoken to you and sent you? There are hundreds of gods . . ." Against these objections "Moses could only legitimatize himself by telling them *the name* of the god of their fathers, his real cult name, not only some secondary epithet." Likewise, it would be necessary for Moses himself to know that the numen in the bush really was the god of the fathers and not a "malicious demoniac being" ("The Name of the God of Moses," *HUCA* 32 [1961]: 122–24).

Moses encountered Israel as a virtual outsider, how could he, as a would-be prophet, validate his mission by announcing or appealing to a previously unheard-of God? Since a previously unheard-of God would presumably have little or no probative value, the name of God for which Moses asks must already have been known to Israel; otherwise the imagined scenario is implausible. The text does not seem to be trying to show simply how Moses came to know the name of God that Israel already knew. (This would make its purpose curiously trivial.) Instead it draws attention to the meaning of the name, both by the question with *mah* and by the answer that is given in 3:14. So the narrative must be portraying Moses acquiring and imparting a new understanding of the meaning of an already familiar name. And Moses' ability to convey such an insight into the character of Israel's God would validate his mission.

This line of argument has undoubted force. Nonetheless it suffers from at least two serious weaknesses. One is that it does not sufficiently address the issue of the genre of the material and so tends to beg the crucial question of what kind of inference may legitimately be drawn from the text. The other is that it does not sufficiently examine the possible theological presuppositions of the narrator. Obviously a major difficulty here is that in our modern context we are so far removed from the literary conventions and theological presuppositions of ancient Israel that we don't know exactly what kind of material we are dealing with. So at best we can only make educated suggestions in the light of prolonged engagement with the narrative traditions of the Old Testament and also comparative literary and historical study. In practice, the best procedure is to see what kind of inferences the text is open to and what ones it is impervious to and to make decisions about genre and presupposition on such an inductive basis. The very difficulty involved in trying to imagine a plausible and coherent scenario may be extremely significant as an indicator that this is not, in fact, an appropriate way to handle the text.

On the one hand, we must take seriously the somewhat abstract and hypothetical character of 3:13, with its likely function as a paradigmatic and didactic text.[48] Although it belongs to

48. Above, p. 20.

the narrative of Moses' objections to his commissioning, it stands out from it, and unless we take this seriously we will likely misconstrue the significance of the text.

On the other hand, the supposition (basic to this whole line of argument) that the people of Israel might perhaps have a problem about the identity of the deity who sent Moses if that deity's name were not already familiar to them introduces a conceptual possibility surely alien to the Exodus writer (and indeed to other Old Testament writers also). Within the immediate context of Exodus, Israel's imagined reluctance to believe that YHWH has really spoken to Moses (Exod. 4:1) is in no sense a theoretical problem of the identity of the deity but is rather a matter of weakness of will that is to be overcome by a demonstration of power. Only the Egyptian pharaoh refuses to acknowledge what Moses is saying on the grounds that he has never heard of the deity in question. And even for the pharaoh the real issue is less one of divine identity than a matter of will (a "hardened heart") that must be overcome by acts of power.

More generally the notion that a test of divine identity might ever be needed is quite alien to the writers of the Old Testament. They simply never raise as a significant possibility that one might need to establish that Israel's God, rather than some other deity, is speaking. Even when the issue of discernment is explicitly raised in the course of debates over true and false prophecy, the issue is never that of discerning YHWH as opposed to some other deity. A non-Israelite prophet such as Balaam speaks at YHWH's behest (Numbers 22–24), while false prophets within Israel are seen either as operating at YHWH's behest in one way or other (e.g., Deut. 13:1-5; 1 Kings 22:19-23; Ezek. 14:9) or as deriving their message from within themselves (e.g., Jer. 23:16-32; Ezek. 13:2-3, 17). Other gods may not always have their existence denied, but the possibility that they might speak to or within Israel or that they might be confused with YHWH is never entertained by any writer of the Old Testament.

Generally speaking, the difficulty seems to lie in trying to treat the realistic and historylike character of the narrative as though it were actually translatable into historical categories such as, How and why might these events actually have occurred? This problem has perhaps been particularly acute in Exodus 3, where a consensus of scholars has felt the basic tradition underlying the text is extremely ancient and most likely rooted in some way in historical fact. Although it has been recognized that this ancient tradition has been overlaid and developed in various ways, a recurrent assumption is that the modern interpreter can still discern certain ancient and unchanged aspects of the tradition.[49]

Much of the problem lies in this assumption, in general terms not in itself unreasonable, that original aspects of the text have somehow, like literary fossils, retained their original nature despite the ongoing tradition process. But although I do not doubt the antiquity of the Exodus 3 tradition relative to its present literary form, I do doubt whether anything in the tradition has escaped the molding influence of the use and interpretation of the tradition within the life of Israel. At every point, therefore, one must respect and seek to understand the text on its own terms. This means, first and foremost, that one must recognize that the whole story is thoroughly imbued with a Yahwistic, indeed in some way monotheistic, perspective. The historical questions of how Israel first came to know God as YHWH, the role of Moses within the origins of Yahwism, and how, when, and why Yahwism became monotheistic are all legitimate questions. But as historical questions they represent concerns to which the text of Exodus 3 is more or less opaque. For the Hebrew writer is writing from a mature Yahwistic and monotheistic perspective in which he takes for granted, and incorporates in the story, assumptions that could not be taken for granted if one tries to imagine the story in its own context as depicted. He takes for granted that (1) YHWH is the one true God, who has been involved in Israel's life from its earliest beginnings with Abraham; (2) Israel's normative life-style began with Moses; (3) what began with Moses was the natural continuation of God's commitment to the patriarchs. The writer's concern is not primarily that of the historian in any modern sense, seeking to give an analytical account of how this came to be. Although he is obviously telling the story of how Israel's faith in YHWH began and

49. The classic traditiohistorical analysis of Exodus 3 is that of H. Gressmann, *Mose und seine Zeit,* FRLANT 18 (Göttingen: Vandenhoeck & Ruprecht, 1913), 21–56.

in that sense is a historian, he is telling it from the perspective of a mature understanding of what Israel's faith in YHWH entails. Particularly in Exod. 3:13-15, which we have argued to be a distinct unit of narrative theology, the writer's concern is in essence entirely simple: to show that Israel came to know God as YHWH in the context of Moses initially coming to Israel to deliver them from Egypt. God told Moses that YHWH was the divine name and this was how God, until now the God of the patriarchs, was to be known from now on by Israel. The practical difficulties Moses might encounter by using a previously unknown name of God are simply of no concern to the writer. Once the paradigmatic nature of the text and its perspective of mature Yahwism are appreciated, the theoretically problematic nature of the imagined encounter between Moses and Israel cannot really serve as an argument against the newness of the divine name that is given.

To summarize and conclude this survey of attempted reinterpretations of Exodus 3 and 6, two basic difficulties with the whole approach must be emphasized. First, the fundamental oddity of one of the presuppositions underlying this whole approach needs to be spelled out. It is all very well as a theoretical position to draw a distinction between knowledge of a name and knowledge of its meaning—to say, for example, "the patriarchs called God Yahweh, but knew Him as El Shaddai; their descendants will both call Him and know Him by His name Yahweh."[50] But the implications of driving a sharp wedge between a name and its meaning are surely peculiar. It means supposing that the patriarchs called God YHWH but that this was essentially meaningless to them, a mere sound without significance (since what they understood about God was represented by El Shaddai). That the writers of either Exodus 3 or Exodus 6 could have supposed, and intended to convey, that the divine name YHWH functioned as a meaningless sound for several centuries prior to Moses seems to me simply incredible. It puts the patriarchal encounters with God, especially those of Abraham where the name YHWH is extensively used, into a very curious light. But also the writers

50. Motyer, *Revelation*, 16.

would surely have considered it at the very least a degrading suggestion about the sacred name. (Admittedly, advocates of this approach do not suggest that the divine name was a "meaningless sound" to the patriarchs, and the wording is mine. But it seems to me that this represents a failure to think through the logic of the position.) The ingenious extension of the Hebrew commonplace that a name has meaning into the hypothesis that you could have God's name without its meaning would never have been thought of had it not been for the need to harmonize the apparent contradiction between Exodus 3 and 6 and Gen. 4:26, etc. The fact that the option has usually been upheld by Jews and Christians opposed to readings of the text that would appear detrimental to their faith has led to a slightly curious result. The desire to resolve one problem (i.e., the integrity of the scriptural text) has given rise to another problem (i.e., the integrity of the divine name). But this has not been fully realized because the suggestion that the divine name could be known without a knowledge of its meaning has only functioned as a problem-solving expedient and not as an option to be seriously and rigorously considered in its own right.[51]

Second, the supposition that what was new in Exodus 3 or 6 was the meaning of the divine name and not the name itself is finally refuted by one simple fact: It is simply not the case that the name is used in Genesis with any difference of meaning from that which it customarily has elsewhere in the Old Testament. In Gen. 15:7, for example, YHWH is the name of divine self-announcement in the context of making a covenant with Abraham. The qualifying description "who brought you from Ur of the Chaldeans" is so similar to the Exodus formula "who brought you out of

51. Of course, attempts have been made to find theological significance in the giving of a new meaning to an already familiar name. Rashi, for example, argued that God's characteristic of keeping faith, such as to fulfil the promises which were not fulfilled for the patriarchs, was what was signified by the divine name in Exod. 6:3 (*Exodus,* 25). Alternatively, Motyer, followed by Glisson, has argued for a kind of progressive revelation in the move from God's self-revelation as El Shaddai to God's self-revelation as YHWH (Motyer, *Revelation,* 24–31; S. D. Glisson, "Exodus 6:3," 141–43). Yet none of these really relate their suggestions to an analysis of the function and significance of the tetragrammaton in its own right in the patriarchal context.

the land of Egypt" (Exod. 20:2) that it gives the divine name precisely the sort of meaning and connotation it has in Exodus and elsewhere. The same can be said of all the other well-known uses of the divine name, both in the primeval stories (e.g., Gen. 2:4ff.; 6:8; 8:21; 9:26) and in the patriarchal narratives (e.g., Gen. 12:1; 15:6; 22:14; 28:13). One might perhaps try to accommodate this by drawing a distinction between traditions in which the divine name has received theological reworking and earlier traditions in which the name was not theologically significant. But any such attempt would not only be intrinsically implausible but would also wholly undermine the premise on which the harmonizing stance rests: that it can explain the usage of the name YHWH in Genesis in a way compatible with a new revelation in Exodus 3. Despite its initial plausibility, the attempt to resolve the familiar problem by a harmonizing reinterpretation of Exodus 3 and 6 must be judged a failure.

TOWARD A NEW PARADIGM: A REAPPRAISAL OF GENESIS 4:26

The inadequacy of the familiar harmonizing option as a way of resolving the problem of the apparent contradiction between Exodus 3 and 6 and Gen. 4:26, etc., still leaves one other approach to the problem—to look again at the meaning of the other problematic text, Gen. 4:26, etc.[52] It is remarkable, given its inherent logic, that this approach has, to the best of my knowledge, never been seriously tried, although an important move in this direction has been made by C. Westermann.[53] This omission is presumably because the usage of the name YHWH elsewhere in Genesis has been considered to be obvious and overwhelming evidence in favor of the understanding, shared alike by exponents of the documentary hypothesis and exponents of the traditional and conservative alternative, that Gen. 4:26 must mean

52. For a fascinating survey of the history of interpretation of this verse, see S. Sandmel, "Genesis 4:26b," *HUCA* 32 (1961): 19–29. Sandmel appropriately characterizes the history as "a history of reading difficulties into a text" (p. 19).

53. C. Westermann, *Genesis 1–11* (Minneapolis: Augsburg, 1984), 339–40, 578–79.

that the name of YHWH was known from earliest times. But a consideration of Gen. 4:26 in its own right, in fact, quickly shows how dubious this interpretation is.

First, the phrase "to call upon the name of YHWH" *(qara' bešem yhwh)* is a regular formulaic expression for worship.[54] It is highly doubtful whether we can legitimately press its wording, as though the usage of YHWH was specially significant and in the context of Gen. 4:26 was chosen in preference to Elohim or El Shaddai. Second, the name YHWH has already been used consistently throughout Genesis 4,[55] and the story has also described Cain and Abel as bringing offerings to YHWH (4:3, 4). Both these facts make it odd to use 4:26b to argue that knowledge or worship of YHWH only began with Seth. Third, Gen. 4:26b makes an odd rival tradition to Exodus 3 and 6 because its genre is so inappropriate. Were it a theophany or at least a divine pronouncement, it would be comparable to Exodus 3 and 6 and would be a plausible literary form for the purpose of showing how God came to be known as YHWH. But a passing editorial comment seems like a distinctly implausible alternative tradition to that of YHWH's self-revelation to Moses at Sinai as in Exodus 3. Fourth, the point of Gen. 4:26b in context is not that people began to worship YHWH rather than, say, Elohim or El Shaddai but that the worship of God is a fundamental constituent of human life and of the beginnings of civilization.[56] Fifth, we must appreciate that the narrator of 4:26 is operating with the same perspective from which the whole primeval history is recounted, that is, the mature Hebrew conviction that there is only one true God, YHWH the God of Israel, and this is the God who has created and sustained all human life from its earliest beginnings. Of course the writers of Genesis 1–11 conflate their own Yahwistic perspectives with those of the primeval traditions which, in their own context at the beginning of Genesis, should, according to our

54. Cf. Gen. 12:8; 13:4; 21:33; 26:25; 1 Kings 18:24; Zeph. 3:9; Ps. 105:1; 116:4, 13, 17. "Name of YHWH" is also used regularly in other idiomatic formulas with verbs such as bless, swear, speak, minister.

55. Gen. 4:1, 3, 4, 6, 9, 10, 13, 15, 16, with the sole exception of *'elohim* in 4:25.

56. So esp. Westermann, *Genesis 1–11,* 339–41.

theory, be in principle non-Yahwistic. But, as we shall argue, an important difference exists between the patriarchal traditions (which are part of Israel's own story and where the pre-Yahwistic context is taken seriously) and the primeval history (which tells of YHWH's dealings with the world as a whole and is entirely shaped by the normative theological perspectives of Mosaic Yahwism).[57] In short, in the primeval history the Yahwistic writers operated as ancient storytellers with little interest in maintaining historical perspective in any modern sense. Thus if the use of the name YHWH in Gen. 4:26 is evidential at all, it is evidential of the perspective of the writer, not of a perspective the writer supposedly attributed to the people of primeval times. And it would be a misunderstanding of the nature of the text to interpret it as showing that the writer thought that people actually knew God specifically as YHWH.

If the above analysis is correct and the apparently most explicit statement that the name YHWH was known in pre-Mosaic times does not, in fact, bear that meaning, then it follows that there need be no contradiction between Gen. 4:26 and Exodus 3 and 6—there is no explicit tradition that the name YHWH was known in pre-Mosaic times.

It may be worthwhile to compare our thesis with that of C. Westermann, who, although he disputes the conventional understanding of Gen. 4:26 for reasons similar to those just given and does relate this to the wider issue of the divine name, does not draw the conclusion we advocate. This is essentially because Westermann maintains the distinctiveness of P over against J as an essential heuristic key to the pentateuchal text (although he is happy to dispense with E). This leads him, however, into a slightly curious position. On the one hand he can say, "J can have seen no contradiction between Gen. 4:26 and Ex 3 because he is talking of something very different in the Exodus passage. There he is concerned with the beginning of the history of the people, whereas here [4:26] he makes a primeval statement in which there is really no point of contact with the Exodus."[58] On the

57. See below, p. 167.

58. Westermann, *Genesis 1–11,* 339.

other hand, because "P knows of a different use [of the names for God] before and after the revelation to Moses in Ex 6:3," he can say that "it is difficult to conceive that the same writer [P in Exod. 6:3] who has the name of Yahweh first revealed to Moses, also uses it in Genesis. And further, one can scarcely imagine that the same writer could have said in Gen 4:26: 'It was then that people began to call on the name of Yahweh,' while the sentence was comprehensible and meaningful in J."[59] Yet, as we have already argued, it is perfectly intelligible that a writer who holds that the name YHWH was first revealed to Moses should nonetheless feel free to use it while telling the story of Israel's forebears. Moreover I simply cannot see why there should be no problem between Gen. 4:26 and Exodus 3, given the meaning of Gen. 4:26 in context and the "very different" concerns of the two passages, and yet there should be a problem between Gen. 4:26 and Exod. 6:3—for exactly the same considerations apply to Exodus 6 as to Exodus 3. To say this does not deny the possible distinctiveness of P among pentateuchal traditions. It questions whether, on the matter of the name of God, there is any reason to suppose that the position of P was different from that of other pentateuchal writers. The parenthetical statement of Exod. 6:3b may simply make explicit the understanding clearly present in Exodus 3 and most likely shared by all the writers of the Pentateuch.

THE ADDITION OF THE DIVINE NAME TO THE PATRIARCHAL TRADITIONS

We may now return to our own thesis, that in principle the use of YHWH in Genesis 12–50 conveys the perspective of the Yahwistic storytellers, who are retelling originally non-Yahwistic traditions in a Yahwistic context, and as they appropriate the stories for Yahwism, so they tend to use the familiar name of their God.

If our thesis about the divine name is correct, one might reasonably expect still to be able to find some indications of the process by which the divine name became part of the Genesis

59. Ibid., 578–79.

stories as they were told, written, and edited within a Yahwistic context. I do not wish to engage in the extensive and complex debate about the tradition-history and redaction of the patriarchal stories in its own right; that would lead too far away from the argument we are developing. Nonetheless, some indication of our basic stance is required, not only because of our thesis but also because the view of the patriarchal stories that it presupposes has recently been called into question. I propose, therefore, to suggest in brief outline the kind of procedures that may reasonably be supposed to have been adopted by the storytellers and editors as they reformulated the patriarchal traditions in Yahwistic terms and to justify the validity of such a hypothesis.

First, we may note that the name YHWH is used in stories that contain other appellations for God. Sometimes this may have no special significance, as, for example, "And YHWH appeared to Isaac the same night and said, 'I am the God of Abraham your father'" (26:24). In other places, however, the name may have been deliberately added. Why it should have been added is a matter for intelligent guesswork. Possibly, the name may have been added sometimes to make clear that the God in question is none other than YHWH. As Genesis 12–50 stands, there is no doubt from start to finish that the God of the patriarchs is Israel's God. And as we have already noted, the idea that a deity other than YHWH might be operative within Israel's story is entirely alien to all Old Testament writers. So any desire to clarify that the deity in question is YHWH would presumably indicate something of the early history of the tradition, perhaps from a time when the stories circulated in relative independence from each other. Alternatively, it may be that the divine name was added for other reasons, such as to emphasize continuity between the stories of the patriarchs and Israel's story.

Instances where the use of YHWH appears to be a deliberate addition to another divine appellation are as follows. On the one hand, it may be part of the narrative framework of stories: "YHWH appeared to Abram and said to him, 'I am El Shaddai'" (17:1). On the other hand, it may appear in speeches, both divine and human: "And behold, YHWH stood above it and said, 'I am

YHWH, the God of Abraham your father and the God of Isaac'" (28:13); "And Jacob said, 'O God of my father Abraham and God of my father Isaac, O YHWH'" (32:10).

Particularly interesting in this latter category is the brief account of Melchizedek (Gen. 14:18-20). Here, even when the story is read in the context of Genesis 12ff., there might naturally be a degree of uncertainty about the nature and identity of the deity, El Elyon (RSV, "God Most High"), by whom Melchizedek, a strange figure standing outside the chosen line of Abraham and his descendants, blesses Abraham. Of course, the story is told with numerous allusions which, read in the light of other Old Testament passages, clarify the nature and identity both of Melchizedek and of his God. Melchizedek is king of Salem, that is, Jerusalem (Ps. 76:2 [Heb. 3]), and was understood to be a prototype for the Davidic kings (Ps. 110:4). Since readers know that Jerusalem is the holy place of YHWH, they would expect that even in the patriarchal context it would already be YHWH who would be known in some way to Melchizedek. Indeed, Elyon is an epithet of YHWH in Israel's worship in Jerusalem (e.g., Ps. 46:4 [Heb. 5]; 47:2 [Heb. 3]). Moreover, the wording of Melchizedek's blessing is revealing, since the maker of heaven and earth could not be a deity other than YHWH and the familiar "Blessed be *(baruk)* . . ." formula is never used in the Old Testament of a deity other than YHWH. Nonetheless, when Abraham says to the king of Sodom, "I have sworn to YHWH El Elyon, maker of heaven and earth . . ." (Gen. 14:22), his words may still be meant to make absolutely clear that it is indeed YHWH by whom Melchizedek blessed him.

Second, in certain passages only the name YHWH and not some other divine appellation occurs, but here it appears likely that YHWH has replaced another name which originally stood in the text. As G. J. Wenham has put it, "The evidence for supposing that the editor sometimes introduced Yahweh instead of El or Elohim is quite clear. For example, Hagar is told to name her son 'Ishma*el,* because *the LORD* has given heed to your affliction. . . . So she called the name of *the LORD* who spoke to her, "You are *El* Roi"' (16:11, 13). Similarly after his vision of the heavenly ladder Jacob awakes and remarks 'Surely *the LORD* is in this place,' yet he goes on to call the place 'Beth*el*' (28:16, 19)."[60]

Third, and perhaps most problematic, some stories use the name YHWH throughout, and in them is no evidence of the use of any other divine appellation. This is particularly the case in the Abraham cycle (e.g., Gen. 12; 13; 15; 18:1—19:28; 24). The consistency of the YHWH perspective in these stories may make one wonder whether they were ever told from any other perspective. Nonetheless, this likely was the case. (In arguing this I am making a general point about the patriarchal traditions, which may not necessarily be applicable in every instance. In particular, I do not wish to prejudge the question of whether some stories may be relative latecomers to the patriarchal corpus, first told only when the corpus had already been recast into a Yahwistic mold, and so their earliest form was Yahwistic. The story of Abraham's servant [Genesis 24] is often considered in this category, as is the Joseph story [Genesis 37, 39–45], since these stories about the divine guidance of individuals lack the depth dimension and resonance of most patriarchal traditions. Such exceptions, however [if they are exceptions], by being atypical only serve to prove the general rule we are seeking to establish.)

The basic assumptions for the approach we advocate have been widely accepted by Old Testament scholars since the work of Gunkel and Alt. Fundamental to Gunkel's work was the recognition that there may be a lengthy tradition-history underlying the stories. This means that material that once might have been expressed in different (i.e., non-Yahwistic) terms has likely been retold so often from within a Yahwistic perspective that it has become imbued with the perspectives of its retellings.

The essential simplicity and plausibility of this hypothesis has often been obscured by supplementary arguments about the nature of the tradition and in particular by its usual combination with the source-critical hypothesis of the Yahwist. This source-critical hypothesis has had two elements that must be carefully

60. G. J. Wenham, "The Religion of the Patriarchs," in A. R. Millard and D. J. Wiseman, eds., *Essays on the Patriarchal Narratives* (Leicester: IVP, 1980), 181.

distinguished. On the one hand, it has been supposed that, although at an original oral stage of tradition reference may not have been made to God as YHWH, by the time the stories were written the deity in them had long since been understood to be YHWH. This meant that the divine name was already integral to the patriarchal tradition, which therefore never existed in written form without the divine name. Generally speaking, this seems to me unobjectionable. On the other hand, it has also been supposed that the writer who used the divine name (i.e., the so-called Yahwist), did so because of thinking the name was actually known to the patriarchs, and thus the writer represented a tradition different from that of Exodus 3 and 6. This particular interpretation of the use of the divine name is mistaken, but it can readily be dispensed with without affecting the substantive point at issue about the written form of the patriarchal stories being different in certain ways from their original oral form.

Although to me this hypothesis does not seem particularly controversial—and indeed seems required by the biblical text—a few words are necessary in its justification and defense, since its basic assumptions have recently been called into question by some scholars. An alternative approach to the patriarchal stories has been advocated, the essence of which is to deny the hypothesis of traditiohistorical development underlying the text. R. N. Whybray and P. Kirkpatrick, for example, have appealed to folklore studies and have questioned in general terms the validity of the assumption that we are genuinely in a position to discern orally transmitted and potentially ancient tradition underlying the patriarchal narratives.[61] M. Köckert has presented a major critique of Alt's seminal essay "The God of the Fathers" and of the scholarly consensus built upon it, which assumed that potentially ancient and orally transmitted tradition underlay the written text of Genesis 12–50.[62] And J. Van Seters is producing numerous studies arguing, among other things, that the Yahwist

61. R. N. Whybray, *The Making of the Pentateuch;* P. G. Kirkpatrick, *The Old Testament and Folklore Study,* JSOTS 62 (Sheffield: JSOT, 1988).

62. M. Köckert, *Vätergott und Väterverheissungen,* FRLANT 142 (Göttingen: Vandenhoeck & Ruprecht, 1988).

not only dates from as late as the sixth century but also contains little if any genuinely ancient tradition.[63] In many ways Van Seters is reviving Wellhausen's contention that the content of the patriarchal narratives is almost entirely a reflection of practices and beliefs contemporary to their writers in the monarchical and exilic periods, which means that the notion of a patriarchal age and patriarchal religion is a wholly anachronistic, and indeed imaginary, construction.[64]

Although the issues here are highly complex, four points may briefly be made. First, the caution and skepticism represented by some of these recent works is to be welcomed. Since for most pentateuchal study the only evidence we have is the written text, it is valuable to be reminded that reconstructions of what might lie behind the text must always be tentative and hypothetical. The confidence of many scholars that extensive and detailed reconstructions are possible, a mood that reaches its apotheosis in Noth's *History of Pentateuchal Traditions,* is simply not justified. However plausible any particular hypothesis may be, the piling of hypothesis upon hypothesis can only lead to conclusions whose likelihood of being correct is minimal.

Second, although much of the critique of traditiohistorical reconstructions is cogent and justified, I do not think that any significant argument has been put forward that would undermine the basic premise of tradition-history, that is, that stories such as those of the patriarchs are likely to have gone through a long process of retelling before they reached their present form. There may be good general grounds for supposing traditiohistorical development to have taken place—which means, after all, no more than recognizing that there probably took place in ancient Israel the practice common to many cultures of retelling stories the content and wording of which were not yet fixed but were open to molding and development by the storyteller. If so, then the basic insight remains valid even if one can do no more than

63. For example, J. Van Seters, *Abraham in History and Tradition;* "The Religion of the Patriarchs in Genesis," *Biblica* 61 (1980): 220–33; *In Search of History* (New Haven and London: Yale Univ. Press, 1983), esp. 361.

64. See further below, pp. 191ff.

point to one or two general features that may have characterized the process.[65]

We must emphasize that an inability to reconstruct the details of a tradition-history does not necessarily mean that the tradition-history did not exist. If the process that underlay the text has left no evidence other than the text itself, then clearly any reconstruction of its details must be highly hypothetical. Generally speaking, any reconstruction works by analogy with literature from other cultures, and the most influential single factor is the decision about the genre of the material; that is, particular types of material (folktale, cult legend, etc.) are assumed to develop in particular ways in order to become what they now are in the biblical text. This fundamental characteristic of all traditio-historical study of the patriarchal narratives is set out and analyzed with great clarity by W. McKane in his *Studies in the Patriarchal Narratives.*[66] Since not only the decision about genre but also the assumptions about the way the genre develops and the applicability of particular analogies are always open to question, it is hardly surprising that the reconstruction of tradition-history should be recognized as a speculative undertaking. But only the attempt to reconstruct any such developmental process in detail has been shown to be unwarranted, not the recognition that such processes may have been at work.

Third, if the above contention is right, then one must confront the important and difficult question of how to distinguish stories with an underlying tradition-history from those without it. In general terms tradition-history is indicated by features within the text which appear to reflect diverse historical contexts. In terms specific to the patriarchal traditions, it is notable that the stories contain many elements that give the appearance of a non-Yahwistic origin distinct from their present Yahwistic stance (as will be argued in the next chapter). Also, the text poses the specific

65. Given the difficulty of finding satisfactory criteria for distinguishing oral from written material, there seems little point in maintaining that the process must have been essentially oral, however likely that may appear in general historical terms. Rather, the process could have been both oral and written, in whichever way was appropriate within the context of Israelite storytelling.

66. W. McKane, *Studies in the Patriarchal Narratives* (Edinburgh: Handsel, 1979).

problem of the divine name. As we are trying to show, this is best explained by the supposition of the retelling of non-Yahwistic material in Yahwistic terms. Ultimately, the test of an approach must be its heuristic fruitfulness. Precisely because I find that the hypothesis of the retelling of non-Yahwistic material in terms of YHWH illuminates the pentateuchal text in many ways, the relatively modest degree of traditiohistorical development it presupposes becomes likely.[67] Moreover, in terms of the work of other scholars, it seems difficult to deny that the supposition of tradition-history has been heuristically fruitful. The quality of interpretation that has been offered on this basis, especially by von Rad and Westermann in their Genesis commentaries, has yet to be matched by those who deny such a depth dimension to the text.

Finally, an analogy that illuminates the present argument for a tradition-history in stories where the name YHWH occurs can be found in the usage of certain place names in Genesis. On the one hand are stories in Genesis that preserve two names for the same place, both the name that the place originally had and the name it came to have in later Hebrew tradition. So, for example, a place that was originally called Luz became Bethel (Gen. 28:19; 35:6), and Ephrath became Bethlehem (Gen. 35:19). This is analogous to stories where the name YHWH has been added to another divine appellation. On the other hand are stories told using a place name we know from elsewhere to be subsequent to the patriarchal period and so technically anachronistic, and yet the name is used quite naturally and unself-consciously by the storyteller as appropriate to the story. For example, Bethel is first mentioned (Gen. 12:8) in a way that might be taken to imply that Bethel was the name familiar to Abraham. Yet we know from elsewhere in Genesis (28:19; 35:6) that the name from Abraham's perspective was, in fact, Luz. Likewise Dan is mentioned in the course of another Abraham story (14:14), yet we know from Judg. 18:29 that the place was called Laish until the migration of the Danites. In both these instances we have a fusion

67. It may be that some other well-known apparent anachronisms in the patriarchal narratives—camels, Philistines—should also be understood in terms of the retelling of a story in categories contemporary to the storyteller.

between the perspectives of the storyteller and the perspectives of the story in a way that was presumably natural in a culture where traditional stories were frequently retold. This usage of place names is analogous to those stories that are told consistently in terms of YHWH (i.e., the perspective of the narrator) but that, it is reasonable to surmise, were once told in other terms (i.e., the perspective of the patriarchal context).

In the light of all these considerations we can reasonably conclude that, when the patriarchal stories use the name YHWH, this is because the patriarchal traditions are being retold from the perspective of Mosaic Yahwism. Although the explicit statement that God was not known to the patriarchs as YHWH (Exod. 6:3b) has usually been considered a notion peculiar to P (and perhaps E), we have argued that there is no good reason to suppose it was not an understanding shared by all the pentateuchal writers, since Gen. 4:26 and frequent uses of the divine name in Genesis are not incompatible with it. Our thesis is that the Pentateuch is, in fact, consistent in its contention that the name YHWH was first revealed to Moses.

In this approach one should reformulate the issue of the divine name and the nature of the tension within the text of Genesis and Exodus when read in their present form. The tension should not be seen as the historical tension of two differing conceptions of when knowledge of God as YHWH first began. Rather it is the theological tension between the particularist conviction that only to Moses and Israel has God been revealed as YHWH and the universalist conviction that YHWH is the only true God and that therefore YHWH is the God with whom both humankind in its beginnings (Genesis 1–11) and the forebears of Israel (Genesis 12–50) had to do.

CHAPTER 3

The Religion of the Patriarchs

In the argument thus far we have sought to establish two basic points. First, Exodus 3 portrays the occasion on which God was first made known as YHWH, a revelation given to Moses on behalf of Israel and reaffirmed in Exodus 6. Second, the Pentateuch is consistent in its understanding that God was first made known as YHWH in God's dealings with Moses, notwithstanding the uses of the name YHWH in Genesis. If these two contentions are correct, then they entail an obvious corollary with regard to Israel's understanding of the period of the patriarchs, that is, that it was a time when God was not known as YHWH. Precisely what this involves is the question to which we must turn next.

Although we have concentrated so far on the name of God, not just because it is a convenient starting point but also because of its importance for understanding the character of God, it would be a mistake not to expand the range of the argument. Religion is not just a matter of a particular understanding of the character of God, as represented by God's name, but of a total life-style involving many interrelated practices, attitudes, beliefs, and values. Such an understanding is so fundamental to the nature of religion that the biblical writers never bother to spell it out, for they simply presuppose it. It is evident, for example, in the book of Exodus, where we have seen that the revelation and interpretation of God's name as YHWH is closely associated with a nexus of other factors all of which relate to YHWH's relationship with Israel as the people of YHWH. If, therefore, it was Israel's consistent tradition that God was not known to the patriarchs as YHWH, then one would expect this to be reflected in the total pattern of patriarchal religion and life-style. Indeed, if there were no significant evidence to this effect, one's initial assumption about the pre-Yahwistic character of the tradition might need to be called into question. Therefore, we must look next to the religion of the patriarchs for evidence to further our thesis.

METHOD AND APPROACH

Discussion of the religion of the patriarchs is common in works of Old Testament scholarship. It features in all studies of Israelite religion, in many studies of the history of Israel and of Old Testament theology, and has numerous articles and monographs devoted to it in its own right.[1] Since our own approach in this chapter will adopt a somewhat different stance from that generally adopted, we must clarify at the outset precisely what this will be.

Most modern discussion of patriarchal religion has worked first and foremost according to the agenda of the ancient historian: What historical understanding of patriarchal religion is possible, given the nature of the literary sources and the traditions embodied in Genesis? This primary question is then customarily followed by discussions of the possible theological significance of the historical reconstruction offered. A wide range of different

1. For a survey of modern scholarly research into this topic, see H. Weidmann, *Die Patriarchen und ihre Religion im Licht der Forschung seit Wellhausen,* FRLANT 94 (Göttingen: Vandenhoeck & Ruprecht, 1968).

The seminal work for twentieth-century scholarship in this area was A. Alt, "Der Gott der Väter" (1929), which was reprinted in his *Kleine Schriften* I (Munich: Beck, 1953) and is conveniently available in his *Essays on Old Testament History and Religion* (Oxford: Blackwell, 1966; ET by R. A. Wilson), 3–77 (recently reissued in The Biblical Seminar series (Sheffield: JSOT, 1989).

The most recent book devoted to the subject, which is a full-scale critique of Alt and the scholarly edifice built upon his foundations, is M. Köckert, *Vätergott und Väterverheissungen*, FRLANT 142 (Göttingen: Vandenhoeck & Ruprecht, 1988). Köckert contains a bibliography and discussion of all significant contributions to the debate since Alt.

For useful short accounts and critiques of the debate (prior to Köckert), see M. Haran, "The Religion of the Patriarchs," *ASTI* 4 (1965): 30–55; G. J. Wenham, "The Religion of the Patriarchs," in A. R. Millard and D. J. Wiseman, eds., *Essays on the Patriarchal Narratives,* 157–88 (Leicester: IVP, 1980).

reconstructions and interpretations has been proposed, with the most obvious unanimity residing in the conviction that the problem is a difficult one, given the fact that the literary sources in Genesis appear to stand at a considerable historical remove from the patriarchal period they depict.

This historical debate is interesting, and we will briefly return to it later.[2] In the present discussion, however, I wish to approach the biblical text in a different way. This approach is interested above all in Israel's own understanding of its foundational traditions: Was there a consistent understanding about the nature of the patriarchal traditions, and, if so, of what did it consist? For the present we will not be concerned either with the extent to which these traditions may or may not be ancient or historically accurate or with the possible processes by which they may have come to have their present form.

I have various reasons for adopting this approach. In the first place, prolonged study of the patriarchal traditions has convinced me of the heuristic fruitfulness of the hypothesis that a common tradition about the distinctively pre-Mosaic character of the patriarchal period was held by all the major pentateuchal writers, as a natural corollary of a common tradition about the initial knowledge of God as YHWH being given to Moses. The non-Yahwistic character of patriarchal religion is indeed a well-known element in many modern discussions since Alt's essay, "The God of the Fathers." But the possibility of the hypothesis in the form we advocate has usually been obscured by the conventional historical orientation toward discerning the differing antiquities and theological outlooks of the various writers and, in particular, the assumption that there is a fundamental difference between the older J/E tradition and the later P tradition. Our concern is not to deny that there may indeed be differences between the outlooks of the various writers but rather to suggest that, whatever their differences, the writers may have held in common certain fundamental assumptions and these may in certain respects be even more important than their detailed points of difference. Our contention is that familiar questions about

2. Below, pp. 191ff.

"early" and "late" levels of tradition may be relativized in significance on the grounds that consistency with a particular character and ethos is the crucial consideration. The point is that, even if particular passages were added to the patriarchal traditions at a relatively late date, they may have been added in such a way as to be consistent with the imaginative context, the "world" of the patriarchs, in which they are set. The question of whether a writer is imaginatively consistent with the world of the patriarchs is crucial. This may relate to the questions of whether the writer is early or late and of whether the tradition has ancient and perhaps historical foundation. But the issues are in principle quite separate, and it is vital not to confuse them.

If this approach to the patriarchal traditions is to be validly carried out, it entails a necessary corollary. If the consistency and distinctiveness of Israel's traditions about the patriarchs is to be meaningful, it can only be so by comparison with some kind of general characterization of Mosaic Yahwism that may serve as a foil for it. How may such a characterization be obtained?

From the perspective of the historian, the origins and development of Mosaic Yahwism raise a host of difficult problems at least as complex as those having to do with patriarchal religion.[3] Although little consensus exists about the history, especially the early history, of Mosaic Yahwism, there is a consensus that the history is more complex than is suggested by the text of Exodus-Deuteronomy as it now stands and that therefore it is illegitimate simply to translate the development of the story in the text into a historical account of Israel's origins. This may be accepted without more ado. Methodological consistency, however, suggests that if conventional historical questions are to be bracketed out of our analysis of the patriarchal traditions, the same should be the case for an analysis of Mosaic Yahwism.

3. For four different approaches, see Y. Kaufmann, *The Religion of Israel* (New York: Schocken, 1960; an abridgment and translation by M. Greenberg of seven volumes in Hebrew, published in Israel, 1937–48); R. de Vaux, *The Early History of Israel,* 2 vols. (London: DLT, 1978; French, 1971); N. Gottwald, *The Tribes of Yahweh* (London: SCM, 1980); N. P. Lemche, *Ancient Israel: A New History of Israelite Society* (Sheffield: JSOT, 1988), esp. chap. 6.

For useful summaries of the kind of position that has generally commanded a consensus, see, e.g., G. Fohrer, *History of Israelite Religion* (London: SPCK, 1973; German, 1968), 66–86; J. Bright, *A History of Israel,* 3d ed. (London: SCM, 1981), 144–62.

Exodus-Deuteronomy is, of course, more difficult to approach in this way than Genesis 12–50, if only because the material is more extensive and more diverse. Nonetheless, the crucial question remains whether certain common and consistent elements in Israel's traditions about its religious foundations may run through the various levels and developments of the Pentateuch as it now stands. Moreover, in order to keep the line of argument reasonably straightforward, we will concentrate primarily on the book of Exodus. On the one hand, the literary juxtaposition of Exodus with Genesis makes a comparison natural. On the other hand, both the content of Exodus (the giving of the name YHWH and divine pronouncements about its meaning together with the exodus and Sinai traditions) and its position within the Pentateuch give the book a fairly obvious function as a fundamental portrayal of the nature of Mosaic Yahwism. We shall, however, also refer to other portions of the Pentateuch for further development of the general characterization of Mosaic Yahwism. The crucial consideration at every point will be the discernment of a common tradition about a fundamental religious ethos, which both has its own inner logic and consistency and is different from that of the patriarchal traditions. Questions about how this religious tradition developed and whether particular practices and expressions may be early or late remain valid historical issues but are beside the point for present purposes.

There remains one final methodological issue to consider. If we are looking for a tradition of a religion distinct from Mosaic Yahwism and yet recognize that the material has already been in some way assimilated to the perspectives of Mosaic Yahwism (at least in the use of the name YHWH), how can we know that any given item genuinely belongs to patriarchal religion rather than Mosaic Yahwism? Is there no danger of the whole argument becoming circular and question-begging? But although from a purely theoretical point of view the epistemological problem may seem hard to resolve, the difficulty may not be too serious in practice, for at least three reasons.

First, although it has been argued that the pentateuchal writers were not interested in maintaining historical perspective in any modern sense and so were happy to merge and blur differing content and contexts, it in no way follows from this that they were unaware of such differences within their material or that they were incapable of imaginative consistency in retaining such differences where they considered appropriate. All we need suppose is that the writers of Genesis and Exodus were able to maintain a sense both of continuity (i.e., one and the same God) and of discontinuity (i.e., one and the same God but known in different ways) in God's dealings with the patriarchs and Israel as they told the stories of the patriarchs from within the context of Israel.

Second, we need not suppose that only what is distinctive in the tradition of patriarchal religion truly belongs to it, for many of its characteristic elements could be shared with Mosaic religion and indeed other religions (for example, the connection between sacrifice and theophany [Gen. 46:1-4; cf. Exod. 24:1-11; Judg. 13:15-20; 1 Kings 18:30-40]). Of necessity, therefore, our method of approach cannot offer a comprehensive picture of patriarchal religion but can only show what is distinctive to it. But all that is necessary for our thesis is to show that there was a tradition of a distinctive patriarchal religion and that, although its overall character may have had things in common with Mosaic religion and some of its particular characteristics may have become blurred through assimilation to Mosaic religion, its distinctiveness was sufficiently recognized and respected so as to be retained by the writers of the Pentateuch.

Third, the real test of our approach must be empirical, inductive, and heuristic. If there is sufficient evidence in the text to build up a cumulative and reasonably consistent picture of a distinctive tradition about the patriarchs, and this can illuminate a reading of the Pentateuch in appropriate ways, then the hypothesis can reasonably be claimed to be well founded.

One final point about method may also be made. Even for the purely historical task of penetrating Israel's traditions about the patriarchs to get at the historical processes and underlying reality that they reflect, it is necessary to begin by considering the nature of the tradition as it was understood by those in Israel who were responsible for its preservation. Since much of the historical task depends on accurately discerning the genre of the text and also detecting different voices within the text (differences reflected in language, style, presuppositions, emphases) and then relating these voices to wider historical contexts, one must be able to establish what are genuine differences within the text and what are legitimate inferences to draw from material of this (whatever) kind. There is a well-known debate about the danger of imposing anachronistic perspectives on, and drawing illegitimate inferences from, the biblical text (as we have already argued with reference to Exodus 3). This debate, by the very nature of things, obviously can never be entirely resolved. Nonetheless some proposals are better than others, and the better proposals will always be those that attempt initially to enter imaginatively into the presuppositions and conventions of the biblical writers who were responsible for the received text.[4]

THE NATURE OF PATRIARCHAL RELIGION

Before beginning our detailed exposition, two preliminary points. First, we must say that few, if any, of the specific features of patriarchal religion that we mention can claim novelty, in the sense that they have not been noted before in existing discussions. Indeed, most of the points are well known, even if often they are only mentioned in passing.[5] What has received relatively little attention is the interrelatedness of the various features. The understanding of specific features in relation to a larger whole is crucial for our thesis. Our concern is to present an analysis of the religion of the patriarchs as portrayed in Genesis in such a way as to suggest the interrelatedness of its various elements and an overall consistency of ethos. Only when patriarchal religion can be seen as in some way a coherent religious system (however

4. This applies particularly to the two most extensive reconstructions of the possible historical processes underlying the pentateuchal text, M. Noth, *A History of Pentateuchal Traditions* (Chico, California: Scholars, 1981), and Gottwald, *Tribes of Yahweh.* Neither scholar seriously attempts to penetrate the dynamics of Israel's own understanding of its traditions, and indeed Gottwald is frankly dismissive of such concerns. But critical conjectures that depend on reading between the lines are always more persuasive if combined with a cogent reading of the lines themselves.

5. I have received most help from C. Westermann, *Genesis 12–36* (London: SPCK, 1986; German, 1981), 105–13 and passim, and the following outline is much indebted to his work, even though my agenda is different from that of Westermann. Initial stimulus for my thinking in this area came from G. J. Wenham, "Religion of the Patriarchs"; also incisive is Th. C. Vriezen, *The Religion of Ancient Israel* (London: Lutterworth, 1967; Dutch, 1963), 103–33.

sketchy the picture may be) can it be validly compared with Mosaic Yahwism.

The second point is that one theoretically significant aspect of patriarchal religion will not be included, that is, the name of God (which is where most historical debate, from Alt to Köckert, has started). There are three reasons for this omission. First, the present regular use of the familiar name YHWH within Genesis 12–50 makes the issue of limited significance. As the text stands, YHWH is the name of the God of the patriarchs. *Ex hypothesi,* the patriarchal designation for God cannot play a major determinative role in any common tradition of patriarchal religion, since the Mosaic name was allowed to predominate.

Second, it is doubtful whether there was any agreed tradition about how God was known if not as YHWH, and the generally accepted use of the name YHWH in the patriarchal context probably means that this particular issue was never much addressed, or if it was, it has receded into the background. The most explicit statement on the subject is, of course, Exod. 6:3, which draws a contrast between God's self-disclosure as El Shaddai and as YHWH and may initially seem to be a general statement about God's self-revelation in the patriarchal period. Two further points may therefore be noted about this verse.

On the one hand, El Shaddai is used rather infrequently in Genesis (17:1; 28:3; 35:11; 43:14; 48:3; 49:25), though other designations are also compounded with El,[6] which might conceivably be taken as implied by reference to the most common El compound. More frequently used in Genesis are the alternative divine designations, "God" *('elohim)* and "God of your father" (both of which are used in Exodus 3). We should remember that Exod. 6:3 is part of a divine speech that seeks to reassure Moses by drawing his attention to aspects of God's commitment to the patriarchs that should strengthen Moses' trust in his present difficult situation. The point, therefore, is not that El Shaddai was the only patriarchal designation for God but rather that it represents a designation of special significance because of its association with the covenant tradition of Genesis 17.

6. El Elyon (14:18ff.), El Roi (16:13), El Olam (21:33), El Elohe Israel (33:20), El Bethel (31:13; 35:7).

On the other hand, although it is not unlikely in general historical terms that El Shaddai (and other El compounds) may once have functioned as a divine name in patriarchal tradition, it is highly likely that the pentateuchal writers thought that, in the light of God's self-disclosure of the divine name as YHWH, YHWH was the only name of God. Any other term, such as El Shaddai, which might originally have functioned as a name, was therefore reinterpreted as a title or epithet. This would appear to be the implication in Exod. 6:3 of the usage of "name" *(šem)* only in conjunction with YHWH and not, as it easily could have been, in conjunction with El Shaddai. (As the Pentateuch stands, therefore, the uses of El Shaddai in Genesis function no differently from other passages in the Old Testament where Shaddai is one divine epithet among others [e.g., Ps. 91:1-2; Num. 24:16]). God has one name, YHWH, which God has made known to Moses and Israel, but God also uses various other titles and epithets.

Third, even if there were an agreed tradition about how God was known if not as YHWH—and the most common term in the patriarchal traditions is the generic title Elohim—any such designation on its own would be of limited significance, since meaning is determined by usage in context. It is the context and associations of what is said about God in the patriarchal traditions that must be determinative for what was thought about God's character, and so to these we must turn.

Patriarchal Monotheism

Although the patriarchs worship only one God, no particular significance attaches to this; there is no implied opposition to the worship of other gods. Although the patriarchs have extensive dealings, and sometimes conflicts, with the native inhabitants of both Canaan and Egypt, the question of religious allegiance is never at stake. That is to say, patriarchal worship of one God is a matter of straightforward religious fact rather than, as in Mosaic Yahwism, a matter of urgent religious choice. The ethos implied by "You shall have no other gods before me" (Exod. 20:3), which is absolutely fundamental to Mosaic Yahwism, is lacking in the patriarchal traditions.

Admittedly, only minimal attention is given to the question of "other gods" (e.g., the passing uncondemnatory references to

Laban's "household gods" [*teraphim,* Gen. 31:19, 34, 35] and to Joseph's father-in-law as the priest of an Egyptian deity [Gen. 41:45, 50; 46:20]), probably because of the consistent monotheistic presupposition of the narrators. Although this presupposition is no doubt in certain ways indebted to mature Yahwistic theology, it nonetheless functions in a way not characteristic of Yahwistic theology. For example, when God speaks to Abimelech, king of Gerar (Gen. 20:3ff.) or to the pharaoh, the king of Egypt (Genesis 41) it is taken for granted that YHWH, the one God, is speaking. It is noteworthy, however, not only that these stories consistently refer to God only by the generic title *'elohim,* probably in keeping with their imagined "pagan" context, but also that such a portrayal of God is essentially impervious to religious polemic. There is no hint that these "pagans" might worship Baal or some other alien deity. On the contrary, God speaks with them as naturally as with the patriarchs. Nor do they pose any threat to the religious allegiance of the patriarchs. The usage of *'elohim,* which Schmidt recognized as problematic in terms of a conventional understanding of the Elohist, is in fact appropriate to and consistent with the open monotheism of the patriarchal context.[7]

One way of appreciating the silence of the Genesis text about "other gods" is to compare its portrayal of Abraham's departure from Ur and Haran with that of Jewish postbiblical tradition. The move from alien territory to the promised land in obedience to God's call would be an obvious context to make a point about religious allegiance, and later midrashim extensively developed the tradition of Abraham's opposition to idolatry.[8] Yet the text of Genesis shows no interest whatever in this.

The one exception to this otherwise consistent ethos is Gen. 35:2 and 4 where Jacob says to his family and those with him, "Remove the foreign gods that are among you, and purify yourselves, and change your clothing," and his family members do

7. Cf. above, pp. 44f.

8. See, e.g., Jubilees 11:14-17; 12:12-24. Cf. M. Zlotowitz and N. Scherman, eds., *Bereishis: Genesis/A New Translation with a Commentary Anthologized from Talmudic, Midrashic and Rabbinic Sources,* ArtScroll Tanach 1 (New York: Mesorah Publications, 1977, 1986), 359–60.

remove "all the foreign gods that they had." Such language is usually characteristic of Yahwistic exclusivism (e.g., Josh. 24:23; Ezra 6:20f.) and seems to be the exception that proves the rule, an occasion when apparently the narrator does not preserve the patriarchal perspective but tells the story in his own Yahwistic terms. Yet even here, the reference to "foreign gods" is not developed and remains somewhat cryptic in light of the lack of other reference. Again the text does not make the move made in later interpretation of saying that the foreign gods were idols taken from native inhabitants of the land, that is, the Shechemites.[9]

The Religion of the Patriarchs Compared with That of the Canaanites

Genesis depicts no antagonism between the patriarchs and the religious practices of the native inhabitants of Canaan. Admittedly, little is actually said in Genesis about the religion of the inhabitants of Canaan, but the very silence suggests a lack of polemical intent. No reference, either explicit or implicit, is made to fertility rites of the sort that are strongly attacked elsewhere in the Old Testament as at variance with Yahwism (e.g., Hos. 2:5ff.; cf. Deut. 11:8-17), and there is little indication of the strongly negative judgment on the Canaanites that runs through the rest of the Old Testament from Exodus onward (implicit in Exod. 3:8, explicit in Exod. 23:23f.).

It is striking, for example, that, although Abraham imagines that the inhabitants of Gerar would have no fear of God (Gen. 20:11), the story explicitly rebuts this assumption with God confirming that Abimelech acted in integrity (20:4-6). The ethos of the story is utterly different from that of, for example, Lev. 18:24-30. Indeed, it is Abraham rather than Abimelech whose relationship with Sarah is at variance with Mosaic law (Gen. 20:12; Lev. 18:9, 11; 20:17).

Again, once the general point has been appreciated, exceptions

9. See, e.g., Ps-Philo, Biblical Antiquities 25:10, and esp. Targum Ps-Jonathan on Gen. 35:2, 4. Later, Rashi's comment on "foreign gods" in 35:2 is "which you have in your possession from the spoil of Shechem" (M. Rosenbaum and A. M. Silbermann, eds., *The Pentateuch with the Commentary of Rashi: Genesis* [Jerusalem: Silbermann], 1972), 169.

may be noted. Although Westermann goes so far as to say, "There is not so much as a single sentence which rejects Canaanite religion or morality,"[10] this overstates the case in light of Gen. 15:16 with its reference to the "wickedness" or "guilt" *('awon)* of the Amorites; also the people of Sodom were "great sinners against YHWH" (13:13).

Within this context, it is interesting to consider the question of intermarriage. How should one assess the emphasis that the tradition lays on Isaac and Jacob not marrying women of Canaan but rather women from among their own kindred (Gen. 24; 27:46—28:9)? How far does this indicate a negative judgment on the inhabitants of Canaan? Generally in the Old Testament, the prohibition on intermarriage with the inhabitants of Canaan is a corollary of a negative assessment of Canaanite religion that views it as a threat to faithfulness to YHWH (e.g., Exod. 34:11-16; Judg. 3:6; Ezra 9–10; cf. the famous judgment on Solomon for his marriages to foreign women, 1 Kings 11:1-10). Does the patriarchal prohibition on intermarriage therefore carry such overtones?

First, it is notable that the prohibition on intermarriage is not consistently carried through. Most notably, Joseph marries an Egyptian woman who bears him Ephraim and Manasseh (41:50-52), but also Judah and Simeon take Canaanite wives (38:2; 46:10). There is no hint of adverse comment against these marriages, and they are not presented negatively in terms of the development of the story.

Second, it is striking that with each prohibition on marrying a Canaanite woman no religious reason is given. When Abraham commissions his servant, the issue that is developed is not the religious danger of Canaanite women but whether Isaac should be taken back from Canaan to Aram if no wife is willing to come from Aram to Canaan (Gen. 24:5, 6, 8). Abraham is emphatic that Isaac must remain in Canaan, so much so that if no wife should come from Aram, the servant would be free from his commission, which would seem to imply that Isaac would then

10. Westermann, *Genesis 12–36,* 68.

be free to marry a Canaanite woman (an implication that, hardly surprisingly, gave rise to debate in postbiblical tradition).[11] When Isaac sends Jacob to Paddan-Aram, the only reason that the story gives is that Esau's Hittite wives make life bitter for Isaac and Rebekah (26:34f.; 27:46; 28:8f.). Although this implies a low assessment of the character of these Canaanite women, this is quite different from seeing them as a temptation to apostasize. Again, the silence of the biblical text may be compared with the development of postbiblical tradition which was quick to characterize Esau's wives as idolaters.[12] Thus, although the Genesis text has a clear sense of the distinctive line of Abraham's descent through Isaac and Jacob, through whom the divine promise is to be fulfilled, it cannot be said that this distinctiveness is expressed in the specifically religious terms that one would expect from elsewhere in the Old Testament.

The Cultic Practices of the Patriarchs Compared with Mosaic Law

The cultic practices of the patriarchs differ in important ways from what the Old Testament presents as characteristic of Mosaic Yahwism (especially in Deuteronomy). In these same ways they are probably similar to the cultic practices of the inhabitants of Canaan which the Old Testament elsewhere opposes. This can be seen in three main spheres.

First, there is no cultic center for the patriarchs, who worship and build altars in a number of places without any suggestion that one place is better than another. This contrasts with the significance that Shechem, Bethel, and supremely Jerusalem have elsewhere in the Old Testament. The importance of Jerusalem as the supreme place of worship is, of course, strongly hinted at in Gen. 22:1-19,[13] and also Gen. 14:18-20.[14] Nonetheless, the

11. See, e.g., Zlotowitz, *Bereishis,* 902–3.

12. See, e.g., Genesis Rabbah 65:16; see Zlotowitz, *Bereishis,* 1112.

13. The links of Genesis 22 with Jerusalem are threefold (cf. my "The Earliest Commentary on the Akedah," *VT* 38 [1988]: 306–7).

First is the emphasis in the story upon "seeing" (*ra'ah,* 22:8, 13), which is then related as a general principle to one place where God supremely sees (22:14a) and is seen (22:14b). This is probably to be connected with the name

way in which the significance of Jerusalem is only implied suggests, among other things, a regard for the distinctive character of the patriarchal period and a recognition that during the period in question Jerusalem did not yet have the official significance it later came to have.

There is, of course, a complex historical question about the development of legislation with regard to cult centers within Mosaic Yahwism. But the essential point is simply that Mosaic Yahwism, with its fundamental requirement of exclusive worship of YHWH, provided a natural context for legislation about legitimate cult centers to develop and that this concern is entirely lacking within the patriarchal material.

Second, it is notable that trees (Gen. 12:6-7; 13:18; 21:33) and pillars (28:18, 22; 31:45; 35:14) play a role of some sort within patriarchal religion with no implication of anything wrong with them. Their precise significance is left undefined (thus permitting widely different interpretations). But the important fact is simply their role within religious practice, because elsewhere such a religious role is explicitly prohibited with little explanation or clarification given (Exod. 23:24; 34:13; Lev. 26:1; Deut. 16:21-22). Admittedly, Abraham builds an altar beside a tree rather than plants a tree beside an altar, and the tree is not described as an Asherah. But there still appears to be a clear general affinity

of the place where the story happens, Moriah (22:2), understood as a noun from the verb *ra'ah* with the sense "Place of Seeing." Within the Old Testament generally are two places, par excellence, where God is seen: the two holy mountains (cf. above, pp. 9–10 & nn. 7, 8): first, Sinai (esp. Exod. 24:9-11; cf. Exod. 33:11—34:35; 1 Kings 19:9-18), and second, Jerusalem (e.g., 2 Sam. 24:15-17; Isa. 6:1; Psalm 84, esp. vv. 5, 8 [Heb. 6, 9]). Since the story envisages a location within the central territory of Israel, three days' journey from Beersheba, it is naturally Jerusalem rather than Sinai that is indicated.

Second, the site of the story is linked with "the mountain of YHWH" (*har yhwh,* 22:14b). Elsewhere in the Old Testament the phrase "the mountain of YHWH" is only used of Jerusalem (e.g., Ps. 24:3; Isa. 2:3), with the sole exception of Num. 10:33 where it is used of Sinai.

Third, the concerns of the story—place chosen by God, sacrifice, place where obedience to God must supremely be shown—all naturally relate to Jerusalem and Israel's worship in the temple.

14. Cf. above, p. 72. The cultic significance of the incident is suggested not only by Melchizedek bestowing a blessing but also by Abraham giving him a tithe, a practice normally only carried out in the presence of a priest at a sanctuary.

between Abraham's and Jacob's practices and those condemned in Deut. 16:21-22.

Again a difficult question arises about the history within Mosaic Yahwism of the prohibition of trees and pillars in cultic contexts. But the essential point is that Mosaic Yahwism naturally lends itself to the development of exclusivist legislation in a way alien to patriarchal religion. Our concern is to grasp the fundamental ethos and character of patriarchal and Mosaic religion (as understood by the Old Testament writers) rather than historically to investigate the ways in which they may have developed and been variously embodied.

Third, what of the three religious observances that from the postexilic period onward came to stand at the heart of Judaism (i.e., circumcision, sabbath observance, and dietary restrictions)? Of sabbath observance there is no hint in Genesis 12–50. Of dietary restrictions, there is also no hint, with the sole exception that it is said the Egyptians do not eat with the Hebrews (Gen. 43:32)—though not vice versa!

By contrast, circumcision is given great prominence in Genesis 17, and indeed Genesis 17 appears to be presupposed elsewhere in the Pentateuch, since no other legislation in Exodus-Deuteronomy requires circumcision. This, therefore, is the law basic to Yahwism. Yet even here, Ishmael, not Isaac, is the son who receives circumcision (17:25, 26). Since the storytellers know that Ishmael does not stand in the line of Israel's ancestors, presumably they would have been able to recast the tradition in such a way as to exclude Ishmael had they considered this appropriate. As the text stands, it seems clear that circumcision in the patriarchal context of Genesis 17 does not carry the kind of exclusive significance that it has in specifically Yahwistic tradition, such as in Judges and Samuel, where "uncircumcised" becomes a pejorative epithet for the Philistines, emphasizing that they are foreign to Israel and YHWH (e.g., Judg. 14:3; 1 Sam. 14:6; 17:26). It should be noted, however, that substantially this Yahwistic understanding of circumcision appears to be present in the unusual story of the massacre of the Shechemites after the rape of Dinah (Gen. 34:13-24).

Patriarchal Religion in Relation to Prophecy and Priesthood

The patriarchs have neither prophet nor priest to mediate between themselves and God, nor do they themselves fulfil the role of either prophet or priest with regard to others. There is a quality of unmediatedness about patriarchal religion, which contrasts with the central roles that prophet and priest hold in Mosaic Yahwism.

In a sense, of course, this is simply a corollary of the fact that Israel as a people does not exist in the patriarchal period, and so the need for mediation between the people and God does not arise. Nonetheless it remains striking that the patriarchs are not depicted in the same sort of way as Moses, who in Exodus is both archetypal prophet and priest, even though God speaks directly to both the patriarchs and Moses. We noted that in Exodus 3 Moses is depicted as a prophet, that is, someone sent to speak in YHWH's name. Quite conceivably, the patriarchs should function in this way to those around them, but the text gives no hint of it. (When the messenger formula, which was basic to classical prophecy, appears it is used only for a human, not a divine, message [Gen. 32:3-5]). Prophecy as supremely exemplified by Moses presupposes YHWH's dealings with Israel.

A partial exception to this is that one of the tasks of a prophet was to intercede in prayer on behalf of others (e.g., 1 Sam. 12:19, 23; 2 Kings 19:1-7; Jer. 7:16), and in this respect Abraham is explicitly said to be a prophet *(nabi')* who will pray for Abimelech (Gen. 20:7). Probably also Abraham's dialogue with YHWH about the fate of Sodom (Gen. 18:22-33) should be seen in this way. But the fact that the one prophetic function Abraham fulfills—intercessory prayer—is one that by its very nature is intrinsically separable from the prophetic role is a reminder that Abraham is not cast in the role of a Moses or a Jeremiah.

With regard to the lack of priesthood in Genesis 12–50, the obvious issue to consider is that of sacrifice. Given the numerous occasions on which it is said that an altar was built by the patriarchs (12:7, 8; 13:18; 26:25; 33:20; 35:1, 7), it is perhaps surprising that relatively little specific reference is made to sacrificial activity (only Gen. 22:1-19; 46:1-2). But the frequent references to calling on the name of YHWH (12:8; 13:4; 21:33; 26:25), in contexts where one would expect an explicit mention of sacrifice, are probably not meant to imply that sacrifice did not take place but rather to emphasize the close relation seen between sacrifice and prayer. Some influence from later Yahwistic perspectives is indeed evident in the text, not least in the fact that the one story of sacrifice told at length (Genesis 22) is implicitly located at Jerusalem and presented as foreshadowing the regular sacrificial worship in the temple. Nonetheless, any suggestion that sacrifice should involve specially qualified personnel with restrictions on function and access—as is indispensable to sacrificial priesthood—is lacking in the patriarchal stories.

Interestingly, the sole priest who appears in the course of the patriarchal narrative (apart from passing references to priests in Egypt [Gen. 41:45; 47:22]) is Melchizedek (Gen. 14:18). Not surprisingly, he is located at Jerusalem, as from a mature Yahwistic perspective this is the most appropriate location for a true priest who blesses Abraham, although the storyteller lays no emphasis on this. Although the blessing he gives is indeed a typical priestly action (cf. Num. 6:22-27; Deut. 10:8), it is an action not restricted to priests; it may be performed by the patriarchs themselves (e.g., Gen. 27:1-45; 47:10; 48:8-22; 49:28). Thus, despite the appearance of a priest connected with Jerusalem, the Genesis text does not convey the sense, which is characteristic of Mosaic Yahwism, that certain religious duties should only be carried out by priests.

Within this general context it is worth noting the "personal" aspect of patriarchal religion, which has featured prominently in most discussions that follow Alt. Alt observed that patriarchal religion "had one essential mark of the later religion of Yahweh. For it stressed above all the relationship between God and man, and between God and whole groups of men, without any fixed association with one place."[15] In one sense this is indisputable, but the language of "personal relationship" needs to be used with some care, since it is potentially so broad and unspecific that it

15. A. Alt, "God of the Fathers," 61.

may obscure importantly differing nuances. In general terms, both patriarchal and Mosaic religion clearly presuppose the kind of encounter between God and humanity that is best described by the language of human relationships. In this sense, as Alt notes, patriarchal religion should be seen as continuous with, and not different from, Mosaic Yahwism, and such a continuity would have been taken for granted by the Genesis writers. (Perhaps some of the significance attached to this personal element in modern expositions has been in reaction to the scholarly phase that once depicted pre-Yahwistic religion as something crude and animistic).[16] It should be remembered, however, that a personal rapport with God may be depicted in differing ways. Thus, for example, although God indeed relates to the patriarchs "without any fixed association with one place," when elsewhere in the Old Testament God's relationship with Israel is closely associated with Jerusalem, the relationship is seen as no less personal or constant for that reason, as far as one may judge the matter from the psalms. The important point is that if the "personal" nature of patriarchal piety is to be useful within analysis it needs to be carefully defined in relation to the other aspects of their religion, such as its lack of formal mediation.

The Patriarchs and the Land of Canaan

Although the patriarchs live in Canaan, there is no suggestion that the land should really belong to them rather than the Canaanites, and they display no aggression with regard to the land. This contrasts sharply with the characteristic attitude of Israel subsequently (Exod. 23:23-33; Deuteronomy 7, etc.). Although there is a sense in which the land is given to the patriarchs themselves (Gen. 13:15, 17; 17:8; 28:13), apparently primarily in the sense of a place to live in for the present, the predominant emphasis is on God's promise to give the land to the descendants of the patriarchs in the future (Gen. 12:7; 13:15-16; 15:18; 17:8; 28:13-14). This means that the Canaanites are regarded as legitimate owners for the present, so much so that both Abraham and

16. See, e.g., W. O. E. Oesterley and T. H. Robinson, *Hebrew Religion: Its Origin and Development* (London: SPCK, 1930), pt. 1.

Jacob buy territory from them (Gen. 23; 33:19). Abraham refers to the land he had come from as "my land" (Gen. 24:4), and he never refers to Canaan in this way. Insofar as the relationship of the patriarchs to the land of Canaan is made explicit, it is always characterized by various forms of the verbal root *gur,* to "sojourn" (e.g., Gen. 17:8; 21:23, 34; 26:3; 35:27; Exod. 6:4). And in the Old Testament the notion of sojourning always implies temporary residence and dependence on the hospitality of others who live in the place permanently.

A consistent corollary of the understanding that the land is not given to the patriarchs except as a place to sojourn is the lack of military activity to take possession of the land.[17] Not that warlike action is entirely lacking. Abraham is depicted as able to command a small army (Gen. 14:14-16), and the sons of Jacob are able to slaughter the inhabitants of Shechem (Gen. 34:25-31). Such warlike abilities, however, are never put toward conquest or occupation of the land, nor is any suggestion made that they should be.

Again, one exception to this general picture is the reference in Gen. 48:22 to Jacob taking territory from the Amorites "with my sword and my bow." This isolated reference to warlike occupation of land is puzzling, not least because Jacob is referring back to something that happened previously, and in the preceding text nothing corresponds to it. We may simply note the exceptional character of the text and surmise that perhaps here, too, the narrator has allowed specifically Yahwistic characteristics to color the presentation of the story.

The Moral Content of Patriarchal Religion

Generally speaking, patriarchal religion lacks moral content or at least moral emphasis in a way that contrasts with the strong moral content enjoined upon Israel by the covenant at Sinai. This can be seen in a number of ways.

First, God gives striking promises of blessing to Abraham, Isaac, and Jacob, and yet little emphasis is laid on moral obedience on the part of the patriarchs, with the exception of Abraham

17. See further below, pp. 186f.

(Gen. 15:6; 17:1; 18:19; 22:16, 18; 26:5), the likely significance of which will be discussed later.[18] When, for example, God appears to the young Jacob God makes a promise with no moral stipulation or any commission attached, either of which, in the light of the Sinai covenant (e.g., Exod. 19:5-6) or prophetic calls (e.g., Isaiah 6; 1 Sam. 3:10-14; cf. Judg. 6:11-16) might have been expected. Moreover, in the course of the narrative Abraham, Isaac, and Jacob each receive a blessing from God (Gen. 21:22; 24:1; 26:12f., 30:27-30, 43). This blessing is portrayed in terms of well-being and prosperity in the same way as blessing is portrayed in the covenant blessings of Deut. 28:1-14. But the relationship between this blessing and the life-style of the patriarchs is left entirely unspecified, except in the case of Abraham (esp. Gen. 18:19; 22:16, 18; 26:5).

Second, as a natural corollary of the first point, the patriarchs are given no warnings of judgment for disobedience to God. The possibility of curse as well as blessing, as regularly presented both in the law codes and in prophetic literature (e.g., Deut. 30:15-20; Hos. 4:1-3), is nowhere alluded to in the patriarchal traditions. Of course, the notion of sin and divine judgment is present in the text, most notably in the story of Sodom and Gomorrah (Gen. 13:13; 18:16—19:29) and to a lesser extent in the story of Joseph and his brothers (Gen. 37, 39–45; esp. 39:9; 44:16). Nonetheless the overall ethos of the story, particularly with regard to Abraham, Isaac, and Jacob, entirely lacks the emphasis upon sin and judgment and the corresponding need for moral choice that is characteristic of Mosaic Yahwism.

Third, it is striking that the patriarchal narratives as a whole entirely lack any framework of moral interpretation (as opposed to theological interpretation in terms of divine promise and typology).[19] This is unique within the Old Testament, for the histories of Israel as a nation (in Exodus-Deuteronomy, in Joshua–2 Kings, and in Chronicles, Ezra, and Nehemiah) all in one way or another present the material within an overarching framework of some kind of moral interpretation. This omission

18. Below, pp. 135f., 142ff.

19. See below, pp. 140ff.

again suggests regard for the distinctive nature of the period of the patriarchs.

The Lack of Holiness in Patriarchal Religion

The exposition of patriarchal religion thus far has attempted to bring out the interrelated nature of the various characteristics observed and to show an overall consistency in the ethos and practice of the religion. The matter-of-fact worship of one God, with its corresponding absence of a sense of urgent religious choice, appears to be the basis for all other features: on the one hand, a lack of conflict between patriarchal and Canaanite religion, seen in similarity of cultic practice, lack of condemnatory attitudes, and lack of aggression; on the other hand, a marked difference between patriarchal and Mosaic religion, seen in differing cultic practice with corresponding differences regarding prophets and priests, differing attitudes to the land of Canaan, and differing moral emphasis. Generally speaking, the distinctive ethos of the patriarchal traditions has been well captured by Gordon Wenham: "There is an air of ecumenical bonhomie about the patriarchal religion which contrasts with the sectarian exclusiveness of the Mosaic age and later prophetic demands."[20]

Our final point can perhaps best be seen as epitomizing both the internal consistency of patriarchal religion and its distinctiveness from Mosaic Yahwism. This is the concept of holiness.

The notion of holiness, which from Exodus onward is a basic characteristic of God and a major requirement for Israel, is entirely lacking in the patriarchal traditions, and this difference is consistently observed in terms of both language and concept.[21] Terminologically, the Hebrew root *qdš* does not appear in Genesis 12–50 except in two insignificant ways—in the place name Kadesh (Gen. 14:7; 16:14; 20:1) and in the depiction of Tamar as a prostitute (*qedešah,* Gen. 38:21f.). Neither God nor the patri-

20. Wenham, "Religion of the Patriarchs," 184.

21. The verbal form of *qdš* is used in an important way in the primeval history (Gen. 2:3). But the primeval history is distinct from the patriarchal history. As already noted, the pentateuchal writers feel free to depict the primeval history in the theological categories of normative Mosaic Yahwism. When Israel's own story begins with Abraham, the content of the tradition exercises significant constraints on the writers.

archs are ever designated by *qdš*. By contrast, the first use of the noun "holiness" in the Pentateuch (*qodeš,* Exod. 3:5) is in the story of the burning bush at Sinai, the context in which God is first revealed as YHWH. And when the people of Israel later arrive at Sinai, the first thing that is said to them is that they are to be a holy nation (*goy qadoš,* Exod. 19:6). The concept of holiness pervades Mosaic Yahwism and is extensively developed in its religious and moral implications in the various pentateuchal laws, more of which are related to holiness than to any other religious concept.

In order to appreciate further the significance of this contrast between the patriarchs and Mosaic Yahwism, it is important briefly to consider the meaning of *qdš* in the Pentateuch. The Pentateuch itself never offers a definition and uses the terminology in a variety of ways, but nonetheless a fundamental sense does become clear. This may usefully be approached via a comparison with the classic modern work on holiness, which has greatly influenced much subsequent literature, that is Rudolph Otto's *The Idea of the Holy.*[22]

Otto argues that the original meaning of holy had nothing to do with morality but rather with a distinctively religious dimension of life which he calls "numinous" and analyzes in terms of a transcendent mystery that is both awesome and appealing. Otto says of the numinous that "there is no religion in which it does not live as the real innermost core, and without it no religion would be worthy of the name. It is pre-eminently a living force in the Semitic religions, and of these again in none has it such vigour as in that of the Bible. Here, too, it has a name of its own, viz. the Hebrew *qādôš,* to which the Greek ἅγιος and the Latin *sanctus,* and, more accurately still, *sacer,* are the corresponding terms."[23] He goes on to say about Mosaic Yahwism that "the noble religion of Moses marks the beginning of a process which

22. Rudolph Otto, *The Idea of the Holy* (Oxford: Oxford Univ. Press, 1924; German, 1917). It is interesting that the most recent study on holiness in the Old Testament—J. G. Gammie, *Holiness in Israel,* Overtures to Biblical Theology (Minneapolis: Fortress, 1989)—builds extensively on Otto's foundations (see esp. pp. 5–8). Unfortunately, this means that most of our criticisms of Otto apply equally (and sometimes more so) to Gammie.

23. Otto, *Idea of the Holy,* 6.

from that point onward proceeds with ever increasing momentum, by which 'the numinous' is throughout rationalized and moralized, i.e. charged with ethical import, until it becomes 'the holy' in the fullest sense of the word. The culmination of the process is found in the Prophets and in the Gospels. And it is in this that the special nobility of the religion revealed to us by the Bible is to be found. . . ."[24]

This is not the place to engage with Otto's main thesis about the universality and validity of religious experience, nor to discuss the conceptual categories in which he traces the historical development of "the holy." Larger questions about the phenomenology of religion must be left to one side. Nonetheless, Otto's basic point about holiness and religious experience will serve as a useful foil for our own analysis.

First, Otto does not note the distribution of *qdš* terminology or its absence in Genesis 12–50. It is not that the patriarchal traditions lack a sense of the numinous. For example, the story of Jacob at Bethel (Gen. 28:10-22) can well convey a sense of the numinous without using the term *qdš* (which Otto ignores in his discussion of the story),[25] and there are various other "numinous" stories where, on Otto's premise, the language of holiness would be appropriate but is, in fact, absent (e.g., Gen. 15; 22; 32:22-32).

Second, Otto does not note the pentateuchal linkage between *qdš* and the revelation of God as YHWH to Moses and Israel. In this conjunction it is worth noting that apart from the patriarchal traditions there is only one other group of writings in the Old Testament where the usage of *qdš* is consistently absent, and that is the wisdom literature (i.e., Job, Proverbs, Ecclesiastes, Song of Songs). Within this considerable corpus of material, the *qdš* root occurs only occasionally (Job 1:5; 5:1; 6:10; 15:15; 36:14; Prov. 9:10; 20:25; 30:3; Eccles. 8:10), always in passing, and never with conceptual significance in terms of the concerns of the book.

24. Ibid., 77.

25. Ibid., 130–32. The influence of Otto's lack of precision at this point may be seen in, for example, J. P. Fokkelman's discussion of the Bethel story in which he routinely refers to Bethel as *'admat qodeš* despite the lack of such language in the Hebrew text (*Narrative Art in Genesis* [Assen/Amsterdam: Van Gorcum, 1975], 63–4).

Given the fact that the fundamental theological premise of wisdom literature is "creation theology" (i.e., reflection on what is generally the case within the world without appeal to the specific traditions of YHWH's dealings with Israel), this linguistic and conceptual absence of *qdš* is entirely consistent with our contention that the Old Testament understands holiness as integrally related to the particularity of Israel's relationship with YHWH.

Third, the pentateuchal texts lay remarkably little emphasis on the numinous and experiential dimensions of *qdš.* Of course, Otto might consider that this reflects an advanced degree of rationalization of the concept, and this may be the case. Nonetheless, the consistency with which, for example, the book of Exodus construes holiness in terms other than Otto's should be appreciated. Apart from the occasional use of *qdš* to designate Israel's religious institutions (Exod. 12:16; 13:2; 16:23), the predominant use is with regard to Sinai, the mountain that is holy because of YHWH's presence there (Exod. 3:5; 15:13, 17; 19:10ff.)—language that elsewhere is used of Mount Zion.[26] In Exodus 19ff. Sinai is portrayed as the archetypal sanctuary, the holy place at which access is restricted and controlled (the first thing said to Moses at the burning bush is "Do not approach"). Moses functions as the archetypal priest who has full access; other select people have limited access, and Israel generally must maintain a distance (Exod. 19:10-24; 24:1-18; esp. 24:1-2). Israel's relationship to YHWH's holy place where YHWH is encountered is regulated by intermediaries, and this corresponds to Israel's own choice, given the overwhelming nature of hearing YHWH's voice direct and unmediated (20:18-21). As the people of Israel worship YHWH at this sanctuary, they are designated a holy nation (19:6) and consecrated as such (24:3-8). This entails their obedience to YHWH's commandments—exclusive worship of YHWH, rejection of alien religious practices, and moral and religious obedience in specified areas; all of which is to be carried out in the land YHWH gives Israel to possess (23:20-33). Moreover, YHWH's holy presence on Sinai continues with Israel in the tabernacle (25:8; 29:38-46; 40:34-38) until YHWH

26. Cf. above, pp. 9f.

chooses another holy mountain in which to have the sanctuary, that is, Mount Zion (e.g., 1 Kings 8:1-13).

This outline sketch, of course, obscures numerous distinctions within the text that are commonly made, but the object of the exercise is to discern an ethos which in one way or another is present in all the various levels of the text. The book of Exodus presents holiness as an exclusive relationship between Israel and YHWH focused upon worship at YHWH's sanctuary.

In summary, then, whatever the possible general value of operating with a broad understanding of "holiness" as a means of religious analysis in the way advocated by Otto and most recently developed by John Gammie, it should be noted that the Old Testament does not present *qdš* either as a universal aspect of religion or as a sense of the numinous. Although Gammie quotes with approval the words of Ernst Sellin, *"God is holy.* Herein we touch on that which constitutes the deepest and innermost nature of the God of the Old Testament,"[27] this is, in fact, inaccurate. The correct wording would be *"YHWH is holy,"* for we have seen that the Old Testament writers can well envisage contexts in which God is operative and yet where holiness, insofar as this is expressed by *qdš,* is not an issue; *qdš* is integral to Israel's relationship with YHWH but is entirely lacking in patriarchal religion (and effectively lacking in the wisdom literature). Moreover, although both patriarchal and Mosaic religions contain awesome encounters with God, in neither case are these usually depicted with the language of *qdš,* nor do they determine the fundamental ethos that in each case is essentially related to a particular kind of monotheism (open for the patriarchs and exclusive for Israel), and a particular kind of life-style (familial for the patriarchs, national for Israel).

SUMMARY OF DISCUSSION

In light of the above, we can see good cumulative evidence to support our thesis that the writers of the Pentateuch shared a common tradition that the patriarchs had lived in a context prior to and distinct from that of Mosaic Yahwism. Admittedly, the

27. Gammie, *Holiness in Israel,* 3.

patriarchal story is occasionally told in terms uncharacteristic of its own ethos yet characteristic of Mosaic Yahwism (Gen. 15:16; 34:14-17; 35:2, 4; 48:22), yet these notes are only sounded in passing and so tend simply to prove the rule. It is perfectly reasonable to maintain that the pentateuchal writers usually maintained an awareness of a distinctive context when they retold the patriarchal stories from within the context of Mosaic Yahwism and yet occasionally lapsed into their own categories.[28]

Finally, we have seen that the difference between patriarchal and Mosaic religion is perhaps most conveniently epitomized by the notion of holiness, as expressed by *qdš*. The concept of holiness, from Exod. 3:5 onward, focuses the exclusive, demanding, regulated, mediated, and sanctuary-centered relationship between YHWH and Israel, while the absence of holiness in patriarchal religion equally epitomizes its open, unstructured, and nonlocated unaggressive nature, its "ecumenical bonhomie."

28. It is not part of our present purpose to examine whether all the passages that portray the patriarchal period in specifically Yahwistic categories are from the same hand. It is interesting to note, however, that Gen. 34:14-17; 35:2, 4; 48:22 have all conventionally been ascribed to P. If there is any significance in this ascription it stands in opposition to the conventional understanding of P as the writer who most scrupulously observed the difference between the patriarchal and Mosaic periods (see, e.g., Westermann, *Genesis 12–36,* 258).

CHAPTER 4

The Old Testament of the Old Testament

We have argued thus far that God's self-revelation to Moses in Exodus 3 is consistently portrayed in the Pentateuch as representing a new beginning, a newness focused in God's self-revelation as YHWH and accompanied by the unfolding of Mosaic Yahwism, which through Exodus and Sinai constitutes Israel as the holy people of YHWH. We have argued also that the Pentateuch more or less consistently portrays patriarchal religion as distinct from Mosaic Yahwism. Yet we have noted that the biblical text takes for granted that the God of the patriarchs is one and the same as YHWH the God of Israel, so much so that the patriarchal story is told with frequent use of the name YHWH. This brings us now to the crucial question for the thesis of this book: What is the nature of the relationship between patriarchal religion in Genesis 12–50 and Mosaic Yahwism in Exodus onward?

The recognition that this is an important issue is, in principle, nothing new. From both source-critical and traditiohistorical perspectives it has been widely agreed that both the E elements in Exodus 3 and the P tradition in Exod. 6:2ff. are making the point of a new beginning with Moses. From a general historical perspective there has been a consensus that Israel's religion did indeed begin with Moses and also that Yahwism as associated with Moses is distinct from the pre-Yahwistic religion still discernible in Genesis 12–50. Given this awareness of the difference between patriarchal and Mosaic religion, the question of the relationship between the different religious outlooks has naturally often been raised.

Since the problem is well known, the crucial factor is not so much the recognition of the problem as such but rather the way it is perceived and discussed. What is striking about most existing literature is that it has consistently treated thc problem as having to do with various facets of religious history. On the one hand, what can we know about the nature of patriarchal and early Mosaic religion, and how did Mosaic religion develop out of its antecedents? On the other hand, what was the religious thought of the Elohistic and Priestly writers? These are, of course, interesting and important (even if often somewhat intractable) questions. Remarkably, however, explicit theological engagement with the issue has tended to be minimal or simply nonexistent. Insofar as theological interest has been expressed, it has tended to be a gloss upon the historical reconstruction. For example, use has been made of Alt's observation about patriarchal religion as a *paidagogos* to Mosaic Yahwism.[1] For the most part, however, interest has been in religious history rather than in theology as such. To say this is not to criticize, for the question of religious history is an entirely proper undertaking for the scholar, and it is hardly appropriate to criticize other scholars for working according to their own agendas and for not doing something other than what they were doing (though one may wonder whether the theological judgment expressed by *paidagogos* was seriously thought through in its own right).[2] Nonetheless, the fact remains that

1. See, e.g., J. Bright, *A History of Israel,* 3d ed. (London: SCM, 1981), 103.

2. For a sharp critique, see H. W. F. Saggs, *The Encounter with the Divine in Mesopotamia and Israel* (London: Athlone; New Jersey: Humanities Press, 1978), 36–38. Saggs comments, "The assumption is commonly made that Mosaic Yahwism represented an advance over patriarchal religion [footnote reference to Alt]; but, insofar as no attempt is made to substantiate this view by evidence, it appears to rest on no more than an evolutionary view of religious development. If one proposes to make value judgements about the matter, it is at least a theoretical possibility that the concept of deity attributed to the Mosaic period was a retrogression from that of the Patriarchs. As soon as Moses appears in the tradition, the concept of God is narrower, less tolerant and more naive. . . . In tradition, therefore, the God of the Patriarchs had quite different qualities from those of the original Mosaic God Yahweh; a tincture of universalism as against ethnic exclusiveness; mercy and tolerance against intolerance and vindictiveness; a calm prosecution of a predetermined plan as against aggressive self-assertion and *ad hoc* reaction."

theology is not simply a matter of religious history and may have an agenda of its own. The difference between theology and religious history is a subject of much debate and disagreement in contemporary biblical scholarship. Since the difference is essential to our thesis, we will preface our own theological discussion with a consideration of a number of existing discussions. These tend to be oriented to a historian's agenda and have created and sustained a scholarly consensus. Only then will we develop our own thesis in the light of them.

MODERN DISCUSSIONS OF THE RELATIONSHIP BETWEEN PATRIARCHAL AND MOSAIC RELIGION

First, Wellhausen. His *Prolegomena* set out the basic categories within which all subsequent pentateuchal criticism has been carried out.[3] In the course of his discussion of the Priestly Code, Wellhausen writes the following:

> It is also a mark of historical pedantry that the mixing up of the period of the patriarchs with a later period is avoided as anachronistic. . . . It is pointed out with emphasis that God was not known to the pre-Mosaic time under His Israelite name, that He revealed Himself to the patriarchs only as El Shaddai, and as Jehovah first to Moses (Exod. vi.2, 3). With a similar intention, which is not far to seek, the time of the patriarchs is kept free of the other Mosaic forms of worship. . . . Now till within a short time ago, there was a great inclination (no one will be found at this date to acknowledge that he felt it) to admire the sobriety and faithfulness of the Priestly Code, as shown in this observance of the different religious stages. . . . How can we regard it as showing historical faithfulness [in the light of Wellhausen's analysis of the history of Israelite religious institutions] . . .? What is it but a theory, that the name Jehovah was first revealed to Moses, and through him to the Israelites, and that it was quite unknown before?—a theory which certainly cannot be upheld, for Moses could have done nothing more irrational than to introduce a new name for the God of their fathers, to whom he directed his people,—and yet a theory which, from the correlation

Even if Saggs' reading of the text is somewhat tendentious, his basic point, about not taking for granted value-laden judgments about the relationship between patriarchal and Mosaic religion, is well taken.

We will return to this issue later (below, pp. 165f.).

3. J. Wellhausen, *Prolegomena to the History of Ancient Israel* (reprint, Gloucester, Mass.: Peter Smith, 1973).

> between Jehovah the God of Israel and Israel the people of Jehovah, readily suggests itself, and is not altogether peculiar to the author of the Priestly Code (Footnote: Exod. vi.2, 3 (Q) = iii.13, 14 [JE]). He had a pattern which suggested certain lines, and these he traces strongly and with a system.[4]

Wellhausen's concern is entirely with the history of Israelite religion. Against those who had argued that the Priestly Code was the earliest pentateuchal source and in many ways historically accurate, Wellhausen argues that the Priestly Code is a late source and, as far as concerns Israel's early religion, historically worthless. The distinction between two religious eras is simply a theory and a mistaken theory at that, although Wellhausen recognizes that its logic is somehow rooted in the earliest portrayal of Yahwism. It is a distinction that does not belong to the history of religion proper but solely to the history of mistaken ideas about the history of religion.

Second, Alt. In his seminal discussion of the religion of the patriarchs Alt treats Exodus 3 and 6 at some length. With regard to Exodus 3 in the Elohist version (which consists of "vv. 1,4b,6, 9–14, 18–23") Alt says,

> The specific function of this story in the plan of the whole Elohist narrative is, on the one hand, to make the reader conscious of the complete contrast in the sight of God between the time of the patriarchs and that of Moses, and on the other hand to compose the difference again in a higher unity by presenting the same God as bearer of the old and new divine names. The story thus becomes the link by which the Elohist sagas of the patriarchs and of Moses can be kept distinct and yet brought into a very close relationship with one another.[5]

Alt recognizes and states the meaning and purpose of the text in a characteristically succinct way; yet, equally characteristically, he does not focus on this meaning and purpose in its own right or the theological implications it contains but rather explicitly brackets out such concerns and instead directs attention to questions of historical reconstruction. Thus he continues:

4. Ibid., 338–39.

5. A. Alt, "The God of the Fathers," in his *Essays on Old Testament History and Religion* (Oxford: Blackwell, 1966; German, 1929, 1953), 11.

> No other narrative work in the Hexateuch contains an exact parallel to this, and the Yahwist, who shows Yahweh in intercourse with men, and especially with the ancestors of Israel, from the beginning, obviously cannot be expected to provide one. . . . The priestly narrative is different again. Its version is like that of the Elohist, in that it combines the revelation of the name Yahweh with the call of Moses in a single act, and thereby contrasts the new name uttered by Yahweh himself with the title revealed to the patriarchs. . . . But in the priestly narrative the title of the God of the Fathers, which is now superseded by the name of Yahweh, is not "the God of Abraham, Isaac and Jacob," as in the Elohist, but *'Ēl Šaddai*. . . . This divergence between the Elohist and the priestly writer at the crucial point of a story which they tell otherwise in the same way, and which has the same important function to fulfil in both narratives, as well as the complete lack of any parallel in the Yahwist, is of fundamental importance for *our study of what they tell us about the tradition behind them.* For it follows that the writers could not have possessed at this point any fixed and unified tradition that they felt bound to follow. . . . *Later theories about the theology of history are here in conflict, and anyone who wishes to sift out the genuine ancient traditions must set these secondary elements aside altogether* [italics added].[6]

With regard to the Elohist conception in its own right, Alt sees it as an artificial and self-contradictory editorial construct. He says of it,

> The Elohist account in Exodus iii . . . can only have reached its present complicated state by the conscious intervention of the writer. As it stands, it contains obvious tensions, which can hardly be conceived of within the simple original saga. . . . If the god who appears to Moses announces himself in his very first words as the God of Abraham, Isaac and Jacob (v.6), there is no need for him to be given a new name. That Moses should expect that his people would ask him the name of the god who commissioned him when he came to them with the message "the God of your Fathers has sent me to you" (v.13) is self-contradictory. Nothing occurs in the story to resolve this tension. . . . The analysis of the passage confirms . . . [that the Elohist] was the first to bring the naming of the God of the Fathers into the story, and his intention in adding this was to reveal to the reader, at the very point where the age of the Fathers passes into the age of Moses, the close connection which ac-

6. Ibid., 11–12.

> cording to his view of the theology of history exists between these two periods.
>
> But if it is the case that the *purely theoretical purposes* of the Elohist led him to place the figure of the God of the Fathers in a position of such emphasis, then the question arises whether the distinctive title God is given here was coined by him in the first place, merely in order to contrast it with the name Yahweh, thus effectively demonstrating the difference between the two main eras in the past. It is not very likely that he invented so freely [italics added].[7]

Alt then proceeds to discuss the historical question of elements in Israel's tradition as used by the Elohist and the Priestly writer that may be genuinely ancient. Since he gives a positive answer to this question in terms of the cult of the God of the Fathers, he necessarily has to return to a consideration of the relationship between this religion and Yahwism. Although the historical problems are exceedingly complex, Alt concludes,

> The ultimate destiny of the worship of the gods of the Fathers must be understood historically as a result of the encroachment of the *national* cult of Yahweh upon the *local* sanctuaries of the Israelite tribes in Palestine, even where this involved the assimilation of fundamentally different types of religion. . . . But we must not overlook the fact that in the case of the God of Abraham, etc., the character of these numina was in one most important respect very well adapted to their identification with Yahweh. For everything that we recognized as truly characteristic of these and similar gods in the Arab and Aramaean areas—their association with particular groups of men, families, clans, or tribes, their providential oversight over the fortunes of their worshippers in the desert, and where they had settled, their concern with social and historical events—all this recurs, only on a higher level and over a much wider field, in the character of Yahweh as the God of Israel. . . . The same fundamental outlook and practice are simply carried on to a higher plane. . . . The gods of the Fathers were the παιδαγωγοί leading to the greater God, who later replaced them completely.[8]

We should note three points about Alt's position (while eschewing any assessment in historical terms). First, as a historian Alt has no place for the theological conception of different religious eras. He recognizes the difference between patriarchal

7. Ibid., 12–13.
8. Ibid., 60, 61, 62.

and Yahwistic religion but does not see this as in any way problematic (except in historical terms), for he is able to explain the difference in terms of historical development and continuity. Second, Alt is consistently dismissive of theological concerns, which he labels as "secondary elements" and "purely theoretical purposes." One gets the impression that theological enquiry is not just different from historical enquiry but also greatly inferior to it. Third, however, Alt evaluates Yahwism as on a "higher plane" than patriarchal religion and borrows the Pauline concept of *paidagogos* (Gal. 3:24) in order to interpret the historical development. This assessment of the developmental process is hardly entailed by the material itself,[9] and indeed Alt thereby introduces a "later theory about the theology of history," which seems to sit a little awkwardly alongside his earlier methodological exclusion of such. Generally speaking, Alt seems to operate in a way characteristic of many religious historians. His explicit stance and method is that of a historian, and he not only excludes but tends to be dismissive of theology as such. But to his historical work is added nonetheless an (admittedly minimal) theological dimension whose methodological relationship to the rest of his work is left entirely unclear. Because of this unclarity the theological dimension is not thought through or developed but essentially functions as an afterthought.

Third, M. Haran. Haran's article "The Religion of the Patriarchs" was a notable attempt to offer a fresh synthesis on the whole issue of patriarchal religion and its relationship to Yahwism in the light of the debate initiated by Wellhausen and Gunkel (of whose traditiohistorical approach Alt offered the most influential example). Haran begins his essay with a quick sketch of a traditional religious view:

> The Bible assumes that the Patriarchal God was identical with the God of Israel in the post-Mosaic era, although He made himself mostly known to the Patriarchs under names other than Yahweh. This view has become deeply rooted in Judaism . . . [and] was passed on to Christianity. . . . This view evolved into an incontestable principle in medieval thought, sometimes influencing, albeit indirectly, even modern research [footnote on certain nineteenth-century movements and on fundamentalism]. Yet, it cannot serve

9. See the criticisms of Saggs [n. 2].

> as a starting-point today, all the more so as it has become obvious that the biblical tradition itself contains decisive evidence against such a view.[10]

One thing is immediately striking about Haran's assertion that the traditional viewpoint "cannot serve as a starting-point today." He makes a fundamental assumption that a theological question about the nature of God is really a historical question about the development of religion. This is, to say the least, odd, since it is by no means self-evident precisely how the evidence of diverse religious beliefs and practices on the part of the patriarchs could disprove the theological understanding of the biblical writers that there is one God who was made known in different ways. Haran is clearly not unsympathetic to the traditional Judaeo-Christian view. Although his overall concern is that of a historian seeking to trace the relationship between Mosaic religion and its precursors, and he emphasizes the diversity and complexity of the likely historical development, he nonetheless draws out the continuity between them in such a way as to be not uncongenial to traditional religious belief (in nonfundamentalist form). He never returns, however, to engage with the theological issue he poses at the outset, nor does he clarify how his historical work affects the theological issue. As such, Haran's formulation of the problem of the relationship between patriarchal and Yahwistic religion is methodologically confused and essentially begs the question as to the relationship between religious history and theology. In this, however, Haran's approach may be typical of a recurrent problem among biblical scholars.

With regard to the name YHWH, Haran considers that it was pre-Mosaic in origin. It "was drawn primarily from the mythological store of the ancient Hebrew tribes" but became "an outstanding symbol of the Mosaic message" via a process of "thorough ideological upheaval."[11] With regard to Exodus 3 his discussion is somewhat obscure but seems to be a variant of the view that the text portrays the giving of a new significance of an already familiar name. His discussion of Exodus 6 is clearer:

10. M. Haran, "The Religion of the Patriarchs," *ASTI* 4 (1965): 30.
11. Ibid., 37.

> The outlook of P, according to which the name Yahweh has absolutely no footing in the pre-Mosaic period, is somewhat exceptional. P draws a line of demarcation between the period of the Patriarchs and the one following: until the end of the former, God made himself known by the name *'El Shaddai* only; from then onward, by the name Yahweh only (Ex. vi,2-3). . . . P identifies *'El Shaddai* with the Yahweh of Moses' message. It is from P that we infer that *'El Shaddai* was the primary God of the Patriarchs. Yet, this source is much more rigid and dogmatic than any other. It sketches the tradition in a most formalistic manner, turning it into a mere symmetrical scheme.[12]

Note two features of this. One feature is the derogatory terminology used about P—"rigid," "dogmatic," "formalistic"—such as one might have expected from Wellhausen. Another is the lack of any serious attention to P's conception in its own right. Presumably Haran adopts such an attitude to P mainly because P denies that the name YHWH is pre-Mosaic, while for Haran the pre-Mosaic origin of the name YHWH is basic to his reconstruction. P was right that *'El Shaddai* was an ancient pre-Mosaic name but wrong to construct a theological scheme that correspondingly denies knowledge of YHWH in the same pre-Mosaic period. P's theological conception is a hindrance rather than a help to the historian and, apart from its valid point about *'El Shaddai,* may be dismissed without more ado.

Fourth, F. M. Cross. Cross may be taken as representative of the many American scholars who, influenced especially by W. F. Albright, have devoted great attention to interpreting Israel's early traditions. Cross's essay "The Religion of Canaan and the God of Israel" is a significant development of Alt's work on patriarchal religion.

Cross begins by summarizing Alt's position:

> Elohistic tradition in Exodus 3:13-15 is crucial to Alt's analysis. . . . In this text there is a clear claim for the continuity between the religion of the Fathers and the Yahwistic faith of later Israel. At the same time the text, precisely in its insistence that Yahweh is to be identified with the god of the Fathers, discloses to the historian that the old religion and the Mosaic religion were historically distinct or, in any case, belonged to two stages in a historical development.

12. Ibid., 38–39.

> The Priestly tradition in Exodus 6:2-3 points in part in a similar direction. . . . In this stratum of tradition there is also the recognition of a cleavage between the ancient time and the Yahwistic era, though again there is the theological affirmation of the ultimate identity of the god of the Patriarchs and Yahweh.[13]

Although there is recognition of the theological dimension of the biblical text, at least in Exod. 6:2f., no attempt is made to explore it. The theological affirmation of divine identity functions simply to alert the historian to diverse religious traditions underlying the text, and the historical explication of this diverse religious development is offered as an interpretation of the text.

Cross proceeds to argue that patriarchal religion was based on the cult of 'El and that YHWH was originally a cultic name of 'El. In the light of this he makes various suggestions about religious continuity between Canaanite religion and the religious practice of both the Southern and Northern Kingdoms in Israel. He concludes:

> Our interests have been directed toward the continuities between the god of the Fathers and Yahweh, god of Israel. We have agreed with Alt to this extent, that Patriarchal religion had special features: the tutelary deity or deities entered into an intimate relationship with a social group. . . . This strain entered Yahwism. Yahweh was judge and war leader of the historical community. He revealed himself to the Patriarch Moses. . . . There is also the second strain which entered Israel's primitive religion, that of the high and eternal one, 'El the creator of heaven and earth, father of all.[14]

Again, the theological issue that Exodus 3 and 6 pose—that is, of one God who is revealed in different ways in different periods of time—receives no attention as such. Rather, the issue raised by the text is seen as a matter of religious history, facing the scholar with the task of showing continuity between different religious groupings, specifically showing how Yahwism developed out of its precursors.

Fifth, N. Gottwald. His *Tribes of Yahweh* is a bold attempt to offer a total reconstruction of Israel's origins.[15] Central to Gott-

13. F. M. Cross, *Canaanite Myth and Hebrew Epic* (Cambridge, Mass.: Harvard Univ. Press, 1973), 5.

14. Ibid., 75.

15. N. Gottwald, *The Tribes of Yahweh* (London: SCM, 1980).

wald's approach is a methodological concern to write a history that takes seriously the sociological dimensions of religious belief and language. Gottwald regards theology as ideology and ideology as a rationalizing projection of sociological reality. Since he is highly critical of those scholars who too easily accept the highly ideological character of the biblical text as it now stands without penetrating to the sociological reality that lies behind the ideology, one would hardly expect Gottwald to give much attention to the theological dimensions of the text in their own right, and this is indeed the case. For our purposes, however, the important question is less whether Gottwald's understanding of theology is questionable than whether and to what extent his account on his own premises accurately characterizes the content of pentateuchal tradition.

The familiar distinction between patriarchal and Mosaic religion is recognized by Gottwald and, in general terms, is understood to show something of the diversity of contemporary groupings within early Israel, a diversity rationalized by the construction of an artificial chronological sequence ("anachronizing periodization"):

> It was known to all the component peoples of Israel that, in spite of its recent mutation as a genuinely novel social system, the various peoples who joined their fortunes in Israel had prehistories of their own. There was a desire that these prehistories not be lost but that their peculiar features be preserved, yet preserved *systematically* in such a way that the peculiarities of each sub-history would affirm and solidify the unity of the whole. . . .
>
> So firmly was the principle established that all prior experiences of any member of unified Israel were to be seen as experiences of all Israel that they were schematized insofar as possible as the experiences of the associated tribes from the bondage in Egypt to the occupation of the land. But there were limitations to continuing such a project of assimilating the discrete traditions. Some of the traditions were permeated by conditions and circumstances which were inconsistent with that unified picture. Specifically, some of the episodes concerned people who were not Yahwists (but rather worshipers of El), and the setting for the episodes was in or near Canaan. Such traditions implied either that they told of events *prior to* the unified history from Egypt to Canaan or of events *subsequent to* the unified history. Of the two temporal conceptions, the latter was clearly impossible to entertain, for it would burst apart the fundamental framework of united Israel if it were granted

> that after entering Canaan from Egypt the peoples were not unified as Yahwists.
>
> It was possible, however, to conceive of a stage before Israel became a large association of peoples in Egypt; when it was a much smaller entity, an entity which could be represented as a large family whose sons became the progenitors of the later, greatly enlarged tribes. Some of the most glaring differences in the social forms of the people, in the population size, and in the religious ideas and practices embedded in the various traditions could be harmonized by grouping the stories into two successive periods: *the period when Israel was in Canaan as a large family and the period when Israel was in Egypt, in the wilderness, and returned to Canaan as an association of tribes.* In this manner, the pronounced contradictions and tensions in traditions which had Canaan as a common setting could be relaxed and harmonized by conceiving two different periods when Israel was in Canaan. The difficulty created by the tension between El and Yahweh worship could be relaxed and harmonized by interpreting El as another name for Yahweh.[16]

As in the other discussions already noted, the theological issue posed by the pentateuchal text is interpreted as a matter of religious history, though of a particular kind. The specifically theological issue about the nature of God is interpreted as an ingenious ideological rationalization of the merging of different social groupings.

Later, Gottwald returns to this issue in a discussion entitled "The Path through Elohistic Israel to Yahwistic Israel." He sees the patriarchal narratives as reflecting the traditions of "pre-Yahwistic proto-Israelites" who lived in Canaan and shared in a common worship of El; these people formed "Elohistic Israel." They made common cause with an incoming Mosaic/Levitical/Yahwistic group and together the combined groups became Yahwistic Israel. This meant that Yahwistic Israel showed elements of both continuity and discontinuity with Elohistic Israel, and Gottwald offers a list of both elements. "Foundational elements of Elohistic Israel retained in Yahwistic Israel" are "militarization, decentralized sociopolitical cooperation, common cult, common name"; "new elements in the reorganized coalition of Yahwistic Israel" are "increase and diversification of member groups, revolutionary cadres, common cult of Yahweh = El."[17]

16. Ibid., 105, 106, 107.
17. Ibid., 493–97.

It is interesting to compare Gottwald's list with our own analysis of the difference between patriarchal and Mosaic traditions.[18] Of course, it must be realized that we are not comparing like with like, since our analysis explicitly eschewed making historical judgments and so did not undertake the kind of critical interpretation of the tradition that Gottwald as a historian undertakes. Nonetheless an appreciation of the internal logic and dynamics of the tradition is, as we argued, a necessary preliminary step for the historian, so that the nature of the source material can be accurately discerned. Moreover, however much the historian may recognize that the material embodies later perspectives for which allowance must be made in critical reconstruction, it still remains necessary to follow the sources to some extent insofar as one believes that the sources genuinely allow some kind of access to historical reconstruction. If, therefore, one uses Gottwald's analysis as a critical heuristic tool for reading the pentateuchal texts and compares it with our own analysis, what emerges?

Essentially, the internal logic of both patriarchal and Mosaic traditions is lost. Historically speaking, the traditions might not originally have had their present logic, and a reconstruction that lacks it might be justified. Nonetheless, one must press the question of the criteria by which the pentateuchal tradition is critically reconstructed. For example, Gottwald can characterize the patriarchal material (Elohistic Israel) as showing militarization and say that "the fighting tradition of the Exodus Yahwists was able to combine with an already tested and experienced military organization among underclass Canaanites."[19] Obviously there are military elements in the patriarchal traditions (Genesis 14, 34), but on what grounds may these be privileged and generalized over against the generally unwarlike character of the traditions as a whole?

Moreover, even with Gottwald's own premises it is difficult to see why a common tradition about patriarchal religion as non-Yahwistic should have been maintained in a Yahwistic context. The pentateuchal text raises the issue of one God who could validly be known in different ways. It is all very well to interpret

18. Above, pp. 87ff.
19. Gottwald, *Tribes,* 495.

this as an ideological representation of the merging of differing groups—with the cult of El in one group being absorbed within the cult of YHWH in the dominant group—and to relate this to the desire to preserve the prehistory of an important subgroup. But this simply translates the problem into a different idiom without in any way resolving it. For the crucial issue concerns the *legitimacy* of non-Yahwistic patriarchal religion that is so clearly implied by the pentateuchal text. Gottwald stresses elsewhere that exclusiveness was a fundamental characteristic of the Israelite confederacy (though he does not relate this to the difference between Elohistic and Yahwistic Israel) and says, for example,

> The Yahwistic cult of Israel's confederacy was both inclusively national and deliberately, even vehemently, exclusive of any other national or tribal or local cult. The multiple forms of Israelite cult all had to be justified and assimilated as modes of worship of the single deity. Moreover, it needs to be emphasized that the considerable versatility of the Israelite cult in adapting forms from the cults of proto-Israelite deities was decisively controlled by the initial purgative, intensely puritanical drive of Yahwism to exclude all those religious concepts and lavish ceremonial practices which served to represent the deity as the guarantor of centralized oppressive politics and thus a support for self-propagating elites.[20]

The notion of versatile adaptation of non-Yahwistic religious forms within exclusive Yahwism would only make sense if there was a corresponding denial of the validity of such forms outside Yahwism. This is indeed the characteristic stance of Yahwism. Precisely this, however, is lacking in Genesis 12–50, where there is respect shown for the non-Yahwistic patriarchal traditions as they are retold from a Yahwistic perspective. Gottwald's understanding of Israel's exclusiveness can allow for the absorption of non-Yahwistic tradition but cannot cope with their respectful preservation. Although his sociological perspective is not without value in many ways, as an explanation of an important and problematic tension within the pentateuchal story it is no more successful than the other historical proposals already noted.[21]

20. Ibid., 382–83; cf. 491, 611ff., 679–80.

21. There is a nice irony about some of Gottwald's polemic against conventional approaches to the biblical text. He says, for example, "Thus we must resolutely struggle against the thoroughly understandable tendency of the

In the work of all the scholars cited thus far, one can clearly see that the agenda of what is significant about the text has been that of the ancient historian. The theological tension within Exodus 3 has been seen as a pointer to diverse historical developments, and interest in these has been the predominant concern. Insofar as the theological concerns of Exodus 3 and 6 have been addressed, they have tended to be treated somewhat dismissively as mere (implicitly somewhat arbitrary) theory; indeed the most explicit statement about the radical newness of God's self-revelation as YHWH in Exod. 6:2-3 has been rather rudely handled as "rigid," "dogmatic," "pedantry," "but a theory." In all this there has been little or no sense either that the theological concerns of Exodus 3 and 6 may actually represent the common tradition of all pentateuchal writers or that the theological tension they portray cannot be resolved by reconstructions (however valid) of religious history.

The fullest existing attempt (that I am aware of) to engage with the theological issues is, not surprisingly, in what is generally recognized to be the outstanding modern treatment of Old Testament theology, the work of G. von Rad.[22] In discussions entitled "The History of the Patriarchs" and "The Revelation of the Name Jahweh" van Rad directly addresses the nature of patriarchal religion and the relationship between it and Mosaic religion.[23] In relation to the exposition of our own thesis thus far, much in von Rad's account has a positive resonance.

First and foremost, von Rad clearly recognizes both the distinctive, non-Yahwistic nature of patriarchal religion and its appropriation by Yahwism. The main thrust of his argument is to show something of the traditiohistorical development of the

biblical traditions, and the less excusable tendency of biblical scholars who too uncritically follow those traditions, to flatten out and to unify the historical discreteness and the sociocultural developmental differentia into an account of a monolithic people under a changeless deity" (*Tribes,* 40). For the central issue posed by the text of Genesis and Exodus is precisely *not* that of a "changeless deity" but almost its opposite, a deity who appears to change in major ways. It is Gottwald whose analysis loses the dynamic of the text and flattens it.

22. G. von Rad, *Old Testament Theology,* vol. 1 (London: SCM, 1965, 1975; German, 1957).

23. Ibid., 165–75, 179–87.

patriarchal traditions with their consequent theological enrichment, and in this he gives prominence to the use of the name YHWH in Genesis:

> The God who supremely controls all that happens in the history of the patriarchs is Jahweh. Regarded from the historical standpoint this is an anachronism, for Israel's ancestors prior to Moses as yet knew nothing of Jahwism—even the late Priestly Document is still aware of the deep cleft and the fresh beginning which were denoted by the revelation of the name Jahweh in the time of Moses (Ex. VI.2f.). Israel's pre-Mosaic forebears had different cultic ties. They worshipped 'the God of the ancestors.'[24]

As the narratives now stand, however, they are told in the light of Israel's God as part of Israel's story:

> The God who led the patriarchs Abraham, Isaac, and Jacob was Jahweh, and the rudimentary divine designations deriving from the now absorbed cult of the ancestors have now simply become designations and predicates of Jahweh. In all that the patriarchs experienced as told in the old traditions Jahwism recognised the hand and the word of its God. . . . Now it is the whole of Israel which relates these far-off happenings to herself and recognises in them what is her very own.[25]

This means that the storytellers felt free not to take undue notice of certain kinds of historical concerns:

> These stories of the patriarchs are not retold in that exclusively historical sense whose sole concern is merely to reproduce exactly what happened at the time: instead, experiences and insights of succeeding ages also found expression in them. The narrators often digest in but a single story of only a few verses the yield of a divine history which in fact stretches from the event spoken of down into their own time.[26]

With all this our own thesis is in complete agreement, as it is also with von Rad's recognition that despite the present Yahwistic stance of the patriarchal traditions an originally non-Yahwistic content can still be clearly discerned:

> The existence of the patriarchs before God, as it is pictured in the stories told of them, contains something unique in the saving his-

24. Ibid., 166.
25. Ibid., 167.
26. Ibid.

> tory. For it is by no means the case that the later Israel simply projected herself and the theological ordering of her life and problems back into the era of the ancestors. Rather she here depicted a relationship to God of a quite peculiar and unique character. This era in the saving history lacks the divine will for justice which was revealed to Israel in the commandments, as it also lacks the revelation of his holiness. It has no regular pattern of cultic practice, and no priests. The patriarchs offer sacrifice on occasion, but the tellers of the stories are simply not interested in questions of the cult or of ritual. In consequence the great problem of cultic antagonism and demarcation from the native indigenous population is still wholly in the background. . . . The unwarlike and indeed "pacifist" attitude in the whole of the patriarchs' existence has often been commented upon. . . . And . . . in respect of the great promise which was the determinant factor in their lives, they still lived before its fulfilment. And it is precisely this which characterises their existence.[27]

Moreover, as the natural corollary of all this, von Rad is in no doubt that the pentateuchal writers portray a new start with Moses:

> Even the traditional picture of the saving history followed by the sources in the Hexateuch recognises that Jahweh was not manifested to his elect from the beginning, but that the revelation of his name only took place at the time of Moses. Oddly enough, it is the latest of the source documents which most strongly emphasises this break in the history of revelation (Ex. VI.2f.,P). It is a surprising emphasis, for to this source's picture of the history, with the strong tendency it has to level out and schematise, the fact must have been an embarrassment. But late though P is, it was, like the other sources, still tied to the traditional material, whose statements in this connexion were unequivocal: all that P could do was to give its own characteristic explanation of the break. J and E take a much harder way of fusing together the two eras in the saving history, that of the God of the ancestors and the time of the full revelation of Jahweh. The narrative in Ex. III, a very complex unit both in substance and style, is designed on the one hand to communicate what was new in the revelation of Jahweh—that is, information about the divine name—and, on the other, to show how this new revelation was very closely linked with the history of the patriarchs. Ex. III is obviously trying to show the continuity between them—what came to pass with the revelation of the name of Jahweh was certainly of incalculable importance for Israel, but it was not the beginning of her God's self-revelation. Jahweh is identical with the

27. Ibid., 175.

> God of the ancestors (Ex. III. 6,13f). [Here von Rad adds in a footnote:] Gen. IV. 26 (J) pushes the beginning of the cult of Jahweh back to a very much earlier time. What comes in question here is an isolated tradition which cannot be harmonised with Ex. III.1f or VI.2f.[28]

Three comments may be made about von Rad's exposition. First, it is interesting to see how dismissive he is of the Yahwistic tradition with its supposed pre-Mosaic knowledge of God as YHWH. In some ways this seems surprising, given von Rad's acceptance of a conventional documentary analysis (in which J is predominant) and also his generally high esteem for the work of the Yahwist. Clearly, however, his sense of the meaning of Exodus 3 and 6 together with the general tenor of the patriarchal traditions as outlined above leads him to this conclusion. It is difficult to resist the feeling that von Rad would gladly dispense with the conventional understanding of the Yahwist as representing a tradition at odds with Exodus 3 and 6. Although he did not reexamine the documentary hypothesis with this issue in mind, it seems reasonable to suggest that our proposed alternative analysis would represent a natural and consistent outworking of the logic of his insights.

Second, von Rad's discussion has a remarkable omission. He nowhere addresses the questions of *why* in the patriarchal traditions Israel should be happy to have "depicted a relationship to God of a quite peculiar and unique character" and *how* this relationship should be understood vis-à-vis Israel's relationship with God. Despite his awareness of the issue of continuity and discontinuity posed by Exodus 3, von Rad shows little interest in pursuing the specifically theological dimensions of this in their own right. Near the outset of his account, when discussing the non-Yahwistic nature of patriarchal religion, von Rad says, "J and E seem to be completely unaware of it [the patriarchal stage in cultic history], and even if memories of it did live on into their time, the story-tellers attached no importance to them." Given the strikingly consistent non-Yahwistic content of the patriarchal traditions and the clear sense of a fresh beginning with the same

28. Ibid., 179–80.

God in Exodus 3—both of which von Rad sees clearly—it is surely far more likely that the distinctiveness of the patriarchal period was a clearly recognized and important issue for the pentateuchal writers and that the reason they presented their material in the initially surprising way they did was their awareness of the theological issue of continuity and discontinuity in God and in God's dealings with Israel.

Third, one other notable passage in von Rad's discussion deserves comment. He returns to the question of the significance of the retelling of the patriarchal stories within Yahwism and the fact that they therefore stand at a considerable remove from their earliest forms. In contrast to the common critical interest in discerning the earliest strata of the stories, von Rad emphasizes that the stories' value resides not in such historical reconstructions, whose returns are meager but in taking seriously the text as it now stands (a remarkable anticipation of much recent debate!):

> But just because there are such very early strata present, it would be a mistake to imagine that a stamp of "authenticity" can be put on these stories. For what we can at most derive from the oldest elements in some of them does not go beyond very general and approximate realities—a little about the living conditions of the men of this period, about their wanderings and the places where they lived, and, beyond this, their "clan religion." . . . Let us keep the idea of "authenticity"—but should we not then in fairness have to admit that, in the form these stories now have, this authentic basic stratum had had superimposed upon it an extremely arbitrary reinterpretation designed to make it serviceable for a later age—this, in some cases, to the point of rendering it impossible to discern the older stratum? The theologian will realise which of the two he has to decide to follow: it is the voice with which the stories speak now, and not the obscure overlaid remains of a much older traditional material, however much interest it may hold—its voice is now silent. [Von Rad then proceeds to illustrate the point by a discussion of Genesis 22.][29]

With von Rad's basic point—that the theologian should follow "the voice with which the stories speak now"—I have no quarrel.

29. Ibid., 173–74. In a footnote, the translator says that for this section, at von Rad's request, he has closely followed von Rad's article "History and the Patriarchs" (*ExpTim* 71 [1961]: 213–16). In this article von Rad does not actually use the phrase "extremely arbitrary."

What does seem to me questionable, however, is von Rad's characterization of the process of Yahwistic reinterpretation as "extremely arbitrary." Of course, he has in mind far more than a relatively simple retelling of stories in terms of YHWH, for he is operating with a highly complex understanding of the development of pentateuchal traditions, as in his famous essay "The Form-Critical Problem of the Hexateuch"[30] and Noth's *History of Pentateuchal Traditions.*[31] Although, as already indicated, I am less confident than von Rad that such extensive tradition-history can genuinely be discerned, nonetheless the crucial issue concerns the possible criteria by which it could be decided whether or not a retelling of a story was "arbitrary," especially when the key issue must be the specifically theological issue of the interpretation of originally non-Yahwistic material in terms of YHWH. Von Rad gives the impression that a complex traditio-historical development is itself sufficient to render the later form of the story "completely arbitrary." This suggests to me that von Rad is here lapsing into the tendency noted especially in Haran, that is, to translate questions of theology into questions of religious history. Of course, questions of religious history are important for theology; nonetheless they are not the only concerns to be borne in mind, and they may not always even be the most important either. This is not the place even to begin to formulate criteria for determining the validity of theological developments (though some will emerge in the course of the argument). The point is that theology may have an agenda and appropriate criteria of its own; regrettably, theological issues are sometimes foreclosed by being treated simply as questions of religious history.

Finally, within recent literature perhaps the most explicit recognition of the theological issue at stake in Exodus 3 and 6 is in the new commentary on Exodus by W. H. Schmidt. Admittedly, Schmidt poses the issue simply with relation to the theology of P rather than that of the Pentateuch as a whole and only poses it in

30. G. von Rad, "The Form-Critical Problem of the Hexateuch," in his *The Problem of the Hexateuch and Other Essays* (London: SCM, 1984; German, 1938).

31. M. Noth, *A History of Pentateuchal Traditions* (Chico, California: Scholars, 1981. ET by B. W. Anderson from German of 1948).

passing without attempting to develop it. Nonetheless, it will provide an appropriate note on which to end this section before we move on to develop our own thesis. Schmidt concludes his discussion of Exod. 6:2-12 as follows:

> Thus Ex 6,2f on the one hand preserves the insight into the diversity of God's way of revelation, and thereby into the change of human worship or even understanding of God, and does not deny a "more" in knowledge of God; and on the other hand confesses the exclusivity of the same one God. In this way the text seeks to hold together discontinuity and continuity, difference and identity, and even in "faith" to declare the unity in change.
>
> Does not this idea and judgment of the Priestly writer's faith spur us similarly to think through and confess that which is common to "Old" and "New Testament" within the difference which the prophet (Jer. 31,31-34) saw?[32]

THE ANALOGY OF THE RELATIONSHIP BETWEEN NEW AND OLD TESTAMENT

Our own approach to the relationship between patriarchal and Mosaic religion will attempt to focus specifically on the theological issue posed by the text of Exodus 3 and 6. In order to be theological, we will necessarily use categories and analogies drawn to some extent from postbiblical theology, especially Christian theology. Of course, this means that there is always a danger of anachronistically reading things into the text; to bring the concepts of Christian theology to bear on the pentateuchal text may have a distorting influence. Later theology, however, may contain precisely or substantially the same dynamic that is present in the biblical text (since both Jewish and Christian theology have deep roots in the biblical material). Perhaps first recognizing an issue in its later form will enable us to recognize it in the pentateuchal text. The fact, therefore, that our categories may be postbiblical does not of itself in any way prejudge their validity for interpreting the text. The test of their validity will be their heuristic fruitfulness.

I suggest that the best way to understand the pentateuchal text

32. W. H. Schmidt, *Exodus,* BKAT 2 (Neukirchen-Vluyn: Neukirchener Verlag, 1988), 292, my translation.

is initially to stand back from it or, in effect, to approach it via an analogy from elsewhere. For if one reflects theologically on the issue that appears to be present in the pentateuchal text—one God who is revealed in two different ways in two different periods—one obvious analogy to this phenomenon readily suggests itself: the Christian understanding of Old and New Testament as representing two different periods of salvation history in which it is one and the same God who is revealed, albeit in different ways. We propose, therefore, that the best approach is initially to consider the phenomenon in its Christian form, where it is well known and much studied, and then apply insights gained here to the pentateuchal text. The less familiar theological problem of Genesis 12–50 in relation to Exodus 3 onward can be illuminated through consideration of the well-known problem of the relationship of the Old Testament to the New Testament (though the illumination may in due course prove to be mutual and reciprocal).

The thesis I wish to propose is that the relationship of patriarchal religion in Genesis 12–50 to Mosaic Yahwism in Exodus onward is analogous to the relationship of the Old Testament as a whole to the New Testament. Or to put the same point differently, the position of the adherent of Mosaic Yahwism with regard to the patriarchal traditions in Genesis 12–50 is analogous to the position of the Christian with regard to the Old Testament. Each case gives the sense of looking back on a previous period of salvation history from the perspective of a new period that has in some ways superseded the old. The dynamics inherent in such a perspective are of great theological interest.

APPROACHING THE OLD TESTAMENT FROM THE NEW TESTAMENT

At the heart of a Christian approach to the Old Testament lie two basic convictions.[33] On the one hand there is a conviction of

33. On the question of the theological relationship between Old Testament and New Testament, see D. L. Baker, *Two Testaments, One Bible* (Leicester: IVP, 1976), and the useful summary discussion with bibliography in H. G. Reventlow, *Problems of Biblical Theology in the Twentieth Century* (London: SCM, 1986; German, 1983).

identity and continuity. YHWH the God of Israel is the God and Father of our Lord Jesus Christ. Any attempt to deny this, such as was most famously made by Marcion, has been vigorously resisted as fundamentally untrue to the New Testament and Christianity. On the other hand there is also a conviction of difference and discontinuity. God has done a new thing in Jesus, through whose life, death, and resurrection humanity can know and relate to God in a way not possible before; a new era of history has been inaugurated which in some ways supersedes what went before.

This somewhat paradoxical combination of identity and difference, of continuity and discontinuity, characterizes a Christian approach to the Old Testament and has always made the appropriation of the Old Testament as Christian scripture less than straightforward. How is the Christian to approach texts that, on the one hand, are true and valid witnesses to the one God and yet, on the other hand, have been in some ways superseded by the New Testament witness to God's salvation in Christ?

If one considers this dilemma in general terms, it can be seen to have at least three constituent components. First is an implicit metaphysical question about the nature of God. How can one God, who is supposed by the Christian to have a particular and consistent, albeit mysterious, character (i.e., understandable, yet transcending understanding), be revealed in two different and to some extent incompatible ways? Both the Mosaic Yahwism of the Old Testament and the Christian faith of the New Testament show a similar conviction that one supreme truth is given by God to humanity, which both reveals God's character and shows people the true way to live. In the Old Testament this centers on Torah, and in the New Testament this centers on Christ. But, although these two ways are not wholly incompatible, since much of Torah can be accommodated within faith in Christ, neither are they wholly compatible, since much of Torah cannot be accommodated within faith in Christ (at least not without substantial reinterpretation). These differences naturally pose the question, put simply, What is God *really* like? Such a question raises fundamental issues about the nature of theology and both Jewish and Christian faith that necessarily lie outside our present task, though we will return to touch on them later.[34] It is worth noting that, although debate about the nature of God and the means by which God's nature may be apprehended is a recurrent issue within Christian theology, this particular form of it has not been common. The general tendency of Christians has been to follow the lead of the New Testament and to argue that it is the understanding of God that comes in and through Jesus that must be primary and normative and all else, including the Old Testament, must be interpreted, or reinterpreted, accordingly. The possible theological implications of the Bible itself normatively presenting God in more than one way have received less attention than they might.

Second is the question of a theological understanding of the course of history. The classic theological term in this context is *dispensation.* In the light of the coming of Christ, history is seen as divided into (at least) two dispensations.[35] The significance of the concept of dispensation can be developed in a variety of ways. Probably its major practical significance lies in the area of biblical interpretation in relation to religious ethos and the practical outworking of that ethos in ritual and practice. On the one hand, why do Christians feel free to dispense with the Old Testament's particularist emphasis on Israel? Of course, the Old Testament is well aware of YHWH's concern for nations other than Israel and sees Israel as a paradigm of divine blessing, but there is, for example, little concern to incorporate other peoples within Israel. The New Testament is also particularist with regard to Christ but understands Christ to relativize the difference between Jew and Gentile and to authorize an active concern to bear witness to all nations with a view to incorporating people of all kinds within the people of God. On the other hand, why is it that Christians do not observe all the religious practices pre-

34. See below, pp. 170ff.

35. The concept of dispensation has become somewhat problematic in modern biblical theology because of the questionable use made of it by some strands of American Evangelicalism (on which, see, e.g., D. P. Fuller, *Gospel and Law: Contrast or Continuum? The Hermeneutics of Dispensationalism and Covenant Theology* [Grand Rapids: Eerdmans, 1980]). Nonetheless, the concept is deeply rooted in classic Christian theology, and so it is important that it should be used, where appropriate, in biblical theology.

scribed by God in the Old Testament, even such fundamental ones as sabbath, circumcision, and Passover? Christians indeed have equivalent practices to all of these—Sunday, baptism, Eucharist; but to observe equivalent practices is not what the Old Testament envisages. From a Christian perspective the classic answer to both these questions lies in appealing to the concept of dispensation, which means that the religious practices of the Old Testament were entirely proper within their own context, but insofar as Christ has initiated a new period of history, the former requirements no longer necessarily obtain. The extensive differences among Christians with regard to religious practice, not least in its relation to the prescriptions of the Old Testament, should not be allowed to obscure the basic logic of a Christian, as distinct from a Jewish, approach to religious practice.

Third is the question about the positive value of those texts that depict the previous dispensation. We have already noted that the concept of dispensation has the negative function of justifying disregard for authoritative religious ethos and practice in the Old Testament and that the Christian, if faced with difficulties, will give greater weight to the New Testament than the Old Testament. Nonetheless, if the Christian approach to these ancient Hebrew texts were purely or even only primarily negative, these texts would not have been revered by Christians as authoritative scripture, as the Old Testament. In fact the Old Testament has generally been considered as having great value supremely in the area of spirituality, or the dynamics of the life of faith. Although in the Old Testament the life of faith is closely tied to particular religious practices and institutions (sacrifice, temple, etc.), the characteristic Christian assumption has been that the life of faith has a dynamic and an integrity of its own which can be expressed in a variety of forms, practices, and institutions. Although different forms will necessarily give a different flavor to the underlying dynamic and will necessarily create a certain distance between the adherents of different forms, the difference need not preclude recognition of a genuinely common underlying dynamic. For example, the Old Testament depicts life under God in categories such as the moral and personal nature of God and the dignity of humanity made in the image of God. It puts forward norms for human life in such terms as trust, obedience, holiness, righteousness, justice, faithfulness, mercy, and forgiveness. And it sets these in the context of a communal life that owes its existence to the gracious initiative of the one true God, a life sustained both corporately and individually through prayer. Insofar as the Old Testament does this, the Christian can identify with the material and appropriate it more or less directly for the Christian life of faith, both communal and individual. Historically, the primary focus of this appropriation has been Christian use of the psalms, but the practice has extended in one way or another to the whole Old Testament. Of course, the appropriation is not always straightforward. With regard, for example, to the well-known problem posed by the imprecatory psalms, Christians have often felt uncertain about the validity of adopting such sentiments and so have tended either to reinterpret (spiritualize) the material or to exclude it (usually by appealing to the dispensation principle). Nonetheless, the basic point that the primary value and use of the Old Testament for the Christian is in the sphere of Christian spirituality remains unaffected.

It should be noted that all these three issues, and indeed the whole problem of continuity and discontinuity, arise out of the decision to privilege certain texts and treat them as authoritative. Whatever, from a historical point of view, the relationship between Israelite religion and the religions of ancient Egypt, Canaan, Syria, and Mesopotamia, these other religions do not raise the same issues for the Christian as does Israelite religion. For the decision to retain as scripture only certain texts that arise out of Israelite religion and were recognized as authoritative within early Judaism gives the theological issues raised by Israelite religion and literature a privileged status for the Christian. The decision to regard texts as scripture is a crucial issue to which we will return in the next chapter.

APPROACHING PATRIARCHAL RELIGION FROM MOSAIC YAHWISM

It is not difficult to see that these basic issues that characterize a Christian approach to the Old Testament apply equally to the relationship of Mosaic Yahwism to the traditions of patriarchal religion. First, despite the consistent difference of portrayal of patriarchal religion from Mosaic Yahwism with its implicit recognition that, in principle, this relates to a non-Yahwistic understanding of God, the pentateuchal writers (who all stand within the context of Mosaic Yahwism) are in no doubt not only that it is one and the same God in each context but also that their understanding of God as YHWH is normative. The possible theoretical difficulty of how one God could be revealed in two different and not wholly compatible ways is not raised as an issue that is meaningful on its own (though we will return to the implicit wider concerns).[36] Essentially, it is simply affirmed that one and the same God is in both patriarchal and Mosaic religion and that the normative understanding of this God is conveyed by God's self-revelation as YHWH.

Second is the question of the status of the ethos of patriarchal religion and also of its corresponding religious practices in their notable difference from those of Mosaic Yahwism. They are neither condemned as improper nor commended as authoritative for the Yahwistic believer—the former of which might naturally have been expected. Although no explicit reason is given for such a silence, it seems reasonable to assume that the theological concept embodied in the traditions the writers portray is that of dispensation. That is, they recognized the patriarchal period as valid in its own right and yet in some ways superseded by Mosaic Yahwism, which meant that practices that may have been entirely proper for the patriarchs within their context were no longer appropriate for Israel within the new dispensation. The new dispensation invalidates certain formal and practical aspects of the old dispensation. The Yahwistic readers of Genesis 12–50 could be relatively unconcerned by the fact that authoritative figures may have shown an openness in association with foreigners and also carried out religious practices inappropriate or forbidden to themselves in the same way Christians sit light with regard to aspects of the ethos and practice of the Old Testament.

Third is the positive use that Genesis 12–50 would have within Mosaic Yahwism and that would be a major factor in the decision to retain these traditions in an authoritative written form.

36. Below, pp. 170ff.

This concerns those components of the patriarchs' life under God—basic assumptions about the nature of God's dealings with people with priorities and goals (if not practices) similar to those of Israel—which could be appropriated by Yahwistic Israel within its own context. Within Genesis 12–50 are three figures whose life is explored at length—Abraham, Jacob, and Joseph—and they all function as in some way paradigmatic for the life of Israel.

Before discussing these in detail, a preliminary general note about procedure will be appropriate. For although recognition of the patriarchs as paradigmatic figures is of long standing, so too are the difficulties such a conception raises. As Childs comments, "How can one ever use the response of the Hebrew patriarchs as an ethical norm when their conduct is filled with flagrant immorality? Abraham lied and traded his wife for personal gain. Sarah was ruthless with Hagar her rival. Jacob was a cheat and Moses a murderer."[37] Childs then goes on to show how the problem has existed for both Christians and Jews from ancient times. Similarly, von Rad comments that "as is well known, a great deal of mischief has been caused by the widespread idea that the patriarchs were patterns of pious behaviour before God. The question whether and where the story-tellers want to provoke 'imitation' is not so very easy to answer."[38] Although both writers are primarily addressing the question of the appropriation of the material within Christian faith today, their observations have an obvious bearing on any appropriation of the stories within the context of ancient Israel.

Having raised the problem, both writers are nonetheless quite clear that the patriarchs are indeed paradigmatic figures. Von Rad continues, "In the stories in Gen. XII.1-9, XIII, XV.1-6, XXII the figure of the ancestor has certainly to be understood as a pattern for the descendants. The clearest case is the Joseph stories, which are certainly didactic."[39] Childs notes that elsewhere in the Old Testament the stories of the patriarchs are "used theo-

37. B. S. Childs, *Old Testament Theology in a Canonical Context* (London: SCM, 1985), 212.

38. G. von Rad, *Old Testament Theology*, vol. 1, 175, n. 16.

39. Ibid.

logically to illustrate God's faithfulness to his promise. . . . The patriarchs are not used as models of morality, but rather to bear testimony to God who in his mercy forgave their sinfulness." Childs argues that in the Genesis narratives themselves "the portrayal of the patriarchs has been refocused about their one role as bearers of Israel's hope. Everything else has been pushed into the background." He concludes that "all the apologetic attempts to explain away the immoralities of the patriarchs operate on the false assumption that the Bible's testimony to Israel's response is in terms of examples of moral conduct." Rather, "the stories of the Fathers are about the faithfulness of God to his word of promise. All human achievement is measured by its trust in God's faithfulness."[40]

Von Rad's discussion leaves one wondering about criteria for determining which stories might qualify to be patterns; Child's theocentric emphasis is valuable but surely underestimates the continuing ethical implications of the portrayals especially of Abraham and Joseph—for "trust in God's faithfulness," if genuine, can hardly be detached from a life-style of obedience and integrity. I suggest that most of the difficulty lies in what appear to be two unspoken, and questionable, assumptions. The first is a narrow understanding of the nature of an ethical paradigm, which effectively reduces morality to moralism. For moralism can be an approach that so stresses obedience to moral requirements that other valid dimensions of human life are discounted, with resultant one-sidedness and unreality. In other words, it seems sometimes to be assumed that if the texts have a moral concern (i.e., for the development of obedient and responsible human life under God), then this is tantamount to the concerns of moralism (or pietism—again, an unduly narrow focusing of piety) that the people of God must always be "good" with no room for learning and growing through, say, mistakes and failures. The other questionable assumption is that an ethical paradigm must always function in a direct and obvious way in the life of believers ("as they, so you"). Of course, there must be an element of this, but it should not be overpressed in such a way

40. Childs, *Canonical Context,* 216, 218, 220.

that it fails to allow the paradigm to function as a total imaginative whole. If one takes the imaginative whole seriously, not only may any direct correlation between paradigm and reader be partial but also readers may be expected to use their judgment and discern differing elements and different kinds of applicability within the paradigm (e.g., examples to avoid as well as to follow, examples to reflect upon as part of a total understanding of life). If one can avoid a moralistic view of spirituality and also allow for the impact of an imaginative whole that calls for judgment and interpretation, the familiar difficulties with using the patriarchs as paradigms largely disappear.

We will start with perhaps the most straightforward of the patriarchs, Joseph, who provides an obvious model for the individual Yahwistic believer. Joseph's life is guided by the good purposes of God throughout (e.g., Gen. 37:5-11; 50:20). Although this may involve enduring unjustly inflicted suffering (37:23-24; 39:20; 40:23), Joseph maintains his integrity before God (esp. 39:9) and continues to trust in God (not made explicit, but clearly implicit). At the same time God is with him and prospers what he does (39:2-6, 21-23) and gives him special insight and wisdom (40:8; 41:16). Ultimately, the recognition of this leads to his being given a position of great honor and power (41:37-45). Toward his family Joseph exercises his power with an inscrutability similar to that of God (chaps. 42–44). But his purposes, like God's, are good and merciful, and the result is reunion and reconciliation (chap. 45).

Abraham and Jacob are more complex characters in that they not only exemplify an individual person's walk with God but also in some way exemplify the corporate life of Israel before God. This is one aspect of the "depth" dimension in their stories—a depth generally understood to be the result of a lengthy history of tradition in which the retelling of the stories imbued their content with overtones of the life of Israel within whose context the retelling took place—a dimension that is lacking in the Joseph story of Genesis 37, 39–45. The Abraham and Jacob stories are regularly suggestive of the traditions of Israel as a nation. Because of the subtlety of the portrayal, it is difficult to offer a neat analysis. Nonetheless, it seems appropriate to approach Abraham and Jacob both as individual figures and as corporate figures.

As noted in our exposition of patriarchal religion,[41] it is particularly around the figure of Abraham that language and concerns suggestive of Mosaic Yahwism most obviously cluster, and Abraham is clearly the major patriarchal figure and the primary concern of later theological reflection.

As an individual figure he is a model of obedient trust, and the specifically Yahwistic elements are less obvious. Abraham lives in obedience to the word of YHWH, even when this is extremely costly (Gen. 12:1-9). He displays generosity toward Lot, allowing him to choose what looks to be (ironically!) the better land, and is blessed by God because of this (13:2-18). He declines possible wealth in faithfulness to a vow to YHWH (14:11, 21-24), and so on. In general, the length of time that Abraham has to wait for the fulfilment of the promise of a son makes him a model for all who "wait for" God. And his willingness to surrender back to God that which is most precious to him in the confidence that "God will provide" (22:8, 14) has generally been recognized by Jew and Christian alike as probing the depths of what life with God may entail. On some occasions Abraham appears to waver with regard to trust in God's promises of land and son (12:10—13:1; 16:1-2; 17:17; 20:1-18).[42] But such wavering does not impair the overall impression of a genuine life of faith on Abraham's part.

41. Above, p. 98.

42. Particularly since the work of Gunkel (see, e.g., his *The Legends of Genesis* [New York: Schocken, 1964], originally the introduction to his German Genesis Commentary of 1901), there has been doubt about the propriety of reading a story such as Gen. 12:10—13:1 in moral terms. Is it not rather the unself-conscious account, told indeed with a certain flourish, of how Israel's ancestor triumphed over the foolish pharaoh? Certainly stories are told in this vein, perhaps most obviously the story of the Hebrew midwives (Exod. 1:15ff.). Nonetheless, two points should be borne in mind with regard to Abraham. First, Gunkel's account is imbued with a romanticist outlook which is open to question, as is his model of traditiohistorical development. Second, even if Gunkel's basic intuition was correct, it would apply mainly to the story in its original, pre-Genesis, form (which was Gunkel's concern anyway) and would need to be carefully justified as still appropriate when the stories were retold from a Yahwistic perspective and the figure of Abraham was interpreted as paradigmatic for Israel in the kind of way we argue for in our discussion.

Rather it shows that even for the most faithful of God's servants the progress and development of the life of faith may contain mistakes and surprises.

As a model for the life of Israel, not surprisingly, Yahwistic dimensions become more apparent in the portrayal of Abraham. Abraham comes to Canaan from Ur, a placc noted to be in Chaldea (Babylonia). This reference to Chaldea makes Abraham's journey parallel to that of Israel in its return from exile in Babylonia. Abraham regularly calls on the name of YHWH, as does Israel in its worship. Abraham receives a divine covenant, as does Israel and the house of David. Abraham has a unique understanding of YHWH's righteousness (Gen. 18:16ff.), as does Israel. Abraham offers worship at Jerusalem,[43] as does (or should) Israel. Abraham is indeed explicitly obedient to YHWH's commandments (Gen. 26:5), as Israel should be. It would not be difficult to extend the list, and indeed we will return to the issue shortly, but the basic point is not in doubt.

Jacob is a more complex person than Abraham, both in intrinsic character and in narrative portrayal. He is the eponymous ancestor of Israel as a people, and the text explicitly draws attention to Jacob as in some sense the embodiment of the nation when at an early stage it tells of his relationship with his brother Esau/Edom (Gen. 25:23; 27:29, where language of national rivalry and dominance is used). But the portrayal of Jacob in general is much less suggestive of the traditions of Israel than is the case with Abraham. Although, for example, it is not difficult to sense historic rivalries between Israel and Edom in Genesis 25 and 27, the generosity of Esau when Jacob returns (Genesis 33) does not resonate with the histories of each nation but surprises the reader who would have expected a rather less warm welcome for Jacob. Apart from the early stages of the story of Jacob, perhaps at the end (Genesis 48) the overtones of the traditions of Israel as a people are strongest. But it should be noted that, in the fullest reference to the Jacob story elsewhere in the Old Testament, Hosea seems to see the whole Jacob story as characterizing Israel in its more questionable aspects (Hos. 12:2-6).

43. See above, p. 92 with n. 13 and n. 14.

As an individual, Jacob in his youth consistently displays an astute and successful cunning (Gen. 25:29-34; 27:1-45; 30:25-43) that seems somewhat problematic from a Yahwistic perspective with its strong moral concerns. Although the writer at times tells the story with a flourish (e.g., 30:43), he does not dispel possible unease as to Jacob's behavior. Jacob's piety is not obvious (unlike that of Abraham), and despite God's appearance and promises to Jacob at an early moment of need and vulnerability (28:10-22), only at a much later moment of fear does Jacob pray for the first time (32:6-12) and have a mysterious encounter with God that changes him and makes him Israel (32:22-32).[44] Only thereafter does he build an altar (33:20) and purge his household of foreign gods (35:1-4).[45] Although Jacob become a more august figure in his old age, his deficiencies as a father are not concealed (37:3-4), and his response to adversity (37:35; 42:36-38; 43:11-14) lacks a sense of either the serenity of Joseph or the trusting obedience of Abraham. Nonetheless, he is the man who is the eponymous ancestor of Israel as a people.

44. Von Rad writes, "The great complex of the stories about Jacob also confronts the reader with the problem of the hiddenness of God's actions with the patriarchs. . . . Compared with the Abraham cycle, the one about Jacob is altogether much less spiritual. If in the stories about Jacob's deceitfulness it was still the blessing that was at stake, for long chapters afterwards the reader completely loses sight of God and his action in the jungle of unedifying manifestations of human nature. Here the picture is really a very, very worldly one. The malice of men, the struggle of the women for the man, the absolutely undignified interpretation attached to the name of each of the ancestors of the race, as due to the momentary situation of a discontented woman—who would take this for more than a fairly trivial piece of entertainment, had it not all been preceded by the divine oracle in Gen. XXV. 23, and, in particular, had there not been the massive blocks of narrative giving the stories connected with Bethel and Peniel (Gen. XXVIII. 10ff,. XXXII.22ff)? These two narratives give the impression of being primeval strangers in the rather worldly context in which they now find themselves, because they concentrate wholly upon God and his direct action towards Jacob. Undoubtedly they are the points where the theme of the Jacob stories emerges to the surface of history in all its power. God is dealing with Jacob. Jacob is to become the ancestor of God's people. God will therefore lead him wherever he goes" (*Old Testament Theology*, vol. 1, 171–72).

45. It may be significant that only after this decisive encounter with God is it possible to trace a certain loose parallelism between the stories of Abraham and Jacob. Like Abraham in Genesis 12–13, Jacob now travels from Shechem, where he builds an altar (33:18-20; cf. 12:6-7), to Bethel, where he builds an altar (35:1-8; cf. 12:8), and finally settles at Mamre (35:27; cf. 13:18). Cf. J. Ha, *Genesis 15*, BZAW 181 (Berlin and New York: de Gruyter, 1989), 198.

The narrative of Genesis 12–50 with its juxtaposition of these three figures suggests a function for the material as a resource for the life of Yahwistic Israel, both corporately and individually. The writers do not moralize, and yet they present their material in such a way that the reader will take it seriously as paradigmatic. The variety and subtlety of portrayal is suggestive of a deep understanding of the varying dynamics of the life of faith as a process of growth which is rarely straightforward. The writers take seriously the weaknesses and difficulties of human personality and the possible limits to its growth (esp. Jacob). They recognize that God's interaction with people is frequently surprising and inscrutable (esp. Joseph) but nonetheless may have recurrent patterns. They recognize the need for patience and for looking at life as a whole. They maintain high expectations of the quality of life under God that is possible (esp. Abraham). And they have a strong sense of the good purposes and the promises of God overarching and undergirding the whole human story. It is not difficult to envisage the pentateuchal writers preserving and molding the patriarchal traditions so that they could function in this way to guide and inform Israel's life with YHWH.

Dispensational Hermeneutics

Beyond this general illustration of the dynamics of interpreting texts from the perspective of a subsequent dispensation, one can take our proposed analogy yet further through a consideration of specific hermeneutical approaches in such circumstances. Within the context of the third of the points noted above—the appropriation of the texts for guidance in the life of faith both corporate and individual—various specific interpretative strategies have been adopted by Christians as they have read the Old Testament. Probably the two most common strategies are the model of promise and fulfilment and the model of typology.[46]

46. For discussion and bibliography, see n. 33, esp. Baker, 191ff., 239ff., 273ff., and Reventlow, 14ff., 47ff. On the subject of typology, one valuable discussion, not noted by either Baker or Reventlow, is A. C. Charity, *Events and Their Afterlife* (Cambridge: Cambridge Univ. Press, 1966), which emphasizes the essentially practical concern of biblical typology—it is not to provide patterning for its own sake but rather is always to provide a pattern and challenge for the life of faith. For a recent brief identification of the main issues, see *Sidic* 21:3 (1988), an issue devoted to the topic "Problems of Typology: Reading the Jewish and the Christian Scriptures."

The basic assumption of promise and fulfilment is that a divine purpose in history culminates and finds supreme expression in Jesus. This means that the Old Testament is in some sense incomplete on its own and looks beyond itself to fulfilment in Jesus. The New Testament writers go to considerable lengths to show God's action in Jesus as the fulfilment of God's ancient promises and purposes for Israel and the world, and in one form or other such an understanding has always been a part of Christian self-understanding. This means that Christian reading of the Old Testament will always have a dimension of interpreting the text as looking beyond itself. Since what is claimed as fulfilment cannot be properly understood apart from the promise of which it is the fulfilment, so the Old Testament retains validity as witness to the divine promise and purpose and also remains a necessary presupposition for an understanding of the New Testament.

The basic assumption of typology is that there is a consistency in the way God acts, such that what God has done uniquely and with supreme clarity in Christ can nonetheless be discerned in similar divine actions and adumbrations in the Old Testament. This, too, may take many different forms, but in one form or another has been a consistent and characteristic element in Christian reading of the Old Testament.

Within a context of expectation shaped by these two hermeneutical assumptions, with a Christian perspective guiding the reader to look for material as significant in particular ways, the Old Testament is read afresh in the light of Jesus. The different hermeneutical models have a tendency to direct the Christian reader to different portions of the Old Testament. Generally speaking, certain portions of prophecy have been seen as fundamental to promise and fulfilment, and certain portions of narrative and psalm have been typologically significant. But in principle they are both applicable to the Old Testament as a whole. For while both hermeneutical models lend themselves to a purely theoretical and speculative approach to the text, which can easily produce far-fetched and bizarre results, the basic purpose of each is practical. Their purpose is to enable Christian readers to enter into the world of the Old Testament text in an appropriate way, recognizing the difference of dispensation yet still finding both models of understanding and practical guidance as they identify themselves and their God with the people and the God of the text.

Our thesis is that precisely these two classic schemes of promise and fulfilment and of typology characterize the specific way in which the patriarchal traditions were interpreted from within a Yahwistic perspective. Of course, this further extension of our analogy has an obvious weakness. This is the fact that the text of the Old Testament was stable by the time of the New Testament. So the rereading from the new perspective could not actually influence the text itself (except occasionally at the level of manuscript copying) but only the way in which it was interpreted, though the relative ease with which much material in the Old Testament lends itself to being read in these ways suggests that such interpretations are not inherently alien to the text. By contrast, at the time of the Yahwistic storytellers and editors the patriarchal traditions were still being retold in such a way that there was not yet one definitive version of them, and so the new perspective could significantly alter the nature of the text itself. This naturally makes it hard to distinguish what constitutes the molding perspective of Yahwism from what was original to the tradition in its own right, and there is room for disagreement as to the respective contributions of each. Nonetheless, our analysis in the preceding chapters gives us an exegetical foundation on which we may build with confidence. Since we have already seen that the language and concerns of Israel and Mosaic Yahwism can be discerned primarily in the portrayal of Abraham, we will limit the present analysis solely to the figure of Abraham.

The Pattern of Promise and Fulfilment

First, then, the pattern of promise and fulfilment. In general terms, Israel saw its existence as a nation in the land of Canaan as a fulfilment of what had been promised to the patriarchs. Since we find that the theme of God's promise to Abraham of descendants, land, and blessing is of central importance in Genesis 12–25, it is intrinsically likely that Israel's self-understanding influenced the way the story has been told and in particular the way in which the promises have been presented.[47]

47. See, e.g., von Rad, *Old Testament Theology,* vol. 1, 170.

Particularly relevant for our purposes is the promise that sets the context for all the patriarchal narratives, Gen. 12:1-3. On the one hand, this promise is integral to the Abraham story on its own terms, for it provides the presupposition without which the story would lose its significance—that Abraham is a model for faith in God, not only in obedience but also in trust with regard to the future, supremely with regard to having a son, but also with regard to a homeland.

On the other hand, the promise looks beyond the immediate story of Abraham and plays a wider role. One should note the strategic location of the promise, serving to introduce the whole patriarchal story and to set it in relation to the story of God's dealings with the whole of humanity in Genesis 1–11. The strategic position of these divine words, coupled with their generalized nature lacking reference to either a specific location or a specific occasion (unlike many other divine addresses in Genesis which are more specifically contextualized) makes it likely that, as they stand, they are the work of a narrator who is thereby setting the context of all that follows within the purposes of YHWH for Israel, whose existence is to be related to YHWH's purposes for the whole world. Gen. 12:1-3 gives the patriarchal narratives a frame of reference which looks beyond them—they cannot be understood adequately on their own terms but must be read in the light of Israel, toward whose existence and significance the stories point. Conversely, Israel as a nation in its land cannot understand itself simply on its own terms but must relate itself to God's dealings with the patriarchs.

One way in which the pentateuchal text makes explicit the relationship between Israel and God's promise to Abraham in Gen. 12:1-3 is in its development of the theme of blessing. The promise envisages Abraham's descendants not only as a great nation in the land of God's gift but also as the recipients of God's blessing in a way that will be determinative not only for themselves but for other nations, too—"I will bless those who bless you, and him who curses you I will curse." This point is reiterated in the two pentateuchal stories which specifically focus on God's blessing of Israel as their central concern. First, the story of Isaac blessing Jacob, in which this appears as the climax of Isaac's blessing and is related to Jacob as a nation (Gen. 27:29). Second, the story of Balaam (Numbers 22–24), in which God's promise to Israel is specifically at threat (22:6). The climax of Balak's three-fold attempt to get Balaam to curse Israel is the reaffirmation of Israel's status of blessing within YHWH's purposes as the climax of the last of Balaam's solicited oracles (Num. 24:9).

Apart from Gen. 12:1-3, many other elements in the story of Abraham most likely reflect Israel's self-understanding as owing its existence to the outworking of God's dealings with Abraham. For example, I have argued this in detail elsewhere as central to the significance both of Gen. 15:6 and of Gen. 22:15-18.[48] And since the basic point is hardly controversial, it needs no further elaboration here.

The Use of Typology

The typological dimensions of the Abraham story are less prominent in modern discussion than promise and fulfilment but featured prominently in much traditional exegesis. Although traditional interpretation often developed the point beyond the limits of the text itself, its foundation within the text is not difficult to discern.

The two fundamental traditions of Israel, which defined and shaped its relationship with God, were YHWH's deliverance of Israel in the Exodus and YHWH's covenant with Israel, centered on the Ten Commandments as the heart of Torah given at Sinai. Abraham has been so portrayed as to embody and personify Israel with regard to each of these.

Consider, for example, the story in Gen. 12:10—13:2. On the one hand, this can readily be understood within the story of Abraham himself. Abraham encounters a foreign king and passes off Sarah as his sister out of fear for his life. This seems a somewhat doubtful action both on its own terms (fear and deception) and in relation to the divine promise (should the pharaoh rather than Abraham beget children by Sarah). But nonetheless God stands by Abraham and brings him out of it with gain rather than loss, a pattern repeated, with variation, in Genesis 20.

48. R. W. L. Moberly, "Abraham's Righteousness (Gen. 15:6)," in J. A. Emerton, ed., *Studies in the Pentateuch,* VTS 41 (Leiden: Brill, 1990), 103–30; idem, "The Earliest Commentary on the Akedah," *VT* 38 (1988): 302–23.

On the other hand, the story of Abraham can be seen to parallel the story of Israel. Abraham migrates to Egypt in time of famine in Canaan (cf. Genesis 42–46), and there he prospers (cf. Exod. 1:7). Subsequently, YHWH afflicts the pharaoh and his house with great plagues (cf. Exodus 7–12), with the result that the pharaoh sends Abraham out of Egypt (cf. Exod. 12:31), and Abraham leaves with wealth and possessions (cf. Exod. 12:35, 38).[49] Both the nature of the story as particular to Abraham and the typical nature of the story with regard to Israel and the Exodus can be discerned.

The story of YHWH's covenant with Abraham in Genesis 15 contains perhaps the most emphatic use of the name YHWH in Genesis (15:7)—the name is on YHWH's own lips and is not accompanied by any other epithet or title. What is immediately striking is the similarity of the formula of divine self-introduction to the regular Exodus formula:[50]

Gen. 15:7 *'ani yhwh 'ašer hotse'tika me'ur kasdim*
Exod. 20:2 *'anoki yhwh 'eloheka 'ašer hotse'tika me'erets mitsraim*

The point of this choice of language is presumably typological. As YHWH brought Israel out of Egypt, so YHWH brought Abraham out of Ur. Abraham's story is seen as parallel to Israel's story, and Abraham in some sense personifies and embodies Israel's experience. Thus both Gen. 12:10—13:2 and 15:7 typologically link Abraham with Israel and the Exodus.

With regard to Sinai and Torah, the theological issue at stake is of great significance. If Torah represents the will of God for God's people, then, however much the distinctiveness of the patriarchal context may be recognized and respected, the Yahwistic storytellers would have a natural tendency to want to show Abraham, the father of Israelite faith, as in some way conforming

49. Cf. U. Cassuto, *A Commentary on the Book of Genesis,* vol. 2 (Jerusalem: Magnes, 1949, 1964), 334–37; M. Fishbane, *Biblical Interpretation in Ancient Israel* (Oxford: Clarendon, 1985), 375–76; J. Ha, *Genesis 15,* 198–99.

50. The parallelism is perhaps even closer in the LXX where in 15:7 (as in 11:28, 31) the text reads not "Ur of the Chaldees" but "land of the Chaldees" (ἐκ χώρας Χαλδαίων—the equivalent of Hebrew *me'erets kasdim*). But Exod. 20:2 in the LXX reads ἐκ γῆς Αἰγύπτου not ἐκ χώρας as might have been expected if the LXX translators had seen significance here.

to Torah. Therefore, not surprisingly, there is one explicit statement to this effect within the text (Gen. 26:5) and another of similar import (18:19). Postbiblical tradition naturally made much of this.[51]

The relationship between Abraham and Torah, however, goes deeper if one considers the supreme story of Abraham's obedience, Genesis 22. Here the two key words, which provide the most explicit interpretation of the story, are *test* (*nissah,* v. 1—the writer's statement of the meaning of the story) and *fear* (*yare',* v. 12—the word which states the outcome, indeed the purpose, of the test, "Now I know that you fear God. . . ."). In this context, *fear* clearly has the sense of moral obedience rather than religious awe, and *fear* in this sense is commonly used of obedience to Torah (e.g., Deut. 5:29; 10:12f.). Moreover, a conceptual linkage between divine testing and Israel's obedience to Torah is well attested elsewhere in the Pentateuch (e.g., Exod. 16:4; Deut. 8:2). What is especially notable, however, is that the specific juxtaposition of *test* and *fear* occurs only in one other passage in the Old Testament (Exod. 20:20). This is a statement of crucial importance for the Sinai tradition as it explains the purpose of those laws (i.e., the Ten Commandments) that stand at the heart of the Sinai covenant. The purpose of the laws is said to be so that God may "test" *(nissah)* Israel and so that the "fear of him" *(yir'ato)* may be before their eyes so that they do not sin. The point of YHWH giving Torah to Israel is to test them so that they will be led into fuller obedience of life. Abraham supremely exemplifies precisely this in his willingness, when tested, to offer Isaac—a total obedience to God that, although in some ways unique, should nonetheless be a model for the response to YHWH that should constantly characterize Israel as a whole. Add to this the observation that Abraham sacrifices to God at the place God selects for him (Gen. 22:2, 3), which is similar to God's requirement for Israel's worship (Exod. 20:24; Deut. 12:5), and that this place is apparently none other than Jerusalem (Gen. 22:2, 14), which is YHWH's chosen place for Israel (e.g., 1 Kings 14:21; Ps.

51. See, e.g., J. Bowker, *The Targums and Rabbinic Literature* (Cambridge: Cambridge Univ. Press, 1969), 235–36 for a succinct introduction to the tradition commonly expressed from Jubilees onward.

132:13), and that Abraham's obedience to God (Gen. 22:12) is what should characterize Israel as it comes to worship (e.g., Psalm 15 and 24; Jer. 7:1-15). Then it is not difficult to see Abraham in Genesis 22 as the typological embodiment of Israel's obedience to Torah.

It is likely that the portrayal of Abraham has been molded in other ways so that he typifies Israel. For example, with regard to Israel's occupation of Canaan, the portrayal of Abraham in Genesis 12–13 is suggestive. The thrice-repeated formula that Abraham "built there an altar to YHWH" *(wayyiben šam mizbeaḥ lyhwh)* in the north (Shechem), center (Bethel, Ai), and south (Hebron) of the land (12:7, 8; 13:18) suggests that the entire land is being symbolically claimed and dedicated to YHWH. In the course of this the narrative draws special attention to Abraham going to a place between Bethel and Ai (12:8; 13:3). Ai is only otherwise mentioned in the narratives of the Old Testament in Joshua 7 and 8 as the area where Joshua and Israel first entered the hill country of Israel.[52] In addition to Joshua going to Shechem at an early stage (Josh. 8:30-35), the conquest narrative continues with a campaign in the center and south of the land (Joshua 10) and a campaign in the north (Josh. 11:1-15), which appear to be symbolic of taking the land as a whole. Abraham's entry into the land appears to have been so molded that it is suggestive of Israel as a nation. Other examples could also be mentioned. But again the basic issue—the likely way in which the story of Abraham has been so told that it resonates with a Yahwistic perspective—is clear.

These two ways in which the story of Abraham was interpreted and appropriated by a Yahwistic perspective are clearly analogous to a Christian reading of the Old Testament. As the Christian perceives the Old Testament in a new way in the light of Jesus, so the Yahwistic narrators perceived the figure of Abraham in a new way in the light of Israel's traditions. In this way the interpretative process primarily works, from Jesus to the Old Testament and from Israel to Abraham; the normative traditions of Jesus and Israel provide the models by which God's earlier

52. Ai is also mentioned retrospectively in Josh. 9:3; 10:1, 2; 12:9.

activity is to be understood. The process, however, is in some ways reciprocal, since the later traditions have themselves grown out of the earlier and had their content formed accordingly. Moreover, the value of the interpretative exercise depends to some extent on the content of the earlier traditions being inherently suitable. Presumably because the tradition already contained divine promises to Abraham and an account of Abraham's leaving Mesopotamia for Canaan, the Yahwistic narrators were able to interpret these traditions as anticipatory of or analogous to Israel's traditions. In a similar way, the Christian finds analogies to the Christian life in the Old Testament precisely because Christianity has many inherent similarities to the Hebraic and Jewish tradition out of which it grew.

SUMMARY OF DISCUSSION

To conclude and summarize our discussion, we can say that within the New Testament and the Pentateuch there is a remarkable parallelism in the concept of different dispensations and the attendant hermeneutical processes. Indeed, so similar are the dynamics of the two interpretative processes that it seems not inappropriate to borrow Christian terminology for the theological concept of the pentateuchal writers and so to designate the patriarchal traditions of Genesis 12–50 as the Old Testament of the Old Testament.

In a recent discussion of the shape of the Pentateuch G. W. Coats asked the question, "What, then, can be said concerning the relationship between the Moses narratives and Genesis?" He went on to observe that "one of the pressing problems, as yet unresolved in the scholarly discussion of the Pentateuch, concerns the relationship between the patriarchs and Moses or between the 'God of the Fathers' dimension of religion in the early tradition of Israel and the religious structure of Yahwism."[53] Our proposal to see the patriarchal traditions as the Old Testament of the Old Testament offers a resolution to this problem.

53. G. W. Coats, *Moses,* JSOTS 57 (Sheffield: JSOT, 1988), 38.

CHAPTER 5

The Old Testament and Jewish-Christian Dialogue

In the light of our thesis about Genesis 12–50 as the Old Testament of the Old Testament, it will be appropriate now to consider its possible bearings upon one aspect of contemporary theological debate, that is, the dialogue between Jews and Christians.

THE MODERN CONTEXT

The growth of Jewish-Christian dialogue has been one of the striking features of recent theological debate in the Western world.[1] For most of the last two thousand years serious theological exchange between Jew and Christian has been minimal or nonexistent. For the most part Christians have operated with stereotypes of the Jew and Judaism which have, to a greater or lesser extent, misrepresented and denigrated much or even all that Jews have stood for. The practical corollary within Western civilization, in terms of ghettos, persecutions, and mass murders, has been of unspeakable horror. Jews, for their part, have mostly shown little interest in understanding Christianity and have been content to operate with their own ill-informed stereotypes. Insofar as Jewishness and Judaism have remained important to them, they have usually wanted from Christians nothing so much as simply to be left alone.

1. An introduction to the issues can be found in M. Braybrooke, *Time to Meet: Towards a Deeper Relationship between Christians and Jews* (London: SCM; Philadelphia: Trinity International, 1990); or in J. Pawlikowski, *Jesus and the Theology of Israel* (Wilmington, Delaware: Michael Glazier, 1989).

In relatively few years a major change has taken place in age-old attitudes. There are perhaps three main reasons for this. First is the Holocaust, or Shoah. The deliberate murder of six million Jews cannot but raise profound and disturbing questions for Christian and Jew, questions not simply about the justice of God but also about the human beliefs and practices that made such murder possible. Second is the establishment of the state of Israel. Although the Zionism that gave rise to modern Israel was not initially a religious phenomenon but an offshoot of nineteenth-century nationalist ideology, the existence of a Jewish state has not only given the Jewish people a new identity within the modern world but has also allowed more specifically religious and theological issues to come to the fore in the attempt to understand the implications of modern Israel for Jews, Jewishness, and Judaism. Third is the decline of Christianity in Western Europe. The reasons for this are less important in this context than the fact of it. The greatly diminished status of Christianity has perhaps encouraged a greater openness and humility in many Christian churches than was the case previously. Similarly, there has been a decline in religious belief and observance among Jews. The parallel decline in both Christianity and Judaism increasingly means that those who have a living faith have common interests in the midst of a largely secular culture. Whatever the reasons, a new (though by no means universal) openness between Christian and Jew has come about, which has led to an unprecedented dialogue.

Christians have perhaps two major concerns in the dialogue. On the one hand is the need to come to terms with, repent of, and renounce the anti-Jewishness and anti-Judaism of so much Christian tradition. On the other hand is the need to develop an accurate and appreciative understanding of Jewishness and Judaism.[2] Within the sphere of biblical study, and in particular recent New Testament study, both these concerns are well represented, and a considerable literature has rapidly grown up. There

2. An important attempt to formulate a systematic theology in this context has been made by Paul van Buren in his three-volume *Theology of the Jewish-Christian Reality (Discerning the Way; A Christian Theology of the People Israel; Christ in Context)* (San Francisco: Harper & Row, 1980, 1983, 1988).

is intense study of the question of the extent to which negative Christian attitudes to Jews and Judaism are inherent in the New Testament;[3] there is also a "quest for the historical Judaism," to understand Jewish material without negative Christian value judgments.[4]

Our present thesis will touch on these issues. Our focus, however, will be on the less well-known problem posed by the "Old Testament," that is, the problem of the shared Christian and Jewish use of the same Hebrew scripture.[5] As already noted, Christian use of the Old Testament has long been seen as an internal Christian problem, a puzzle posed by the logic of scriptural witness to God in two dispensations. All too often, however, it has been seen *only* as an internal Christian problem, as though the continuing existence of Jews and Judaism and their use of the same scripture were of little or no significance.[6] Insofar as Christians take Jews seriously, they must take seriously Jewish use of the "Old Testament." If they do so, one corollary will be to face, with a new sharpness, the question of the grounds on which Christians lay claim to Jewish scripture as in some way Christian scripture. That is to say, the real issue may be not so much Jewish use of Christian scripture ("What should Christians make of Jewish use of the Old Testament?") but rather Christian use of Jewish scripture ("In what way is it legitimate for Christians to appropriate the Hebrew scriptures of the Jews?").

Because of both the importance and the difficulty of the issues

3. See, e.g., W. Klassen, "Anti-Judaism in Early Christianity: The State of the Question," in P. Richardson, ed., *Anti-Judaism in Early Christianity,* vol. 1, *Paul and the Gospels* (Waterloo, Ontario: Wilfrid Laurier Univ. Press, 1986), 1–19.

4. The recent works of E. P. Sanders and J. Neusner are particularly important in this context; e.g., E. P. Sanders, *Paul and Palestinian Judaism* (London: SCM, 1977); J. Neusner, *Studying Classical Judaism: A Primer* (Louisville: Westminster/John Knox Press, 1991).

5. For a recent discussion of the issues, see R. Brooks and J. J. Collins, eds., *Hebrew Bible or Old Testament?* (Notre Dame: Notre Dame Univ. Press, 1991).

6. In standard Old Testament theologies that explicitly discuss the theological issues posed by the relationship between Old Testament and New Testament, the possible significance of a Jewish perspective is usually passed over. See, e.g., G. von Rad, *Old Testament Theology,* vol. 2 (London: SCM, 1965, 1975; ET from German), pt. 3; C. Westermann, *Elements of Old Testament Theology* (Atlanta: John Knox, 1982; ET from German), pts. 1 and 6.

at stake, it will be appropriate initially to stand back a little. The context for our discussion may be set by reminding ourselves initially of what it means to regard certain texts as scripture and what it means to do theology with regard to these texts.

THE PRIVILEGED STATUS OF THE BIBLE

The question of the nature of scripture and of biblical theology may be approached via reflection on the privileged status of the Bible. Obviously, Christians and Jews accord privileged status to the Bible, but it is important to probe some of the reasons why and their possible implications. Why should biblical scholars accord a significance and, in principle, contemporary relevance to the theological content of the Bible that they do not accord to the theological content of other religious texts of antiquity?

In the following discussion I will write explicitly from a Christian perspective. I will make no more than passing reference to Judaism and its privileging of scripture because, despite obvious and important similarities to Christian approaches, the dynamics of the varying relationships between Jews and their scripture are often importantly different from those of Christians. Any attempt to do justice to this would necessitate endless qualifications to the argument. To take two examples. On the one hand, the way in which many Jews privilege scripture because of their sense of historical continuity with biblical Israel introduces considerations that are not characteristic of Christians (except perhaps for those Jews who are also Christians). J. D. Levenson has noted the "profound involvement" with Hebrew scripture that is a fixture of modern, secular Israeli culture, and he comments that "most modern Jews are inclined to find their identity in Jewish history, not in Jewish theology."[7] On the other hand, the possible relationships between scripture and contemporary Jewish lifestyle are generally different from those possible for Christians. As M. H. Goshen-Gottstein has put it, "On the practical level of observance, rabbinic Judaism has effectively cut itself off from further direct dependence on Scripture. . . . The system of

7. J. D. Levenson, "Why Jews Are Not Interested in Biblical Theology," in J. Neusner, B. A. Levine, and E. S. Frerichs, eds., *Judaic Perspectives on Ancient Israel* (Philadelphia: Fortress, 1987), 294.

halakhic observance and the structure of Tanakh meaning have hardly anything in common."[8] In the light of these differences, I hope that the omission of a Jewish perspective in the following discussion will not be taken to imply disregard for the role of Judaism in establishing its own privileged understanding of scripture.

It is important to raise and press this question of privileged status. From the point of view of the ancient historian concerned to understand the religious beliefs and practices of the ancient world, it is hardly self-evident that these biblical texts—however weighty, memorable, and profound much of their content may be—should qualify for special treatment as a separate collection of texts. Some of the content is not obviously special; much of it can be paralleled in other ancient texts. And on general moral and religious grounds the content of certain other ancient texts may be at least as worthy, if not sometimes more so, as the content of some of the biblical texts. The historian may, of course, reckon with the privileged status accorded to these texts insofar as it became a historical fact within ancient Jewish and Christian religion. But that is more an issue of the afterlife of the texts which, while significant in its own right, may legitimately be set aside insofar as the historian seeks to understand the texts within the historical context in which they were first written. The rhetoric of modern biblical study has made much of a historical approach to the biblical text, seeking to recover the authentic meaning of the text in conscious distinction from the interpretations put upon it by later ecclesiastical dogma. So the fact that biblical scholars have generally continued to accord privileged status to the biblical texts, which is the very essence of a later ecclesiastical perspective, has sat somewhat uneasily alongside the claim to offer straightforward historical interpretations of the text.

Ancient history is not, of course, a wholly objective discipline.

8. M. H. Goshen-Gottstein, "Tanakh Theology: The Religion of the Old Testament and the Place of Jewish Biblical Theology," in P. D. Miller, Jr., et al., eds., *Ancient Israelite Religion* (Philadelphia: Fortress, 1987), 626, 627. The essay is an illuminating attempt by a Jewish scholar to formulate a Jewish approach to scripture analogous to the kind of Christian approach advocated here.

Insofar as history is a discipline concerned with in some way understanding the past and is to be distinguished from antiquarianism, which delights simply in the compilation and contemplation of data from the past as an end in itself, the past must be interpreted with categories, analogies, and insights from the historian's own understanding of thc world. And insofar as historians discuss material that in some way relates either to basic judgments of belief and value or to people's sense of identity in the contemporary world, their discussion of the past will both be informed by, and will potentially inform in return, contemporary debate about beliefs, values, and identity. Since the Bible almost inescapably raises questions about beliefs, values, and identity, at least within the Western world, any good historical account of its contents is likely to have implications for contemporary debates on such issues. Nonetheless, the potential implications of informed historical insight into the history of Israelite, Jewish, and Christian religion is not what has been classically understood by the term *theology.* Theology classically is concerned with constructive questions of what belief and practice *can* be and *ought* to be as a living reality in the present rather than simply descriptive, albeit suggestive, accounts of what it *has* been in the past. As such, theology involves dimensions that relate somewhat obliquely to the concerns of historians qua historians, insofar as they conform to the conventions of historiography as a modern academic discipline.

To put the matter another way: since ancient history may not be without implication for contemporary understanding, biblical theology as a scholarly discipline in the last two centuries has faced a constant struggle to distinguish itself from a history of the religious beliefs, practices, experiences, and interpretations of ancient Israel, nascent Judaism, and early Christianity. There is a general feeling that biblical theology should not just be religious history but should have something more, and this something more is commonly expressed in terms of biblical theology being not just descriptive but also prescriptive as well.[9] This is all very

9. See, e.g., these introductory essays: J. A. Ziesler, "New Testament Theology"; N. W. Porteous and R. E. Clements, "Old Testament Theology," in A. Richardson and J. Bowden, eds., *The Westminster Dictionary of Christian Theology* (Philadelphia: Westminster, 1983), 398–403, 406–13. A particularly

well, but *why* should it be prescriptive? The point is more often assumed or asserted as an obvious fact—the Bible is authoritative for Christian faith—than it is argued. The importance of focusing explicitly on this issue lies in the fact that unless one does so the question of the relationship between the authority of the text and the way Christians read it is likely to be begged. Instead of an exploration of the dynamics entailed by the privileged status of the text, the issue is assumed to be obvious or unproblematic, which it isn't.

An analogy may be helpful. The question of the privileged status of the Bible may perhaps be illuminated by comparing the Bible with Homer. I choose Homer for two reasons. First, Homer still has the status of a literary classic in our culture, that is, a work whose breadth and depth give it enduring value. Much work has been done recently on the concept of the "classic," not least as a possible model that might account for the contemporary significance of the Bible while escaping from familiar puzzles about theology, history, and biblical authority.[10] Nonetheless, although the Bible is indeed a classic and may be acknowledged by those with no interest in Christian faith as having various kinds of value (not least that of enduring insight into the human situation), the kind of insight the Bible may offer qua "classic" is very much less than that usually associated with the notion of "scripture" where explicit and prescriptive teaching and guidance—"the word of God"—is expected to be found. Scripture entails a status and authority that a classic lacks.

Second, in antiquity Homer was a classic with something like the kind of "scriptural" status for Graeco-Roman culture that the Bible has for Christian culture. Of course, "scripture" is not a Graeco-Roman category, and Graeco-Roman religions were diverse and had a great diversity of sacred traditions. But the

sharp and stimulating account is H. Räisänen, *Beyond New Testament Theology* (London: SCM; Philadelphia: Trinity International, 1990). Räisänen focuses on the same issues that concern us here but prefers to move in a very different direction.

10. See, e.g., K. Stendahl, "The Bible as a Classic and the Bible as Holy Scripture," *JBL* 103 (1984): 3–10. The concept of classic may be operative even when the terminology is not used, as in G. Josipovici, *The Book of God* (New Haven and London: Yale Univ. Press, 1988), or D. J. A. Clines, *What Does Eve Do to Help?* JSOTS 94 (Sheffield: JSOT, 1990), esp. 47–48.

analogy is still perhaps sufficiently close to be illuminating. Although the Iliad and the Odyssey are not religious works of the same kind as the Bible, they nonetheless contain much suggestive material about the gods and humanity. The Homeric portrayal was given privileged status within Graeco-Roman culture and for centuries shaped many people's perceptions and expectations about the gods and their relationships with humanity.[11]

Today nobody would dream of treating what Homer says about the gods in the sort of way that Christians treat what the Bible says about God (or if they did, they would be regarded as extremely strange and idiosyncratic). One may indeed find studies of Homer with sections devoted to "theology." But such studies will be concerned to offer a historical description of religious thought and practice within the Homeric world, with no implication that such thought and practice might be a valid option to be adopted by a person today.[12] Insofar as Homer has value and meaning for today it is because of its status as a classic and because its literary qualities and aspects of its portrayal of life still resonate with and can enhance the contemporary reader's understanding and intuition. It is not because of specific items of religious belief or practice that the reader might be expected to appropriate. Belief in Zeus and the Homeric pantheon is not a contemporary option. Belief in YHWH, understood by Christians as the God and Father of our Lord Jesus Christ, is. Wherein lies the difference?

I suggest that the basic reason for the difference is the fact of a continuous existence down the centuries of communities of faith whose understanding of God and humanity has been profoundly informed, indeed fundamentally shaped, by these biblical texts. The continuing vitality of such communities gives rise to the presupposition that a continuing truth content is in the scriptures of those communities. This leads to giving the text privileged status and reading it in a particular "committed" kind of way, that is, with the expectation that it will speak to and guide people today. Of course, if the content of the Bible was not, in fact, of

11. See, e.g., R. Lane Fox, *Pagans and Christians* (Harmondsworth: Viking, 1986), chap. 4.

12. See, e.g., C. M. Bowra, *Tradition and Design in the Iliad* (Oxford: Clarendon, 1930), chap. 10.

great breadth, depth, and power, disappointment would long since have eroded its privilege and undermined the communities of faith. Nonetheless the point remains that without continuing communities of faith it would cease to be meaningful to privilege the Bible (except as a classic) in the way that Christian theology customarily does.

It seems to me that a corollary of this is to recognize that if Homer had continued to be read as "scripture" outside the context of Graeco-Roman culture until the present day, then Homeric theology in the same sort of sense as Christian biblical theology would be a feasible option. Conversely, if Christianity ceased to function as a living religion, then biblical theology would cease to be an option or rather would only be an option in the sense that Homeric theology is currently an option, that is, as religious history. Indeed, for many today, for whom Christian faith is no longer a viable option, biblical theology is clearly little different from Homeric theology—interesting as history, curious and misguided as a way of life today.

The recognition that the privileged status of the Bible is dependent upon the continuing vitality of the Christian church is hardly novel, but it is often obscured by the widespread willingness in Western culture to accord some kind of privileged status to the Bible for general cultural reasons. Perhaps because the privileged status of the Bible has generally, at least until recently, not been seen to need justification, its potential implications for what counts as reading the Bible well have not been allowed into the foreground of most studies of biblical theology. If this argument be allowed, its implications are enormous and for the most part lie beyond the scope of the present study. For present purposes the important point is that if the Christian church privileges scripture and so makes its contemporary theological use possible, then the basic categories by which the church interprets scripture must necessarily be of primary importance. In this context we can begin to consider some of the possible implications of Jewish and Christian use of the same scripture.

OLD TESTAMENT AND NEW TESTAMENT

We may proceed by focusing on the term *Old Testament* and exploring its logic and implications. To some extent we have already touched on this in the previous chapter, but it will be helpful to develop it further.

We should note at the outset that *Old Testament* and *New Testament* are terms of Christian theology, which encapsulate the privileged status of the biblical texts. The privilege is implied primarily by the noun *Testament* while the Christian perspective is contained in the adjectives *Old* and *New*.

The linguistic origins of *testament* as a rendering of Hebrew *berit*, Greek *diatheke*, and Latin *testamentum* (the biblical origin being Jer. 31:31), together with the historical origins of the use of the term within Christian theology are important issues in their own right but need not be our concern here. For present purposes, the important point is that *testament* has become part of the universal vocabulary of Christian theology and presupposes an understanding of the biblical material as canonical writings that bear authoritative witness to God and the nature of human life.

With regard to the adjectives, we should note that the terms *Old Testament* and *New Testament* are correlative and interdependent. That is, to refer to the Old Testament as *Old* Testament makes the Christian assumption that there is a *New* Testament in the light of which the Old Testament becomes Old. To refer to the New Testament as *New* Testament makes the Christian assumption that there is an Old Testament in the light of which the New Testament becomes New. In the terms *Old Testament* and *New Testament* the epithets *old* and *new* are not primarily chronological judgments, as though Old Testament were equivalent to "Ancient/Older Testament" and New Testament equivalent to "More Recent Testament," though of course such chronological assessments would be entirely accurate. Rather, the terms are first and foremost a theological judgment to the effect that the content of the Old Testament belongs to a period and mode of God's dealings with the world that has been in some ways superseded by the coming of Jesus Christ in the New Testament.

Now although such presuppositions are valid for a Christian, they are not necessary presuppositions. The same material may be approached in more than one way. For the present we must leave aside the interesting and important question of those who wish to approach the material without prejudice as to questions of faith and theology, from the perspective of, for example, either ancient history or literary criticism. (I sometimes wonder whether many of the problems and misunderstandings about modern biblical criticism may not be encapsulated in the tendency to retain the names Old/New Testament that are theological and privileged while wanting to treat the content in a way that is nontheological and nonprivileged.) Rather, our concern is with those who may still have theological presuppositions but of a different kind. This is most obviously the case for the Jew for whom the greater part of the Christian Bible is also scripture.[13] Jews revere as scripture the same material that Christians call Old Testament, but they do not call it Old Testament. (Or if they do acquiesce in the term out of deference to Christian or general cultural usage, then they will tend to understand *Old* simply as *Ancient*.) Rather, Jews call their scripture [Hebrew] Bible or Miqra (that which is read out) or Tanakh (an acronym of its constituent parts: *Torah, Nebiim, Ketubim*). The difference of name epitomizes a difference of presupposition and approach.

Of course, the Jew's relationship to Tanakh is in many ways as indirect and problematic as is the Christian's relationship to the Old Testament. In each case there is a history of religious faith and practice subsequent to the Hebrew scriptures, a history with perspectives of its own within which the believing interpreter stands. For most practical purposes, the later interpretative perspectives represented by Mishnah, Talmud, Targum, and Midrash function, broadly speaking, in the same sort of way that the New Testament and the creeds function for the Christian. They provide a content that takes priority over the Hebrew scriptures for the regular life of the community of faith and provide an interpretative context within which the ancient Hebrew text is read. As a result, Tanakh is not usually read without reference to its history of interpretation, that is, its ongoing use within communities of faith in postbiblical times. The crucial difference of principle, however, is that the status of the later interpretative

13. Unfortunately it lies beyond the scope of this study even to attempt to engage with the issues of Islamic appropriation of Judaeo-Christian scripture.

perspective differs for Jew and Christian respectively. For the Christian the New Testament represents a qualitatively new divine revelation, in some ways superseding what went before. But for the Jew the status of Talmud, etc., is that of *commentary*: expounding, elaborating, developing, and applying the existing material but in no way superseding it. For the Christian there is a new dispensation; for the Jew there is not. This basic difference of principle leads in practice to subtly but profoundly differing interpretations by Jew and Christian of the same Hebrew scripture.

To put this same point differently: Judaism is *not* the same as the religion of the Old Testament but is a rich and complex system based as much, if not more, on postbiblical developments (Oral Torah, according to the familiar rabbinic designation) as on Hebrew scripture (Written Torah). For all the difference, however, there remains a fundamental continuity, for the category of Torah, which is primary and normative within Hebrew scripture,[14] is also normative within Judaism. For the Christian, by contrast, the primary and normative category of the religion is Christ, not Torah, which means that Christians necessarily stand in a position of discontinuity with regard to Hebrew scripture. For the Jew there is a continuity where for the Christian there is a discontinuity. This difference is reflected in differing nomenclature for the same material.

We can see, then, that the assumption that the Bible has special significance for today depends on the presence of communities of faith whose identity is in one way or another defined in relation to the Bible and who stand in some kind of continuity with previous such communities of faith, whose life-style and understanding down the ages has been informed by the Bible as a fundamental norm. Further, the familiar terms Old Testament and New Testament are explicitly Christian terms which encapsulate a Christian understanding of how Christian faith relates to the content of the Bible. Specifically, the terms Old Testament and New Testament presuppose the fundamental stance of Christian faith, that Jesus is the key to understanding God and

14. This is, of course, an assessment of the material in its canonical form, without prejudice as to the underlying history of Israelite religion.

provides the focal point from which all else should be evaluated and understood.

THE VALIDITY OF OLD TESTAMENT AS A CONTEMPORARY THEOLOGICAL CONCEPT

In the light of this basic point—that Old Testament is a specifically Christian term that implies a judgment with at least some negative connotations about the content of Hebrew scripture—what place, if any, should it have in Jewish-Christian dialogue, especially with reference to scripture? The crucial question is, Do its negative connotations entail a negative assessment of Jews and Judaism such as to make any genuine dialogue impossible until the term is expunged from Christian vocabulary?

The consensus of Christians engaged in recent Jewish-Christian dialogue has been to answer this question in the affirmative. The point may be expressed more or less strongly. Recent assessments of the term Old Testament range from its being "improper"[15] to its being "anti-Semitic."[16] But a common concern to get rid of an apparently pejorative term is increasingly evident.[17] For example, M. Braybrooke, in his recent introduc-

15. Br. John of Taizé, *The Pilgrim God: A Biblical Journey* (Washington, D.C.: Pastoral Press, 1985), 4.

16. See, e.g., E. L. Dachslager, "Getting Rid of the 'Old Testament,'" *Reconstructionist* 44 (1978): 7–10. Dachslager comments that "to refer to the Hebrew Bible as an 'Old Testament' is a prime example of what Solomon Schechter called 'the higher antisemitism'" (p. 8). My nearby colleague Prof. J. F. A. Sawyer of Newcastle University consistently refers to Christian use of "Old Testament" as anti-Semitic. See his recent article, "Combating Prejudices about the Bible and Judaism" (*Theology* 94 [1991]: 269–78) in which he describes use of the term Old Testament as damaging, arrogant, oppressive, symbolic of a rejection of the Jews, and theologically indefensible.

17. Theological engagement with this issue reaches a nadir in a recent Christian study of anti-Judaism: C. M. Williamson and R. J. Allen, *Interpreting Difficult Texts: Anti-Judaism and Christian Preaching* (London: SCM; Philadelphia: Trinity International, 1989). Here (p. 115) preachers are urged to abandon use of the language of Old Testament/New Testament on the ground that it contributes to anti-Judaism. It is said (quite rightly) that "congregations need to be educated as to the effects of the adjectives 'old' and 'new' when applied to the parts of the Bible and to Judaism ('old covenant') and to Christianity ('new covenant')." Yet the entire argument in favor of dropping the language of Old Testament/New Testament is this: "In our culture, 'old' is often a negative word denoting that which is wearing out, outmoded, no longer desirable. Our culture usually values more highly the new, which is regarded as fresh, interesting, desirable. The new home, the new car, the new job—these

tion to Jewish-Christian dialogue, makes a passing reference to the issue of Old Testament and says, "The use of 'old' and 'new' of covenant, testament or people of God is best avoided, because it carries with it, especially to Jewish ears, the implication that the church has replaced the Jewish people and that God abandoned them because they killed Jesus."[18] Too often, however, such comments about the undesirability of the term Old Testament are not consistently worked through. For though it is easy enough for Christians to take the point that Old Testament is a term that Jews can take exception to, we must point out that there are few obvious alternatives to it, primarily because of its being correlative with New Testament. Although many Christians might be willing to abandon the term Old Testament on its own, they might show a somewhat greater reluctance to cease referring to the New Testament. Some consistent proposals have, of course, been made. Paul van Buren, for example, has proposed replacing *Old Testament* with *Scripture/The Scriptures/The Hebrew Scriptures,* and replacing *New Testament* with *The Apostolic Writings.*[19] Perhaps most elegant is the language of *First Testament* and *Second Testament* as proposed by J. A. Sanders and adopted as editorial policy by the *Biblical Theology Bulletin.*[20]

From the perspective of Christian theology, two essential questions must be put to all such proposals. First, do the terms Old Testament and New Testament express insights essential to Christian faith such that the integrity of Christian faith would be threatened by their abandonment, or are they really somewhat arbitrary and so able to be replaced without loss (supposing that cultural inertia against doing so could be overcome)? Second, if the terms are essential to Christian faith, do they necessarily imply a negative assessment of Jewish faith?

According to our thesis—it will be no surprise by now—

represent advances. Advertisers describe products as 'new and improved.' This simple word-association suggests that an *Old* Testament (as well as the religion which it contains and its followers) is worn-out, outmoded, no longer functional, especially in contrast to the New (and improved) Testament."

18. Braybrooke, *Time to Meet,* 171 n. 16.

19. P. van Buren, *Discerning the Way,* 23, 120ff.

20. J. A. Sanders, "First Testament and Second," *BTB* 17 (1987): 47–49.

answers to these questions may best be considered if the issue of Christian terminology of Old/New Testament is set alongside what we have argued to be a parallel phenomenon in the very heart of Hebrew scripture, what we have presumed to call "the Old Testament of the Old Testament." On the one hand, this provides a close analogy to a problem until now generally considered unique and so offers the possibility of shedding fresh light upon it. And on the other hand, the fact that the parallel phenomenon is integral to the Hebrew scriptures of the Jews offers the possibility that the whole issue can be understood in a way acceptable to a Jewish perspective.

In the light of our analogy, it is, I think, clear that the answer to the first question must be that the language of Old/New Testament *is* essential. It is as necessary for the Christian that the faith centered on Jesus in some ways supersedes the religion of the Old Testament as it was for the adherents of Mosaic Yahwism that their faith in some ways superseded patriarchal religion. As we have seen, each time a sense of a new beginning introduces a new dispensation. In this new dispensation the assumptions and structure of the resultant religion have a consistent logic and identity of their own. Although each time there is a deep sense of continuity with what went before, there is nonetheless a major change of ethos and of religious practice. The new religions, respectively centered on Christ and Torah, have normative status for their adherents and relativize the significance of the former dispensation. However much the texts of the former dispensation may be appropriated by, and to some extent be molded to, the perspectives of the new dispensation, the very fact that this process goes on presupposes the normativity of the new perspective and the impossibility of continuance in the old as it once was. Whatever, therefore, the apparent initial attractiveness of abandoning the language of Old Testament, it is simply not possible for the Christian to do so and still to explain the logic of a Christian, as distinct from a Jewish, position.

The whole problem with looking for religiously neutral language, such as First/Second Testament, is that it evades the basic theological issue of different dispensations posed by the biblical text. For the ancient historian who approaches the biblical material without prejudice as to its possible relevance for today, such religiously neutral language is indeed appropriate. For the Christian theologian, whose self-understanding, identity, and life-style are all in some way bound up with an understanding of the meaning of scripture, the exclusive adoption of religiously neutral language is at best a dereliction of duty and at worst a deception (as much of self as of others). We must be clear about this point. It is not the case that Christians must always and only use the terms Old/New Testament. For a good number of practical purposes, such as either Jewish-Christian dialogue or many facets of academic biblical study, it may be preferable to adopt terminology that is common to all parties, terminology such as *scripture* or *Bible,* so as to facilitate discussion of common ground. But it would be a mistake to allow such conveniently neutral terminology to disguise fundamental underlying differences when it comes to matters of the use of the Bible in the life of faith today. For Christians have to account for the fact that Mosaic Torah is as divinely prescribed as their own way of life in the New Testament, and yet they disregard most of its formal requirements. This is no more neutral an issue than is the position of Mosaic Yahwism vis-à-vis patriarchal religion. J. A. Sanders talks of the need to "avoid the supersessionism of old Christendom implicit in the terms Old and New Testament" but leaves "supersessionism" as an unanalyzed bogey word.[21] But the inescapable fact is that in some ways there must be a superseding of existing religion if Christianity is to distinguish itself from the

21. Ibid., 48. Similarly, when D. M. Bossman comments on the editorial policy of *Biblical Theology Bulletin* in adopting the language of First and Second Testament, he cites as a factor in its favor that "'Old' Testament has suggested that the Christian 'New' Testament supercedes what is past" (*BTB* 17 [1987]: 46). In like manner P. D. Hanson comments on traditional Christian typology that "the end result of such supersessionist typology is that Judaism is regarded as essentially dead, whereas God's whole future is seen bound up with Christianity." He goes on, however, to insist "that larger patterns of meaning, be they historiographic, ideological, or theological in nature, must be demonstrated as being in harmony with the biblical materials themselves, though by virtue of the dialogical nature of all interpretation, they will of course move beyond ancient settings and meanings by participating in the world and setting of the interpreter and his or her community" ("Biblical Interpretation: Meeting Place of Jews and Christians," in G. M. Tucker, D. L. Petersen, and R. R. Wilson, eds., *Canon, Theology, and Old Testament Interpretation* (Philadelphia: Fortress, 1988), 42.

Torah-centered religion of the Old Testament or Mosaic Yahwism from patriarchal religion.

The crucial issue is what the notion of superseding does and does not involve in these two instances. We have argued that in each case there is a change of basic ethos and of formal religious practice, such that important aspects of the previous religious system are set aside as no longer appropriate and are replaced by an alternative pattern. With this, however, goes a continuity of general spirituality, in terms of the values and goals of life under God, together with the sense that the new system represents a fulfilment toward which the previous system was pointing.[22] We have consistently referred to the new system as "in some ways superseding" the old, because there is a subtle and complex blend of both continuity and discontinuity. It is vital that the terminology to be generally used in a theological context should capture this sense of combined continuity and discontinuity. Although, therefore, the language of Old Testament, being Christian in origin, may initially appear tendentious when applied to the heart of Torah, it is, in fact, the only conceptual language available in theological parlance that accurately captures the dynamics of the pentateuchal text and likewise the dynamics of a Christian stance in relation to the Torah-centered religion of Hebrew scripture. Thus the crucial question becomes, not whether the language of Old Testament should be retained, but rather what implications and resonances such language should have—which leads us to the second question.

In answer to the second question, the force of our analogy is that the Christian should no more denigrate the Torah-centered religion of the Old Testament, or the Judaism that grows out of it and stands in basic continuity with it, than that Torah-centered religion (i.e., Mosaic Yahwism) itself denigrated patriarchal religion. Although Mosaic Yahwism made exclusive demands on Israel and could be strongly polemical against other, especially Canaanite, religious systems, Mosaic Yahwism has no polemic against patriarchal religion even though patriarchal religion is open toward the Canaanites and appears to have certain affinities

22. Above, pp. 129ff.

with Canaanite religion. On the contrary, Mosaic Yahwism respected and preserved the distinctiveness of patriarchal religion, saw it as the foundation for its own existence, and recognized the continuing validity of God's dealings with the patriarchs. In a similar way, therefore, the Christian should respect and recognize both the content of Mosaic Yahwism as its own antecedent of continuing validity and also the religious system of Judaism that in its own different way develops from it. This is obviously a major issue deserving a fuller treatment, but the basic point we wish to make should be clear.

This means that although the language of Old Testament has negative implications about the validity of important aspects of ethos and practice for those living in the perspective of New Testament—whether Christianity vis-à-vis Mosaic Yahwism, or Mosaic Yahwism vis-à-vis patriarchal religion—it is not or at least should not be a value judgment of inferior as opposed to superior. The language is essentially an indicator of *difference* between systems that are closely related and yet in certain ways incompatible, with no necessary implication about the relative value of the different systems. Or to put it more accurately, there are indeed value judgments internal to Christianity about the propriety of Christian observance of certain aspects of a Torah-centered ethos and practice, in both biblical and Jewish forms, just as there are similar judgments internal to Mosaic Yahwism with regard to aspects of patriarchal religion. Yet such internal value judgments do not of themselves prejudge value judgments as to the relative merits of each system taken as a whole.

For example, Christians can respect and, as guests, join in the observance of *kashrut,* which Judaism has developed and maintained in continuity with biblical precept (as interpreted rabbinically). But it is impossible for Christianity itself to adopt *kashrut,* precisely because the dietary laws symbolize the unique status of Israel as distinct from other peoples, while Christianity is by definition open to Jew and Gentile without distinction (see esp. the paradigmatic narrative of Acts 10). Alternatively, in terms of initiation, Jews practice circumcision, again in continuity with the precept of Tanakh, while Christians baptize in continuity with the precept of the New Testament. From an internal Christian perspective, circumcision (as religious initiation) is unacceptable, but this unacceptability does not mean that Christians cannot respect the practice of circumcision in a Jewish context.

This point about the function of the language of Old/New Testament as primarily an indicator of difference between religious systems, with value judgments only internal to the adherents of those systems, is perhaps best appreciated by a Christian if we turn away from familiar comparisons between Judaism and Christianity and consider instead patriarchal and Mosaic religion. It is commonly considered that Mosaic religion represents an advance on patriarchal religion—a point we noted in relation to Alt's use of *paidagogos* to express the relationship.[23] And certainly much in the content of Mosaic Yahwism, perhaps most obviously its high moral content, must command respect and admiration. Yet equally we noted that Saggs was able to rate Yahwism as a retrograde development in relation to patriarchal religion.[24] And again, much in the tradition of patriarchal religion, perhaps most obviously its combination of commitment with openness, has great appeal. From a Christian point of view, it is not possible simply to pronounce on the superiority of one system and the inferiority of the other. Rather, both systems have strong points and both have weak points. Moreover we should note that the strengths of each system are to some extent incompatible. The emphasis on commitment, holiness, and morality and the possible responsibility to speak and act on God's behalf are closely tied to the strongly structured, mediated, and exclusive nature of Yahwism that makes it so different from the ritual simplicity and "ecumenical" openness that make patriarchal religion attractive. Despite these differences, even incompatibilities, between the two religious systems, each can be appreciated positively in different ways. Although more could be said, the basic point should be clear.

None of this means that it is never possible to make value judgments between different religious systems, though such judgments can rarely be easy or straightforward, not least because

23. Above, p. 106.

24. Above, p. 106, n. 2.

there is no neutral, value-free ground on which anyone can stand. Moreover, because of the self-involving nature of religious language, any responsible critique of another religious system must involve a commitment to live in a way consonant with that critique. (All too often Christians have argued for the superiority of Christianity and yet at the same time have behaved in ways that denied and undermined the very values they have purported to uphold in their argument.) For present purposes, however, the concern is *not* to try to argue the relative merits of Jewish and Christian faiths but rather to try to remove a source of misunderstanding in dialogue between them. The essence of our argument is that although the language of Old Testament is necessary to Christian self-definition, it need not carry the overtones of a negative judgment of inferiority with regard to the Torah-centered religion of the Old Testament and the Judaism that has grown out of it and for which Torah remains the central concept.

LIMITATIONS IN THE CONCEPT OF TWO OLD TESTAMENTS

Having put forward our basic case on the strength of our proposed analogy, we must now admit that the analogy has certain weaknesses that prevent the parallelism from being as complete and helpful as it might be. They do not invalidate the analogy, but they do necessitate a certain restraint in its use.

First and foremost is the fact that patriarchal religion has no known continuation other than Mosaic Yahwism, but Mosaic Yahwism led to both Judaism and Christianity. From the perspective of Mosaic Yahwism, the patriarchal dispensation represents an internal theological problem, analogous to the Christian approach to the Old Testament in isolation from the continuing existence of Judaism. Whatever the historical complexities that underlie both patriarchal religion and Mosaic Yahwism as they are presented in the text of the Pentateuch, the text gives no hint that Mosaic Yahwism faced alternative continuing religious communities that lived and worshiped God within the ethos and practice of patriarchal religion in contradistinction to Mosaic Yahwism. There is, of course, polemic against Canaanite religion. But on the one hand, the relationship between patriarchal and Canaanite religion appears to be one of certain affinities rather than identity, and on the other hand, anti-Canaanite polemic does not take the form of laying claim to continuity with the patriarchs in opposition to alternative claims to continuity with them. There is therefore no biblical parallel to the phenomenon of Judaism and Christianity as rival claimants to a common tradition.

Second, even if Genesis 12–50 is "the Old Testament of the Old Testament," it is still not quite analogous to Hebrew scripture as the Old Testament for Christians. This is not because it is so much smaller, since quantity of material does not affect the basic theological issue of different dispensations. The point is rather the lack of independent status of Genesis 12–50. We have already noted how the interpretative perspective of Mosaic Yahwism is already embodied in the text of Genesis 12–50, unlike the interpretative perspective of Christianity, which can only be a way of reading the Old Testament text whose content was fixed before Christianity came into being.[25] This difference is furthered by the way in which Genesis 12–50 is placed in the context of Genesis 1–11. For although we have argued that the consistent ethos of Genesis 12–50 is non-Yahwistic, in such a way as can still be seen without difficulty despite its present relatively light (in general) Yahwistic molding, the same is not the case with Genesis 1–11. Here it seems clear that all the stories have been thoroughly imbued with the classic concepts of Yahwistic theology. In work elsewhere I have argued that the story of the Garden of Eden in Genesis 2–3 is a study of the nature of life under Torah.[26] I have also shown how some of the central theological concerns in the story of the flood have an exact parallel in the story of Israel's disobedience and restoration at Sinai in Exodus 32–34.[27] The strong historical likelihood is that Israel developed its theology in the context of its own history and traditions and then applied this theology to retelling the widespread and often-told stories of the origins of humanity and the flood in its light. The point is that the primeval stories of Genesis 1–11, unlike the patriarchal stories of Genesis 12–50, have no inherent outlook of their own which can be discerned independently of

25. Above, p. 140.

26. R. W. L. Moberly, "Did the Serpent Get it Right?" *JTS* 39 (1988): 1–27.

27. R. W. L. Moberly, *At the Mountain of God: Story and Theology in Exodus 32–34,* JSOTS 22 (Sheffield: JSOT, 1983), 91–93.

their Yahwistic presentation; the Yahwistic presentation is all. This means that the patriarchal stories are set in such a thoroughly Yahwistic context, even in Genesis, that they can no longer function as a distinct voice independent of Yahwism in the way Hebrew scripture can function as a distinct voice independent of Christianity. The patriarchal stories still have a voice that is distinctive and needs to be heard, for reasons already given. But from the point of view of reading the material as scripture, the voice is necessarily somewhat muted. This is perhaps the main reason why Judaism has never recognized the phenomenon of an Old Testament within the heart of Torah.

One final point should be made in this context, which to some extent touches on looseness in my proposed analogy but which also raises larger issues about the mode of argument adopted. This is the fact of a certain deliberate fuzziness of historical perspective. For example, both Judaism and Christianity as religious constructs are, arguably, products of late antiquity, particularly the fourth, fifth, and sixth centuries. Prior to that, even though there were distinct communities with recognizably distinct and diverging beliefs and practices, both Jewish and Christian, they did not acquire their classic historic identities until movements and tendencies developing over several centuries came to a fruition and exercised a leavening effect on subsequent self-perception, both Jewish and Christian. Because we are moderately well informed, particularly about developments within Christianity in its first few centuries, we know about the gradual and often confused processes by which the insights of the New Testament were developed into a religion with an identity that was indeed rooted in the New Testament but that focused issues in ways that may not have been so in the New Testament itself. To talk of Christian perceptions of the New in some ways superseding the Old in the rather general way adopted throughout the present argument presupposes a mature Christian perspective which may be difficult to pin down to a precise historical context. In particular it tends—deliberately—to obscure two facts. The first is that the obvious biblical precedent for the language of Old and New Testament has clearly pejorative implications about the continuing value of what is represented by Old as opposed to New (Jer. 31:31-34; Hebrews 8; 2 Corinthians 3). The second is that by the time Christianity had reached its own classic self-understanding and had also defined itself in relation to Judaism, it actually had an overwhelmingly negative view of Judaism as a continuing phenomenon.

This raises important issues about method. The point I wish to make here is the legitimacy and value of an argument that resolutely focuses on the wood rather than the trees. The study of differing Christian perceptions of the Old Testament and, for example, the numerous different ways in which typology has been understood and practiced would be an extensive undertaking of great interest. It would, however, be all too easy to end with a fascinating array of historical material which simply overwhelmed by the sense of its diversity. What I have sought to do throughout the present argument is to focus on the inner logic and internal dynamic of related religious traditions and to recognize that living religious traditions will have certain constant characteristics which will appear in many and varied forms in different historical circumstances—whether it be the lack of holiness with its corresponding lack of religious polemic in patriarchal religion, the exclusivist nature of Yahwism as a natural context for restrictive legislation about the practice of worship, or the logic of typology as an appropriate mode of dealing with the difficulties posed by different dispensations. Of course, any such general analysis must take seriously the varied historical forms in which these characteristic tendencies display themselves and be open to modification in the light of them. The point is simply that modern biblical study has already amassed a vast amount of material about the details of ancient religious history but still has relatively little in the way of consistently principled theological appropriation of this material in relation to the dynamics of the life of the various communities of faith.[28] This task can only be undertaken responsibly if points of historical

28. This may sound somewhat surprising, given the fact that modern Old Testament theologies have consistently been written by scholars concerned to relate their work to the contemporary life of the Christian church. But because of fundamental methodological unclarity, particularly with reference to how their work differs from a history of Israelite religious thought and practice and how Christians may responsibly appropriate Old Testament material in their modern context, these theologies have tended to have rather limited impact outside the context of specialist biblical scholarship.

detail are consistently related to the internal dynamic of the religious tradition as a whole. In particular, we must not suppose that the polemical language characteristic of the period of Christianity's struggle to define itself in distinction from Judaism is necessarily the best guide to appreciating either the inner dynamics of or the continuities and discontinuities between the two faiths.

Our particular concern here is how Christian theology should reformulate itself in the light of the new openness to and appreciation of the rich traditions of Jewishness and Judaism. One indispensable element in any responsible approach must be to seek a fresh understanding of the internal logic and inner dynamics of Christian faith. Only in the light of this can one see whether the negative attitudes toward Jewishness and Judaism that have generally characterized Christianity are, in fact, necessary to the faith or whether they are really perversions and distortions of it. The contribution of the biblical theologian is to grasp what is at the heart of the dynamics of the biblical faith upon which Christianity is based and to use it toward reshaping contemporary faith accordingly. I have tried to show in this study that the concept of Old Testament is necessary to Christian faith and indeed has far deeper biblical roots than has hitherto been appreciated. But the very fact of this deeper biblical rootage has enabled a fresh perspective on what the concept need and need not imply and has made it possible to argue that a pejorative assessment of a religious system centered on Torah is not a necessary part of the concept of Old Testament.

RELIGIOUS LANGUAGE AND COMMUNITIES OF FAITH

Finally, it will be appropriate to try to draw together certain implications of our argument. Basic to our argument in this chapter has been a consideration of the privileged nature of the biblical text (an issue usually dealt with under such headings as *inspiration* and *authority*). Only because it is thus privileged does it become meaningful to relate what the text says to life today. The basic reason for this privilege is not just the inherent quality of the content of the Bible, vital though it is, but also the historic and contemporary existence of communities of faith whose identity, understanding, and life-style is by definition related to the content of the biblical text. In terms of conventional discussion, the church is a necessary presupposition for the inspiration and authority of scripture to be meaningful concepts.

It follows from this that the theological categories by which the church interprets scripture have a status not always appreciated. Those whose sole interest in the Bible is historical or literary are free to abandon theological categories and their related assumptions about the contemporary significance of the text. But Christians who wish to retain the privileged status of the text cannot be permitted to abandon some of the categories that are integral to that privileged status. It is no good to saw off the branch on which you sit, even for the best of intentions.[29] Of course, the issues posed by the granting of privileged status to the Bible in a modern pluralist society are complex, but some resolution is not impossible.

In the present context, the issue has been the relationship between Christians and Jews, distinct yet related communities of faith who have each privileged the Bible in different ways. The growing concern of Christians has been to purge their faith of those elements that have been hostile and destructive toward Jews. One recurrent factor in this has been proposals to abandon the language and concept of Old Testament on the grounds that it inherently denigrates Jews and Judaism. Yet I have argued that this is not an appropriate step, precisely for the reason that such language expresses something that is necessary to the logic of a Christian, as distinct from a Jewish, position. And I have tried to

29. It should be clear that I am in fundamental disagreement with the widespread view, conventionally traced back to Gabler, that Old Testament theology is primarily a historical and descriptive enterprise (i.e., a history of Israelite religious thought), whose appropriation within Christian faith is not for the biblical scholar but for the systematic theologian. This entirely fails to do justice to the kind of hermeneutical concerns that have been basic to our thesis and that actually operate in practice. For recent discussions which try to break new ground but which simply fall back into a "Gablerian" dichotomy, see J. Hogenhaven, *Problems and Prospects of Old Testament Theology* (Sheffield: JSOT, 1988); W. E. Lemke, "Is Old Testament Theology an Essentially Christian Theological Discipline?" *HBT* 11 (1989): 59–71. More genuinely radical, and correspondingly more promising, is A. K. M. Adam, "Biblical Theology and the Problem of Modernity: *Von Wredestrasse zu Sackgasse,*" *HBT* 12 (1990): 1–18.

show that when the logic of the language is analyzed, it need not, in fact, carry the kind of pejorative connotations that are commonly attributed to it.

In all this, I have been trying to explore something of the logic of what it means for Christians to live in the light of scripture. It is important, therefore, to relate the discussion of this chapter to that of the previous chapter where the same basic issue was at stake. In the discussion there about the logic of different dispensations we noted three major issues: the nature of God as one, yet revealed in different ways; predominant discontinuity of formal religious ethos and practice; predominant continuity in the values and goals of personal (communal as well as individual) spirituality.[30] We noted that all these three issues, and indeed the whole problem of continuity and discontinuity, arise out of the decision to privilege certain texts and treat them as authoritative.[31]

The crucial point to appreciate as we round off our discussion is the interrelatedness of all these issues. Questions about the nature of God are inseparable from questions about human communities of faith that live in relation to God. Questions about these human communities of faith are inseparable from questions about their history and identity as they are expressed supremely in those texts that they privilege as scripture. Questions as to why Jews and Christians privilege their scriptures are inseparable from questions of how they have encountered God and lived life under God down the ages. Questions as to why Jews and Christians are distinct cannot be understood apart from questions about the content of their scriptures, which they largely hold in common and yet in which Christians have a crucial extra part relating to Jesus. Questions about how Jews and Christians should regard each other today cannot be separated from questions about the nature and logic of scripture and their corresponding communal commitments.

Of course, to put matters thus is in one sense a gross oversimplification, since it does no justice to the history and traditions of

30. Above, pp. 126ff.
31. Above, p. 130.

Jews and Christians as they have developed—each with enormous variety and complexity—in postbiblical times. And since it is essential to our argument that one takes seriously the continuing life of communities of faith as the context for engagement with the Bible as scripture, these later developments cannot be dismissed as theologically irrelevant. Nonetheless, our concern is still with the fundamental dynamics of each religious tradition. Once the dynamics of the scripture of each is appreciated, it is not difficult to see why each tradition developed in the way it did—Jews always relating in one way or another to the implications of Torah and Christians always relating in one way or another to the implications of Christ.

The essential point we wish to make is that metaphysical and epistemological questions about the nature of God, raised by the contention that there is one God who is revealed in different and not wholly compatible ways, are inseparable from questions about the values, ethics, and life-style of particular human communities and that the crucial linkage between these two sets of questions is provided by the biblical texts privileged as scripture. If this is not recognized, the whole argument is likely to be skewed. Or to put the basic point differently, both Jewish and Christian theological language about the nature of God and humanity is only meaningful if the language is recognized to be self-involving and to entail a commitment to live in a particular way which is at heart defined by the content of scripture.[32]

To argue for the inseparability of theology and life-style in this way is not, of course, to concede to the reductionist suspicion that claims about God are in reality *merely* claims about humanity, that theology is nothing but an elaborately coded ideological way of expressing preferences for particular kinds of human life-style. It is simply to recognize that reality has many dimensions and that these dimensions are interrelated. It is simply to reaffirm an understanding about the nature of theology that used to be taken for granted but which has all too easily been lost sight of since the epistemological revolution that began with Descartes.

32. An important and stimulating discussion of many of the issues at stake here is N. Lash, *Easter in Ordinary: Reflections on Human Experience and the Knowledge of God* (Virginia: Virginia Univ. Press; London: SCM, 1988).

In traditional Christian terminology, you cannot love God unless you also love your neighbor.

If we consider the relationship between Jews and Christians in the light of this, certain points become clear. First, in a real sense both Jewish and Christian faiths are at heart scriptural. However differently Jew and Christian may use scripture in practice (and differ among themselves) and however much their faith may for most practical purposes be mediated in nonscriptural ways, the basic content of the faith is biblically defined in terms of Torah and Christ. Without this basis the faith becomes ultimately vacuous.[33]

Second, for both Jew and Christian, identity is defined by membership in a community, a community whose identity is itself defined by, among other things, appeal to the content of scripture. Again, Jew and Christian may understand their communal membership in strikingly different ways (and differ among themselves on the issue). But insofar as they understand God and humanity as Jews and Christians, they do so in the categories provided by their communities. These communities in practice exhibit almost endless diversity and interrelate with other human communities, commitments, and understandings in almost every possible way. Nonetheless, insofar as Jewish and Christian faiths retain an integrity of their own (i.e., faith is not reduced to mere categories, the social or economic, for example), membership in such communities will encourage some and discourage other aspects of life in ways that otherwise would not be the case.

Third, for both Jew and Christian, language about God is inseparable from commitment to particular life-styles within their communities. Again, the dynamics of this may vary greatly (and the historic formal appropriation of Christianity by Western culture has made the relationship between belief and practice highly problematic), but a fundamental similarity is clear. If, therefore, Jews and Christians are to talk to each other meaning-

33. An interesting recent discussion of biblical authority, which is doubtful about the propriety of seeing Christians as a "People of the Book," is J. Barton, *People of the Book? The Authority of the Bible in Christianity* (London: SPCK, 1988). This is not the place to engage directly with Barton's argument, but it will be clear that our argument would suggest a somewhat different emphasis.

fully about God and life, they will do this best not by diluting their traditions in a search for a lowest common denominator but rather by entering more fully into their traditions. For it has been central to my thesis that the biblical material shows deep similarities in the dynamics of each tradition and makes possible the sharing of considerable common ground. Of course, the similar dynamics are bound up with practical expressions of such differing nature that the different traditions can never coalesce, and those engaging in dialogue cannot (unless they choose to convert and embrace another system in its entirety) do more than become temporary guests in religious systems that are not their own. The challenge for Jews and Christians is so to appropriate their own traditions that they can recognize and enter into the dynamics of life under God in all the richness and the fullness that their traditions make possible. As they do so, they may increasingly recognize what is held in common with one another. This can open up the possibility that they may be able to transform the pain of distance and separation into a joyful acceptance of the diversity of valid ways of living life under the one God.

CHAPTER 6

Paradigms for Pentateuchal Criticism

The thesis of this book has been advanced. In the course of it I have tried to keep to the point and to resist going into interesting related issues except where they have seemed to me to bear directly upon the thesis. At this stage, however, it might be helpful at least to touch on a number of issues raised explicitly or implicitly in the preceding argument. The aim will be both to clarify the bearing of our thesis upon some well-known debates and also to suggest directions for further study.

THE DOCUMENTARY HYPOTHESIS

As has already been observed, the whole of pentateuchal criticism is in something of a turmoil at present. There is widespread dissatisfaction with the conventional paradigm built upon the work of Wellhausen and Gunkel.[1] R. Rendtorff, for example, is able to say that "the question of the future of pentateuchal criticism, at least for German Protestant theology, is at the same time the question of whether scholars can free themselves from the burden of the documentary hypothesis."[2] Certainly, when re-

1. See the works cited above, chap. 1 nn. 34, 35; chap. 2 nn. 11, 12; also A. de Pury, ed., *Le Pentateuque en Question* (Geneva: Labor et Fides, 1989). In my judgment the most telling critique is that of Whybray. His main weakness is that he has little to offer by way of positive alternative and attempts no exegesis and interpretation of his own; it should also be noted that he makes no attempt to deal with pentateuchal law, and yet the interrelationship between narrative and law was a major element in Wellhausen's synthesis.

2. R. Rendtorff, "The Future of Pentateuchal Criticism," *Henoch* 6 (1984): 3. The article is a useful summary statement of Rendtorff's approach.

sponsible scholars can disagree about the very existence of pentateuchal sources and can differ by half a millennium over their possible dates, one may reasonably wonder whether the best questions are being asked in the best way. It must be admitted, however, that the dissatisfaction is by no means universal,[3] and no alternative paradigm of comparable comprehensiveness and explanatory power has yet been advanced that has been able to command a new scholarly consensus. The task for dissatisfied scholars, therefore, is to work toward a new paradigm on the basis of numerous detailed studies of specific issues. This present thesis is one such study. Although it would be premature to build a whole new paradigm on the basis of this thesis, it may be possible to lay a few foundations.

First, our argument raises the issue of the propriety of any continued use of the term *the Yahwist.* The problem is that the basic distinguishing characteristic of the Yahwist, as traditionally understood, was that the Yahwist maintained that the name YHWH was known to the patriarchs, in opposition to E and P who introduced the name only in the time of Moses. However many other features have been considered also to distinguish the Yahwist, the issue of the divine name has been basic and has given the writer this name. If our thesis is correct, this distinguishing characteristic is unwarranted, for we have argued that all the pentateuchal writers shared a common and undisputed tradition that the name YHWH was first revealed to Moses, but they all felt free nonetheless to use the name YHWH in the patriarchal context for the reasons given.

To say this does not in itself prejudge the question of whether there may not have been some process in the composition of the Pentateuch (writer, editor, school, tradition, or whatever) that corresponds to much of what has generally been associated with

3. For defenses of the conventional paradigm, see, e.g., the works cited in chap. 1 n. 36, n. 37, and W. H. Schmidt's *Introduction to the Old Testament* (London: SCM, 1984; German, 1979, 1982) as well as his *Exodus* commentary. Also, with regard to the flood narrative, one of the classic examples of the strengths of a documentary analysis, see J. A. Emerton, "An Examination of Some Attempts to Defend the Unity of the Flood Narrative in Genesis, Part I" *VT* 37 (1987): 401–20; idem, "An Examination of Some Attempts to Defend the Unity of the Flood Narrative in Genesis, Part II," *VT* 38 (1988): 1–21.

the Yahwist and that may be distinct from the Elohistic and Priestly processes within the Pentateuch. We have restricted our study to an exegesis of Exodus 3 and 6, an examination of the divine name in Genesis, an analysis of the traditions about the nature of patriarchal religion, and an exploration of certain aspects of the appropriation of the patriarchal stories within Mosaic Yahwism. Although we have found that for understanding the text in all these areas a documentary analysis is, in effect, either an obstacle or an irrelevance, this still leaves significant dimensions of the text unexamined, such as the well-known consistencies of vocabulary, style, and emphasis attaching particularly to P but also to some extent to J and E. The problem, however, is not that we simply need to find a new name for a process we recognize and understand. Rather, the crucial issue is precisely the nature of the processes at work in the composition of the Pentateuch and the conceptual model(s) we should use to envisage and describe them.

With regard to the patriarchal narratives, for example, our study has suggested two factors of primary importance, neither of which receives sufficient attention in conventional documentary analysis. The first is the distinction between the world of the patriarchs and the world of Mosaic Yahwism, which cuts across the usual major distinction between the earlier JE and the later P traditions. Future studies will need to take seriously the world of the patriarchs and possible significant distinctions within it (people, place, time) if analyses of differences within the text are to be well founded. The second factor is the nature and extent of Yahwistic appropriation and editing of the patriarchal stories, which we have suggested varies not only between the Abraham, Jacob, and Joseph cycles but also to some extent within them.

For example, one of the many distinctive features of the Joseph cycle in Genesis 37–50 is its almost complete nonuse of the name YHWH (a fact that has not usually prevented much of the cycle being ascribed to the Yahwist).[4] The occasional uses can

4. In referring conventionally to the Joseph cycle in Genesis 37–50 I do not intend to prejudge questions about the possible inclusion of elements from the Jacob cycle. See C. Westermann, *Genesis 37-50* (London: SPCK, 1987; German, 1982), 22–24.

be categorized as follows. First, the divine name appears in Gen. 49:18 in what is an obvious gloss, a psalmlike interpretative comment on Jacob's prophecy. Second, it appears in two moralizing comments in the story of Judah and Tamar (Gen. 38:7, 10), a story whose precise relationship to the surrounding Joseph story is unclear. Third, it appears eight times in comments by the narrator at the beginning and end of the story of Joseph and Potiphar's wife (Gen. 39:2, 3, 5, 21, 23). On the one hand, may the primary reason for the general nonuse of the name be that the storytellers wish to maintain the distinctive context of the Joseph story, both the temporal context (pre-Moses and the burning bush) and the geographical context (almost entirely Egypt, where God would most naturally be referred to by a general generic term, *'elohim*)? On the other hand, may the use of the name in Genesis 39 signify a storyteller specifically interpreting the story at a key moment (beginning of Joseph's time in Egypt and of his suffering despite maintaining faithful integrity) so as to appropriate it for Yahwistic readers so that they can see that YHWH may be present with the believer even in times of unmerited adversity? It is not that the language and content of the story of Genesis 39 is distinctive (as against, e.g., chaps. 40 and 41), for in the course of it (39:9) Joseph is concerned not to sin against God (*'elohim* rather than YHWH). Thus a conventional ascription of the story to J obscures the crucial point of a Yahwistic appropriation of a story told in terms that are not specifically Yahwistic (although still characteristically Hebraic). One can discern something of the differences and possible compositional processes within the narrative. But it is highly doubtful whether J, E, and P offer the most appropriate conceptual model for analyzing and explaining them.

The problem of an appropriate conceptual model is one that has already been raised by other scholars, especially R. Rendtorff. As conventionally conceived, J, E, and P were independent accounts of Israel's traditions that were redactionally merged. The basic model that was used in the formulation of the documentary hypothesis was that of historical source documents, each telling Israel's foundational story in its own way, which were combined because, despite their differences, there was a reverential desire to preserve each. This is a perfectly plausible and intelligible model. But how far is it still coherent and useful? Although the model was straightforward for Wellhausen, for each writer simply told Israel's story as a retrojection of contemporary conditions, once Gunkel showed the likelihood of greater depth and antiquity in the material, the situation became more complicated. How far is it genuinely possible to distinguish between tradition (the basic content of the story as originally told), literary source (the retelling of the story in written form), redaction (the further reworking of the stories and their linkage to a wider literary context), and supplementation (the addition of yet further material)? Although Noth, building on the work of von Rad, offered a comprehensive account of these questions,[5] we have already noted the strong objections against supposing that we are in a position to analyze the traditions with the kind of confidence that Noth showed.[6] It is extremely difficult to be at all precise about the various stages of tradition, composition, redaction, and supplementation. The result is that the use of J, E, and P often functions somewhat vaguely to designate differing kinds of material rather than to indicate clearly conceived stages in a compositional process.

Another difficulty relates to the supposition of conventional documentary analysis that J, E, and P are continuous narrative traditions running through Genesis, Exodus, and Numbers. There has been a tendency to group J and E together as distinct from P and to formulate the main difference within the narrative traditions as the difference between the early traditions of JE and the later traditions of P. Even if the distinction between earlier and later traditions remains historically justified, this way of posing the issue has had the unfortunate effect of cutting across and obscuring what we have argued to be the crucial distinction for the pentateuchal writers, that is, the distinction between the time of the patriarchs and the time of Israel. In this context the arguments of Rendtorff, Blum, and Thompson that one should understand the growth and composition of the Pentateuch in

5. In his *History of Pentateuchal Traditions* (Chico, California: Scholars, 1981).
6. Above, p. 75.

terms of distinct and independent blocks of tradition rather than continuous parallel literary sources are in many ways a useful corrective.[7] It is important not only to be able to see patriarchal tradition as distinct from Yahwistic tradition but also to appreciate the distinctiveness of each of the three major patriarchal cycles. Of course, threads run through the different blocks and link them together. But the questions that have been brought to the fore for understanding the growth and nature of the Pentateuch are, on the one hand, the respective nature of the blocks and the links, and on the other hand, their respective importance.

In short, there are at least three major difficulties with the continued use of the language of J, E, and P. First is the general point that the language of J, E, and P presupposes that we are in a position to distinguish clear antecedent stages in the composition of the Pentateuch, when it is doubtful that this is genuinely the case. Second is our specific point that the terminology of "the Yahwist" is no longer warranted, which means that its continued use will simply make for confusion. Third is the general point that the language of J, E, and P begs the question of the best conceptual model for envisaging the development of the Pentateuch. In the light of these points, it must surely be best to look for fresh language and conceptual models. I recognize that it will not be easy to drop such convenient and well-established terminology as that of J, E, and P. But such a move should best enable genuinely fresh engagement with the pentateuchal text.

In my judgment, it would be most helpful to adopt categories that are descriptive of the content of the text: patriarchal traditions (subdivided into Abraham, Jacob, and Joseph cycles, with further subdivisions as appropriate, such as Isaac stories and Edomite traditions); similarly Mosaic traditions (subdivided into Exodus, wilderness, Sinai traditions, again with further subdivisions as appropriate, such as Passover traditions, Balaam

7. See Rendtorff, *The Problem of the Process of Transmission in the Pentateuch,* JSOTS 89 (Sheffield: JSOT, 1990); E. Blum, *Die Komposition der Vätergeschichte,* WMANT 57 (Neukirchen-Vluyn: Neukirchener Verlag, 1984); E. Blum, *Studien zur Komposition des Pentateuch,* BZAW 189 (Berlin: de Gruyter, 1990); T. L. Thompson, *The Origin Tradition of Ancient Israel,* JSOTS 55 (Sheffield: JSOT, 1987).

cycle, etc.). Then within these various traditions one can analyze what is peculiar to them, what they have in common with others, factors suggestive of internal history, factors suggesting that one story has been molded in the light of another, and so on. The point of this is not to abandon a critical-historical perspective, for it will always be appropriate in any analysis to draw attention to factors such as common language and concepts in different stories and to formulate corresponding explanatory hypotheses. But categories of analysis that relate in the first instance to the Pentateuch as it stands, rather than to hypothetical stages of its possible prehistory, will provide a firmer foundation for studies of every kind, historical as well as theological. In any case, until such time as we understand better the processes embodied in pentateuchal narrative and have demonstrated that understanding in convincing exegesis and interpretation, a certain reticence in the formulation of overarching hypotheses about the composition of pentateuchal narrative might not be inappropriate.

METHODS OF READING PENTATEUCHAL NARRATIVE

Doubts about the heuristic value of conventional documentary analysis lead conveniently into a consideration of the wider debate about appropriate ways of reading biblical narrative.

An extremely simplified account of the current debate might run along the following lines. On the one hand is the familiar historically oriented study of the text in terms of sources, tradition-history, redaction, etc., which works on the premise that a text can only be properly understood when it is related to the historical context in which it originated. On the other hand is a growing body of literary studies that tend, in one way or another, to be concerned not only with the text as significant in itself, often irrespective of its history, but also with the modern reader and the modern reader's interests and concerns as an essential constituent in the determination of what a text means. The relationship between these historical and literary approaches is generally unclear. And how a theological approach to the text might fit in with them is even less clear.

Obviously, much of the debate revolves around the basic point with which we started that *how* we read the text depends on *why* we read the text. Scholars quite legitimately have differing concerns as they come to the biblical text, and it is futile to argue that one is right and the other is wrong. Scholars with one set of concerns can recognize and respect good readings of the text by scholars with different concerns without feeling obliged to adopt the agenda of those other scholars. Nonetheless this does not mean that all approaches have equal ability to penetrate to the heart of biblical narrative, nor does it excuse all interpreters (whatever their concerns) the task of suiting their questions and methods to the nature of the text. I propose to try, at least in outline, to relate the reading of the text in this present work to wider methodological debate and thereby to reflect on my own methodological assumptions and their bearing on how we have read the text.

Given the basic premise that the meaning of the text cannot be determined without reference to the concerns of the modern reader, my own stance has been explicitly that of a Christian theologian. This has guided our reading in several ways.

First, it has determined the essence of what I understand to be a theological approach to the biblical text. All too often theology is seen as secondary to historical or literary readings of the text; scholars may study the text according to the agenda of the ancient historian or the literary critic and then make some comment about the possible theological significance of their findings. This may not be without value, but it can easily lead to methodological confusion. A truly theological approach should be theological from the outset. The question is who sets the agenda. That is to say, the theologian allows the fact that the Bible is privileged as scripture by the Christian church to set the agenda for how it is studied. This means, in general terms, that the concern is so to read the text that it will in some way illuminate the contemporary community of faith. In particular, we have suggested that the primary contribution of Old Testament theology (and I would maintain the same for New Testament theology also) is in the area of spirituality, whereby contemporary patterns of living—ethics, values, assumptions about the nature and purpose of life—are informed by the biblical text. The explicit adoption of this basic stance is, in my judgment, the distinguishing characteristic of doing biblical theology.

Admittedly, to allow the needs of the community of faith to set the agenda does not of itself give much clue to the best ways of reading the text, for different communities of faith will esteem different kinds of reading as most helpful to the contemporary situation, and there will always be a certain pluralism of approach. But I take it as fundamental for a Christian (Protestant) scholar in the modern Western world that, if scripture is to function as a norm for the life of faith and if the reading of the text is not to be sectarian or privatized, then, whatever else one may do with the text, its historical integrity must be respected. Precisely what the "historical integrity" of the text means is itself a matter of debate, so I will simply indicate certain factors I take to be basic.

First, I have been concerned to be attuned to the kinds of meaning appropriate to ancient Hebrew language and thought, that is, to be historical in a general cultural sense without being unduly concerned about all the questions proper to the agenda of the ancient historian. Second, I have been concerned to take seriously the literary context of the Pentateuch within which the Genesis and Exodus narratives stand. This means recognizing that stories may no longer be in the same form or have the same meaning that they once may have had (in their original historical context), but they may have been subject to reinterpretation and given a particular meaning in their present literary presentation. Third, I have assumed that, since the pentateuchal text was apparently composed and preserved so as to function within ancient Israelite and Jewish communities of faith as an authoritative portrayal of Mosaic Yahwism, specifically theological concerns (among others) were important within the ancient context. Indeed, given the special significance of the Pentateuch, it seems to me particularly important to pay close attention to those theological perspectives that have been brought to the forefront by those who arbitrated on the processes of tradition and interpretation underlying the text of Genesis and Exodus.

Perhaps, however, the crucial methodological decision was to try as far as possible to enter into the world of the pentateuchal story in its own right and on its own terms. I envisage this process as follows.

Generally speaking, it has almost always been recognized in

modern biblical study that the date of writing of the pentateuchal narratives is probably at a considerable remove (whose precise extent is admittedly debatable) from the context of the stories themselves. This means that the stories of both Genesis and Exodus have been told from within the context of a possibly mature and theologically sophisticated Yahwism (though the precise nature of Yahwism at most periods is again debatable). Yet the interpretative potential of this recognition for reading the stories as stories has all too often been left unrealized—though there have been notable exceptions, as for example in von Rad's *Genesis* and Childs's *Exodus*. For the insight has generally been made to serve historically oriented interests of one kind or another rather than the illumination of the story in its own right.

Sometimes the interest has been to recover the earliest form of the story; Gunkel's creative insights in his Genesis commentary were consistently oriented in this direction, on the assumption that the stories in their most ancient form were somehow superior to their later retellings. His concern with Genesis 22 was to read it as the cult story of a Canaanite sanctuary at Jeruel, not as a story about Abraham as a model for Israel's obedience to Torah at Jerusalem.[8]

Sometimes the depth dimension of the text has been assumed to represent an unintended historical fragment. An example is the common recognition that the reference to a hitherto unmentioned place as "the mountain of God" in Exod. 3:1 presupposes that the mountain already has a significance in relation to God. As noted, this has regularly been interpreted as evidence for the pre-Mosaic significance of Sinai, rather than being read as a reflex of the rich Hebrew tradition of Sinai and Zion, from which perspective, in some form, the story is surely told.[9]

Sometimes, indeed very often, the emphasis of the text has been interpreted in terms of the supposed historical context and concerns of its writer. Attempts to do this in a theologically constructive way were particularly evident in once-fashionable studies of the Kerygma of the Yahwist, Elohist, and Priestly

8. H. Gunkel, *Genesis*, 5th ed. (Göttingen: Vandenhoeck & Ruprecht, 1922), 236–42.

9. Above, p. 8ff.

writers.[10] For example, H. Wolff collected the various references to the "fear of God" that he saw as the distinctive theme of the E fragments in the Pentateuch and related this to a composition in the Northern Kingdom sometime in the century between Elijah and Hosea when Israel was tempted by Canaanite religion to abandon its commitment to YHWH. His concern was explicitly to recover "an originally independent documentary source, with its own technique of composition and an independent message" and to "consider toward what situation in Israel this new proclamation of the canonical tradition might have been directed."[11]

None of these concerns are in principle illegitimate. But they all mean that important aspects of the text are left unexamined. Perhaps the most important aspect that is left unexamined is how the perceived emphases of the text relate to the internal logic and dynamic of the story that is being told. We have already noted this with regard to the use of Elohim in the patriarchal stories.[12] Three further examples may illustrate the point. First, in our discussion of patriarchal religion, we noted that a consistent corollary of the understanding that the land is not given to the patriarchs except as a place to sojourn is the lack of military activity to take possession of the land.[13] This lack of military activity is a well-known point, and it is commonly assumed that this particular emphasis is in some way a reflection of the historical context within which the text was composed and is to be understood primarily in relation to that context. So, for example, Y. Kaufmann observed that "the patriarchs live in almost idyllic peace" and deduced from this that "the post-Hyksos—indeed, the post-el-Amarna—age seems to be indicated. The stories presuppose an extended period of peace in Palestine, such as the reign of Seti I and Ramses II, most of whose wars were waged in

10. See H. W. Wolff, "The Kerygma of the Yahwist," *Interpretation* 20 (1966): 131–58; idem, "The Elohistic Fragments in the Pentateuch," *Interpretation* 26 (1972): 158–73; W. Brueggemann, "The Kerygma of the Priestly Writers," *ZAW* 84 (1972): 397–413. Cf. Rendtorff's comment that "the theological interest for German Old Testament scholars is almost totally based on the theology of the different sources" ("Future," 2).

11. Wolff, "Elohistic Fragments," 161.

12. Above, pp. 44f., 88.

13. Above, p. 97.

Syria."[14] Alternatively, M. Rose argued that the patriarchal traditions have been deliberately demilitarized and that this is evidence that the Yahwist cannot be Solomonic but must come from a later period when particular weight was put on the family, probably in the seventh or sixth century.[15] Lacking in these proposals is any serious engagement with the way the lack of military activity is part of a consistent ethos in the patriarchal portrayal as a whole and so may need to be understood initially in terms of the internal logic of the tradition. At the very least, the emphases of the text cannot be properly related to a possible historical context until they have first been understood in their own right.

Second, J. Ha in a recent study sees Genesis 15 as a theological compendium of the entire pentateuchal history, written in the time of the Exile.[16] He argues that a major purpose of the exilic author was the desire to strengthen the faith of the exiles. One central means of doing this was the depiction of a unilateral oath by YHWH which was meant to reinterpret and replace the bilateral Sinai covenant after Israel's failure to maintain the latter.[17] I choose this as an example because it is similar to arguments frequently advanced about P's reinterpretation of covenant in the exilic period.[18]

Even if, for the sake of argument, one allows not only that Ha is right about the date of Genesis 15 but also that he is right about the concerns of its author, his thesis depends entirely on reading

14. Y. Kaufman, *Religion of Israel* (New York: Schocken, 1960, 1972), 219.

15. M. Rose, "'Entmilitarizierung des Krieges?' (Erwagungen zu den Patriarchen-Erzählungen der Genesis)," *BZ* 20 (1976): 197–211.

16. J. Ha, *Genesis 15,* BZAW 181 (Berlin and New York: de Gruyter, 1989).

17. Ibid., 164–68; cf. 196, 211.

18. See, e.g., W. Zimmerli, "Sinaibund und Abrahambund," *TZ* 16 (1960): 268–80 (reprinted in his *Gottes Offenbarung,* 2d ed. [Munich: Kaiser, 1969], 205–16). Zimmerli summarizes his position in his *Old Testament Theology in Outline,* where he says, "P's elimination of any explicit covenant made in the Mosaic period has as its consequence the fact that the age of Israel becomes exclusively the age in which the promise to Abraham is fulfilled. This notion is probably based on a conscious theological reflection that is understandable from the perspective of the postexilic period. In the preexilic period, Israel foundered on the law that was associated with the 'covenant' of the Mosaic period. P no longer looks upon the age of Israel's national history, which begins with Moses, as an age characterized by the covenant defined in the law. This age, too, is dominated by the promise given to Abraham" (p. 57). The critique we formulate with reference to Ha applies equally to Zimmerli.

the chapter against its supposed historical background in complete disregard of its actual place and function within Israel's story. If the story is read in its pentateuchal context, it must be understood as part of the story of the patriarchs. Since, as we have seen, it is fundamental to Israel's story that the period of the patriarchs is in some ways superseded by the advent of Mosaic Yahwism, it is meaningless in terms of the story to argue that the patriarchal covenant in some ways superseded the Mosaic covenant. Of course, the story of Genesis 15 could have been told from within the Yahwistic context in the time of the Exile in such a way as to show that what is narrated there is of continuing validity and significance for the story of Yahwistic Israel.[19] But that is essentially to make the point pentateuchal tradition consistently makes: despite discontinuity there is abiding significance in God's dealings with the patriarchs and continuity between them and God's dealings with Israel. Ha's way of reading the text turns the logic and dynamic of the pentateuchal story upside down.

A third example is Wolff's discussion of the "fear of God" in E, as already mentioned. One obvious criticism, already made by Westermann, is that Wolff does not give sufficient weight to the expression having different meanings in different contexts.[20] This can be developed further. Of the various uses of "fear of God" in E (Gen. 20:11; 22:12; 42:18; Exod. 1:17, 21; 18:21; 20:20), two are set in particularly weighty and memorable contexts (i.e., the Akedah [Gen. 22:12] and the Ten Words/Commandments [Exod. 20:20]). The latter is especially significant, since Exodus 20 is the account of YHWH giving Israel those precepts that are to be at the heart of the covenant between YHWH and Israel, and Exod. 20:20 explains the purpose of God speaking the Ten Words—the commandments from heaven must find their response in Israel's obedience on earth. Conceptually there is an integral relationship between YHWH com-

19. This is part of my argument about the significance of Gen. 15:6 in my "Abraham's Righteousness," though I see it as a retelling and reappropriation of an older story.

20. C. Westermann, *Genesis 12–36* (Minneapolis: Augsburg; London: SPCK, 1985, 1986; German 1981), 362.

manding and Israel obeying. It is not just that Exodus 20 gives a fundamental account of the fear of God in terms of obedience to Torah but that this is where language about fear as obedience to Torah is intrinsically at home.

How then should the usage in Genesis 22 be understood in relation to this? Wolff simply takes the text in a straightforward way: "When God began to speak to Israel his will was the same as it was when he declared it to Abraham. . . . God's normative word from Mount Sinai to all Israel is directed toward the same goal that he had set for the Patriarchs: fear of God."[21] On one level such a reading is fine. But it leaves untouched the logic of pentateuchal tradition that the quality of obedience indicated by "fear of God" is particularly at home in a Sinai/Torah context and that therefore the use of the language with regard to Abraham is best seen, as already indicated, as a typological molding of the Abraham story in terms of the normative concept of Torah.[22] This in turn means that one should distinguish between "fear of God" in a general sense as a moral and upright way of living, open in principle to anyone (Gen. 20:11; 42:18; Exod. 1:17, 21; 18:21)—which in Abraham's case was not in doubt prior to Genesis 22—and "fear of God" in a specifically Yahwistic sense as Israel's obedience to Torah through which YHWH "tests" *(nissah)* Israel (Gen. 22:1; Exod. 20:20; cf. Exod. 16:4; Deut. 8:2, 13:3 [Heb. 4], Jdg. 2:22, 3:4). Now while such language and concepts would no doubt have been appropriate in ninth- and eighth-century Israel and conceivably could have originated there, the point is the importance of first of all understanding the language in terms of the logic of Israel's story in which it stands.

The hermeneutical model for the theologian need not just be the reconstruction of an ancient context toward which some particular emphasis in the text may originally have been addressed and then the application to some similar modern context by analogy (a process that tends to be circular, since the ancient context is usually proposed on the basis of the modern historian's general sense of the kind of situation toward which such an

21. Wolff, "Elohistic Fragments," 167.
22. Above, p. 142ff.

emphasis would be appropriately directed). It may be equally important (and, especially with pentateuchal narratives, much more important) to grasp a story or group of stories as a total imaginative whole and to allow the resultant picture to inform the reader in a way that may be less immediately directive but that may have intuitive and imaginative potential that is more formative in the long run.

The relationship between Gen. 22:12 and Exod. 20:20 leads on to another issue, one made much of especially by scholars oriented toward literary criticism. This is the possible need for readers to reformulate their initial assumptions, including those assumptions arising out of an initial reading of the text, in the light of further reading of a wider narrative context.[23] For we have found that a careful reading of the text of Genesis and Exodus in its own right has forced us to reread Genesis and to address questions about its composition and tradition-history. Precisely because the portrayal of the revelation of the divine name in Exodus 3 stands in obvious tension with the frequent usage of the name in Genesis, one is forced to study the nature of this tension and possibly reformulate one's original understanding of the text.

The most natural way of approaching the text is along the lines of the traditional and conservative position, assuming that the name YHWH was indeed known to the patriarchs but that it was given a new meaning in the context of Moses and the Exodus. The plain sense of the Genesis text is that YHWH is the God of the patriarchs. If in the light of Exodus 3 and 6 this is found to be inadequate—as we have argued it must be—one must rethink the nature of the text. The conventional modern approach, which construes the tension as a historical problem of divergent traditions, we have also argued to be inadequate. The interpretation we have offered instead has arisen out of the effort to rethink familiar categories and to become attuned to the logic of the ancient text. In essence, the aim has been to recapture something of the logic of ancient storytelling where a given content will

23. One of the most stimulating works in this area is M. Sternberg, *The Poetics of Biblical Narrative* (Bloomington: Indiana Univ. Press, 1985).

naturally be assimilated in varying ways to the perspectives of the storyteller and yet may still remain recognizable on its own terms. An important part of this has been recognition of the particular influence exercised over the retelling by the theological perspectives of Mosaic Yahwism. The result is that reading Genesis and Exodus is not a straightforward matter because, depending on perspective, YHWH both is and is not the God of the patriarchs. One must understand Israel's way of interpreting the novelty of God's self-revelation to Moses as YHWH and appreciate the theological perspective that holds in tension the particularity of YHWH's revelation to Moses and Israel with the universality of YHWH's activity as the one God. Even though anyone who wishes to make theological use of the patriarchal stories must affirm that, as the plain sense of the text still says, YHWH is the God of the patriarchs, this will no longer be understood in the same way as in an original reading of the text. Initial understanding must be reformulated and become more sophisticated through rereading.

One could express this general process in a historical way and say that, unless the historical depth and multilayered nature of the text is appreciated, it will not be accurately understood. One could express it in a literary way and talk of the dynamic interaction between text and reader with consequent reformulation of the reader's understanding. Or one could express it in a theological way, in terms of the traditional Christian and Jewish affirmation that the Bible, as holy scripture, is not like any other book. A fuller understanding of the nature of God and God's dealings with the people of God may only become apparent as the communities of faith consistently read, reread, study, and reflect upon the meaning of the sacred text.

THE HISTORICITY OF THE PATRIARCHAL PERIOD

Throughout our discussion, our concern has been to try to understand the dynamics of the pentateuchal text, without prejudice as to the questions of what kind of history underlies it. Certainly it would be a fundamental error to make any straightforward move toward historical reconstruction solely on the basis of a careful reading of the text. Too many unknown factors about the nature of the tradition are embodied in the text. Nonetheless, I do not think this means that nothing can be said on historical questions, and it will be appropriate briefly to consider the bearings of our thesis upon two well-known historical problems.

First, the historicity of the patriarchal period. At present the view that the patriarchal traditions represent genuinely ancient material with historical foundations has become somewhat unfashionable (though, of course, whether a view is in or out of fashion bears no necessary correlation to its likely correctness).[24] For example, N. P. Lemche says in general terms that "the OT historical tradition is revealed to be a fiction written around the middle of the first millennium."[25] Specifically with regard to the patriarchal narratives he says that they "were composed in a society which no longer possessed any clear idea as to the patriarchal age, for which reason its narrators composed their stories as narratives about a distant fairytale past."[26] Alternatively, Miller and Hayes, in their recent history of Israel, simply do not engage with the patriarchal period.[27] The fashionable tendency is to assume that all the material in Genesis–Joshua is equally impervious to the modern historian. Miller and Hayes nowhere even raise the once widely held view that Genesis 12–50 may be accessible to the historian precisely because of its distinctive content.

The most substantial general critique of the historicity of the patriarchal traditions, T. L. Thompson's *The Historicity of the*

24. In some quarters it has become so unfashionable to make historical claims on the basis of Old Testament texts that it is apparently possible to label any such move as fundamentalist (though precisely what that means in such a context, apart from being something undesirable, is unclear). See B. O. Long, "On Finding the Hidden Premises," *JSOT* 39 (1987): 10–14. Such sweeping judgments do not greatly assist the difficult task of relating Israel's literature to the reconstruction of its history. Insofar as one is interested in Israel's history, then, despite all the various difficulties it presents, Israel's literature must be a primary source for that history.

25. N. P. Lemche, *Early Israel: Anthropological and Historical Studies on the Israelite Society before the Monarchy* (Leiden: Brill, 1985), 412.

26. N. P. Lemche, *Ancient Israel: A New History of Israelite Society* (Sheffield: JSOT, 1988), 60.

27. J. M. Miller and J. H. Hayes, *A History of Ancient Israel and Judah* (London: SCM, 1986), chap. 2.

Patriarchal Narratives, certainly makes a strong case against once-popular attempts to relate the patriarchal traditions to particular periods and wider movements in modern reconstructions of the history of the second millennium. In terms of the canons of modern historiography it is not at present possible to write a history of the patriarchal period. But from the fact that, because of insufficient evidence, modern scholars are not in a position to date the patriarchal traditions and relate them to a wider historical context, it in no way follows that the stories have the timelessness of myth or that nothing related in them ever happened, even though Thompson does appear to want to draw such a conclusion. It is also an omission in Thompson's discussion that patriarchal religion receives no sustained treatment.

J. Van Seters, in his *Abraham in History and Tradition,* argued that the Abraham narratives are a creation of the period of the Exile. In this work there is no discussion of patriarchal religion, but in a later article Van Seters turned to this and argued that the distinctive content of patriarchal religion in Genesis does not warrant any confidence in the antiquity or historicity of the traditions.[28] The relative brevity of his discussion suggests that he sees no real difficulty here. He mostly discusses the El epithets, which, in the light of the use of El as an epithet for YHWH in exilic texts, especially Second Isaiah, he argues to be part of an exilic interpretation of YHWH as a universal God. As for trees, pillars, and altars, these simply show the continuity and prevalence of a popular piety such as the Deuteronomic reform was aimed against.

The recent work of Köckert is a major analysis specifically of the religion of the patriarchs and is a sustained critique of the whole debate subsequent to Alt.[29] It is a valuable discussion, and many of Köckert's criticisms are certainly on target. Yet one major weakness in the book is that nowhere is there an analysis of Köckert's own working premises, particularly as these relate to the question of the dating of texts and the practices they contain. Köckert consistently argues that the patriarchal texts are not

28. J. Van Seters, "The Religion of the Patriarchs in Genesis," *Biblica* 61 (1980): 220–33.

29. See above, p. 80, n. 1.

early and the practices depicted in them are not distinctive, but his major tool of analysis is comparison with linguistic usage and practices referred to in texts that can be fairly confidently dated sometime within the seventh or sixth century. If similarity of linguistic usage and religious practice can be shown, then a common period of origin is the explanation, and the antiquity of the patriarchal traditions is thereby disproved. Yet this is clearly a *non sequitur* unless one can also disprove the possibility that the similarity could be explained by later texts drawing on the language and content of earlier texts. Of course, Köckert shows that it is extremely difficult to prove that the patriarchal traditions are early, since the evidence usually appealed to could also be interpreted in the way he proposes. But this simply means that a methodological impasse has been reached in which we do not have sufficient evidence to prove anything about patriarchal religion. It has not been shown that the traditions of patriarchal religion may not be early, any more than Thompson has shown that the content of the patriarchal traditions could not originate in the second millennium. All that has been shown is that modern scholars are not in a position to demonstrate such early origins or to do other than propose early origins as one possible, but always arguable, interpretation of the evidence.

Our thesis adds a new factor to the debate with our picture of a patriarchal religious ethos and practice that is both self-consistent and different from Mosaic Yahwism, or rather develops a feature already present in the work especially of Westermann.[30] Although we have allowed that some of this content could have arisen in a Yahwistic context on the premise of imaginative consistency with the world of the patriarchs, it is highly unlikely that all the material had its origins thus. Given the extreme unlikelihood that such a religious "world" could simply have been invented, least of all by adherents of Mosaic Yahwism, it presumably has some kind of historical origin. But of what sort?

Van Seters, as already noted, regards the material as originating in Israel's popular piety prior to the Deuteronomic reform. In many ways this is a restatement of Wellhausen's position. The

30. Cf. above, p. 85, n. 5.

classic interpretation popularized by Wellhausen was to assimilate "unorthodox" patriarchal practice to "unorthodox" practice in Samuel and Kings and to argue that this simply shows the character of Israelite religion prior to Deuteronomy and Josiah's reform. Köckert in a not dissimilar way sees patriarchal religion as a family religion that existed alongside official Yahwistic religion.[31] This interpretation of patriarchal religion as a disguised form of pre-/non-Deuteronomic Israelite religion presumably represents the kind of move likely to be made by anyone who attempts to lower the date of pentateuchal composition and content to the seventh and sixth centuries.

The difficulties with such an approach are considerable. First, neither Van Seters nor Köckert attempt to explain the privilege and respect accorded to the traditions of patriarchal religion by the writers of the Pentateuch. If patriarchal religion was in reality popular or family piety contemporary with but outside the mainstream of official Mosaic Yahwism, it is difficult to see why the pentateuchal writers, who are effectively the definitive exponents of official Mosaic Yahwism in Exodus-Deuteronomy, should have done what such a hypothesis requires. They have given traditions depicting non-Yahwistic ethos and practices the considerable luster of inseparable association with the ancestor of Israel's faith, Abraham, and the eponymous ancestor of the whole nation, Jacob/Israel. They have refrained from all adverse comment. And they have gone to considerable lengths to relate such material to Mosaic Yahwism in the way we have shown above. One would have thought that straightforward suppression would not only have been easier but also more in keeping with the generally exclusive and polemical nature of Yahwism in Exodus-Deuteronomy.[32]

31. M. Köckert, *Vätergott und Väterverheissungen,* FRLANT 142 (Göttingen: Vandenhoeck & Ruprecht, 1988), 141–47, 161, 309–11. Köckert builds especially upon the work of R. Albertz, *Persöniche Frömmigkeit und Offizielle Religion: Religionsinterner Pluralismus in Israel und Babylon,* Calwer Theologische Monographien 9 (Stuttgart: Calwer, 1978); see esp. pp. 77–91 for Albertz's main discussion of patriarchal religion.

32. It is important to press this point, because failure to do justice to it is a common feature of recent pentateuchal study. To take one (admittedly extreme) example, G. Garbini wishes to bring the date of the final (apparently substantive) redaction of the Pentateuch down to the third century. A major

Second, any account of patriarchal religion must explain its internal consistency. The assimilation of "unorthodox" patriarchal practice to "unorthodox" practice in Samuel and Kings on the assumption that this simply shows the character of Israelite religion prior to Josiah's reform obscures crucial distinctions. Figures like Samuel and Elijah may indeed have done things at odds with pentateuchal legislation, but that they stand within the context of Yahwistic exclusivism is not in doubt. The generally consistent lack of such exclusivism in patriarchal religion must be accounted for. Neither Van Seters nor Köckert shows much appreciation of the kind of coherence within patriarchal religion that we have sought to demonstrate. Köckert's extensive discussion for the most part focuses on the agenda set by Alt (pre-Yahwistic divine appellations, possible religiohistorical analogies, the promises to the patriarchs, the role of Genesis 15), none of which (except to a limited extent the use of Elohim) feature significantly in our analysis of the character of patriarchal religion.[33] That popular or private family religious practice could have achieved considerable coherence is not impossible. But that it should have achieved the kind of consistency we outlined in chapter 3, both internally coherent and consistently different from Mosaic Yahwism, is highly unlikely. If, moreover, the supposition is correct that material may have been added to the patriarchal traditions at different periods but almost always in such a way as to be imaginatively consistent with the patriarchal world, such a persistent tradition about the patriarchal world hardly seems to be explained by the supposition of popular or family religion.

Third is the significance of the use of El in the patriarchal traditions, both in various divine appellations compounded with El (El Shaddai, El Elyon, etc.) and in the names of people and

element of his argument is that "we can easily see that Genesis is characterized by a markedly anti-Egyptian attitude which is at the same time philo-Babylonian, and also by the repudiation of all the traditions which cast doubt on the ideological purity of Abraham" and that the text reflects the developed ideology of the postexilic Jerusalem priesthood ("Between Egypt and Babylon," in his *History and Ideology in Ancient Israel* [London: SCM, 1988; Italian, 1986], 133–50, esp. 145–46).

33. Köckert does briefly note a few of the distinctive traits of patriarchal religion (e.g., pp. 160–61) but sees no difficulty in fitting them into his hypothesis of family piety.

places compounded with El (Israel, Ishmael, Bethel, etc.). Both Van Seters and Köckert are dismissive of the likely antiquity of the divine appellations using El, and Van Seters sees the use of El in exilic texts, especially Isaiah 40ff., as part of an exilic interpretation of YHWH as a universal God. In essence, therefore, their approach is to argue that Yahwistic traditions in Genesis 12–50 were interpreted in terms of El, rather than El traditions interpreted in terms of YHWH. The implausibility of this as an explanation of the El usage in Genesis 12–50 is indicated by the correspondence of divine appellations in terms of El with names such as Israel, Ishmael, and Bethel, whose antiquity is undoubted. It is particularly the El aspect of the name Israel itself that is striking. Here I am in agreement with Gottwald who writes, "Given the overwhelming importance of Yahweh as the proper name of Israel's god, we should have expected the divine name Yahweh, probably in the short form Yah, to have appeared in the people's name, yielding "Israyah," or the like. The simplest explanation of this anomaly, I believe, is that Israel must have been a pre-Yahwistic entity. . . ."[34]

The cumulative force of these three factors—Yahwistic respect for patriarchal religion, the coherence and distinctiveness of patriarchal religion, and the undoubted antiquity of names compounded with El—makes an explanation of patriarchal religion as a disguised form of non-Yahwistic religion in the seventh or sixth centuries extremely implausible. By contrast, little difficulty attaches to the supposition that the patriarchal traditions were accommodated within Mosaic Yahwism precisely because of their antiquity and because they were recognized to derive from a period that was the precursor to Mosaic Yahwism.

To have said all this does not entirely resolve the methodological impasse outlined above, for on almost any given point of textual detail it may still be possible to argue for affinities of one kind or another with texts of the seventh or sixth (or other) century. And the methodological difficulties inherent in any reconstruction of patriarchal religion mean that there will always be severe limitations on the extent to which we can be confident in correlating the Genesis traditions about the patriarchs with

34. N. Gottwald, *The Tribes of Yahweh* (London: SCM, 1980), 494.

any underlying historical context. Nonetheless, the above considerations indicate that a choice between seeking early and possibly historical origins for patriarchal tradition and offering explanations that see it as originating in the seventh and sixth centuries is not simply arbitrary. However much one may recognize some elements in the patriarchal stories as most likely originating from their interpretation and use in the context of the Exile,[35] there is a clear general presumption in favor of an early and historically rooted context for the patriarchal traditions as a whole. This basic point is put strongly by Westermann, whose detailed work on the patriarchal narratives has received perhaps less attention than it deserves because of the attention given to the proposals of Van Seters and Thompson. Westermann comments, "We will never achieve complete certainty as to which texts in Gen. 12–50 may come from the patriarchal period, and which traces in texts of later origin may go back to it. . . . We can, however, be quite certain that one cannot contest the possibility that texts, narratives, and motifs in Gen. 12–50 reach back into the patriarchal period."[36]

THE ORIGIN OF THE NAME YHWH

Questions also arise concerning the origins of the name YHWH. If it is the consistent Old Testament tradition that the name first came to Israel through Moses, is this historically accurate? And how does it relate to possible occurrences of the name in non-Israelite texts?

With regard to the biblical material, the classic move is to attempt to penetrate behind the text and tradition of Exodus 3. I am doubtful, however, whether ultimately we are in a position to do more than repeat or paraphrase the Old Testament tradition that the name YHWH was revealed by God to Moses in the Sinai desert. We may suspect that the historical reality was more complex and speculate as to what this might have been—the Kenite hypothesis (that Moses learned the worship of YHWH from the Kenite tribe into whose priestly family he married) being the best

35. Cf. my "Earliest Commentary on the Akedah," *VT* 38 (1988): 302–33, and "Abraham's Righteousness (Gen. XV 6)," in J. A. Emerton, ed., *Studies in the Pentateuch* VTS, vol. 41 (Leiden and New York: Brill, 1990) 103–30.

36. Westermann, *Genesis 12–36,* 40.

known and most widely advocated theory. But whether the text of Exodus provides the right sort of material to sustain such hypotheses seems to me questionable for reasons already given.[37] To say this is not to deny the legitimacy of historical reconstruction, nor is it to make covert claims about the historicity of the text and tradition of Exodus 3 in its present form—though many scholars have been prepared to accept the historical likelihood of the tradition that the origins of the name YHWH should be associated with Moses. It is simply to recognize that we have neither the evidence nor the tools to enable effective historical penetration behind the Exodus text. The choice is either to repeat Israel's tradition, making clear its status as Israel's tradition, or to say that we know nothing.

The historical question has other dimensions, however, because of the discovery of second millennium names, possibly compounded with the name of Israel's God, and also possible references to the name of Israel's God in texts from Ugarit and Ebla which would antedate Moses (whenever exactly he is to be dated). G. Garbini, for example, has surveyed this issue and has castigated biblical scholars for ignoring extrabiblical evidence which apparently disproves the biblical tradition of the name YHWH originating in the context of Moses. He states,

> If we want to draw any conclusion from the extra-biblical evidence relating to Yahweh we can state that the texts show a divine figure worshipped in the region of Syria and Palestine from the beginning of the second millennium B.C. on, both by sedentary people and by nomads: a divine figure connected with the local pantheon but in no way pre-eminent; a divine figure, in short, the form of whose name fluctuates remarkably: Yah, Yaw, Yahweh. . . . What is certain is that traditional Yahwism has lost its starting point: Yahweh existed before the Hebrew people existed and was worshipped in the land of Canaan when the Hebrew tribes were still practising the cult of their "fathers."[38]

Unfortunately, Garbini does not reflect upon his point that the name "fluctuates remarkably." Or to put it differently, he does not discuss the crucial issue of how to determine what counts as a

37. See above, p. 8ff., 64f.

38. G. Garbini, *History and Ideology in Ancient Israel* (London: SCM, 1988), 57.

genuine occurrence of the name of Israel's God. On the one hand, although he says that A. Finet has "demonstrated convincingly the formal identity between *yahwi/yawi* and the name of the Hebrew God,"[39] the fact still remains that as yet no example of the tetragrammaton has been found in any pre-Mosaic extrabiblical material. On the other hand, although the tetragrammaton could certainly be abbreviated, usually when compounded in a name, it hardly follows from this that forms such as *yah, yaw, ya* should always be seen as abbreviations of the tetragrammaton unless other contextual factors also point in this direction.

It is important, however, not to allow the argument to become skewed by focusing solely on the use or nonuse of the tetragrammaton, for it remains possible that the tetragrammaton might appear in pre-Mosaic extrabiblical material. The crucial factor must be the significance and meaning attached to the divine name, and meaning is determined by usage and context. We have shown above how the book of Exodus ties the divine name into a nexus of interrelated traditions—YHWH, Moses, prophecy, Israel, Sinai, holiness, Exodus, Torah. For Israel, the meaning of the name is that meaning it has within the context of Israel's life and worship as a whole. If the tetragrammaton were to appear in a wholly different context of meaning, how far would it be meaningful still to call it the same name? Even if, for the sake of argument, one allowed Garbini's point that non-Israelite peoples in the second millennium worshiped a deity whose name was formally identical with that of Israel's God, I do not see how it is possible to give any significant content to his supposed corollary that "traditional Yahwism has lost its starting point: Yahweh existed before the Hebrew people existed and was worshipped in the land of Canaan when the Hebrew tribes were still practising the cult of their 'fathers.'" For what is meant by "traditional Yahwism" and "Yahweh"? Garbini trades on the familiar meaning of these terms as applicable to a non-/pre-Israelite context in a way that is tendentious.[40]

39. Ibid., 56.

40. W. Johnstone comments that "on the significance of a possible non-Israelite origin of the name Yahweh, S. R. Driver has already said all that is necessary (*Exodus,* li): 'The *source* from which either this or any other divine

In short, we are not in a position to offer a critical historical account of the origins of the name YHWH that differs significantly from Israel's own account. We may indeed recognize that matters are likely to have been more complex than the account of the book of Exodus suggests, and extrabiblical material may possibly indicate some antecedents of Israel's faith. But insofar as we are concerned with the name YHWH as a substantive term with anything like its familiar connotations, then the historian will most likely not go far wrong in recognizing Israel's tradition to be well grounded in Israel's history.

In conclusion, two final points may be worth making. First, I have considerable sympathy for those scholars who argue that much in modern critical reconstructions of Israel's early history is unwarranted, not least because of insufficient attention to the genre of the material and the question of the use to which it is legitimate to put such material. I do not disagree with N. P. Lemche when he writes that *"our most important duty is to acknowledge our ignorance.* By this I mean that we are obliged to avoid composing hypotheses about Israel's prenational existence in the absence of adequate sources."[41] Where I part company is in the fashionable corollary of a sweeping dismissal of all historical worth in Israel's early traditions largely on the basis of a few loose and sometimes tendentious genre classifications—saga, legend, fairytale (!).[42] It is of little value to criticize scholars as "relentlessly conservative" and as "clinging to the OT narrative" when the fact remains that interesting and unexpected features within many texts require explanation, perhaps most appropriately

name was ultimately derived by the Hebrews, matters little or nothing: the question which is of importance is, What did the name *come to mean* to them? . . . We can await with perfect calmness whatever the future may have to disclose to us with regard to its ultimate origin, or its pre-Israelite use" (*Exodus,* OT Guides [Sheffield: JSOT, 1990], 103).

41. Lemche, *Early Israel,* 414.

42. Ibid., 414, 417; cf. T. L. Thompson and D. Irvin, "The Joseph and Moses Narratives," in J. H. Hayes and J. M. Miller, eds., *Israelite and Judaean History* (London: SCM, 1977), 149–212. Astonishingly, the term *fairytale* is clearly deliberate, as it is used in *Ancient Israel* not only of the patriarchal stories (p. 60) but also of certain narratives in Judges and Samuel (pp. 121, 216). One would like to know precisely what Lemche means by fairytale and what characteristics in these Old Testament narratives qualify them specifically for this, rather than any other, genre designation.

some kind of historical explanation.[43] Indeed, the genre of pentateuchal narratives is far removed from that of modern historiography. It has been central to our thesis that the nature and purpose of the stories is best understood, and the stories are best appropriated for biblical theology, when the agenda and priorities of the ancient historian are laid aside. And we have argued that modern historical concerns have simply misconstrued the pentateuchal text with regard to the problem of the divine name. But all this does not exclude the possibility that aspects of the text are accessible to historically oriented enquiry, as long as one recognizes the severe limitations inherent in such an undertaking.

Finally, although it remains the case that all historically oriented questions about the content of the narrative traditions of the Pentateuch are intractable, they are intractable in different ways. In particular, it may be easier in some respects to sharpen a historical focus on the traditions of Genesis than on those of Exodus, even though the basic content of Genesis 12–50 is apparently more ancient. This is essentially because it is still possible to discern both non-Yahwistic and Yahwistic perspectives in Genesis 12–50 and so in some way analyze the historical depth of the text. In the call of Moses the material has been so thoroughly assimilated to the mature perspectives of its own Yahwism (Yahwistic monotheism, Moses as prophet) that it is much harder to find any firm basis for distinguishing between earlier and later dimensions of the tradition. It may appear paradoxical to suggest that the historically oriented reader can in some ways find firmer footing in Genesis 12–50 than in Exodus. But the paradox may, in fact, do justice to the differing characteristics of the patriarchal and Mosaic traditions.

43. Lemche, *Ancient Israel,* 31; idem, *Early Israel,* 414.

Epilogue

Our thesis has been advanced, and some of its possible implications have been briefly explored. In conclusion, one final point.

In the words of Ecclesiastes, "There is nothing new under the sun." That is to say, my thesis that there are two different dispensations within the Old Testament and that this is an issue of fundamental theological significance is, in one sense, nothing new. It is precisely this that features prominently in Paul's arguments about justification in Galatians 3 and Romans 4, where he draws a sharp distinction between the time of Abraham and the time of Moses.

Paul's perception of the significance of the distinction is remarkable because it goes against the predominant consensus in Jewish biblical interpretation from as early as the book of Jubilees (perhaps written around the time of the Maccabees or in its aftermath). Here the difference between patriarchal practice and Mosaic Torah is clearly perceived but is an evident source of embarrassment, with the result that the stories are so rewritten that patriarchal practice is made to conform to Mosaic Torah. And we have seen that the Pentateuch itself, in much more restrained and subtle manner, also conforms the patriarchal period to the patterns of Mosaic Yahwism in certain limited but important respects. Thus the Jewish tradition of emphasizing continuity rather than discontinuity between the patriarchs and Moses is a natural extension of a hermeneutical model already present within scripture.

Why should Paul, by contrast, emphasize the discontinuity?

The short answer would appear to be his engagement with the significance of Jesus, which has, among other things, caused him to reread scripture and ask a new set of questions about its possible meaning and significance. Particularly in his wrestling with the question of the relationship between Jewish Torah and gentile standing and life-style before God, he found precisely the scriptural precedent that he sought in the stories of Abraham. For here is the acknowledged forefather of Israel, and yet what is significant about him is his relationship with God by faith (ἐκ πίστεως) rather than his observance of Mosaic Torah (and even though he practised circumcision, one of the crucial markers of Judaism, this was a secondary factor in his story). Generally speaking, it is hard to deny an obvious plausibility in Paul's approach of highlighting the discontinuity between Abraham and Moses in order to show that on Judaism's own scriptural premises the status of Torah may be relativized. Of course, only the extra factor of Jesus can give the argument real force and show why one might wish to go against the otherwise natural consensus interpretation.

This leaves us with the recognition that the same phenomenon may be interpreted in different ways. Or more precisely, we have seen that the theological relationship between two dispensations is by definition a matter of both continuity and discontinuity, and we have different parts of the biblical canon stressing now the continuity and now the discontinuity. Although this suggests that within the canon there is no one way to handle the fundamental problem of different dispensations within salvation history and that the inherent tension cannot be definitively resolved, the issue nonetheless deserves careful consideration. For example, although major writers both in the New Testament and among the church fathers emphasize the discontinuity between Old and New Testament, when issues of Christian self-definition vis-à-vis Judaism are at stake, in contexts where Christians have been concerned primarily to read and appropriate the Old Testament as scripture in its own right, they have generally emphasized the similarity and continuity between the testaments.

In short, one of the major tasks facing Christian biblical theology is to take seriously the presence of three dispensations within the canon of scripture and to probe their implications for the understanding of God and for normativity and pluralism within communities of faith today. Toward that task this present work is but a beginning.

Bibliography

Abba, R. "The Divine Name Yahweh." *JBL* 80 (1961): 320–28.

Adam, A. K. M. "Biblical Theology and the Problem of Modernity: *Von Wredestrasse zu Sackgasse.*" *HBT* 12 (1990): 1–18.

Albertz, R. *Persönliche Frömmigkeit und offizielle Religion: Religionsinterner Pluralismus in Israel und Babylon.* Calwer Theologische Monographien 9. Stuttgart: Calwer, 1978.

Alt, A. "The God of the Fathers." In his *Essays on Old Testament History and Religion,* 3–77. Oxford: Blackwell, 1966, recently reissued, Sheffield: JSOT, 1989; ET of "Der Gott der Väter," BWANT 12, 1929. Reprinted in his *Kleine Schriften* I, 1–78. Munich: Beck, 1953.

Andersen, F. I. *The Sentence in Biblical Hebrew.* The Hague: Mouton, 1974.

Auffret, P. "The Literary Structure of Exodus 6.2–8." *JSOT* 27 (1983): 46–54.

Baker, D. L. *Two Testaments, One Bible.* Leicester: IVP, 1976.

Bar-Efrat, S. *Narrative Art in the Bible.* JSOTS 70. Sheffield: Almond, 1989. ET from Hebrew of 1979.

Barton, J. *People of the Book? The Authority of the Bible in Christianity.* London: SPCK, 1988.

Bigger, S., ed. *Creating the Old Testament: The Emergence of the Hebrew Bible.* Oxford: Blackwell, 1989.

Blum, E. *Die Komposition der Vätergeschichte.* WMANT 57. Neukirchen-Vluyn: Neukirchener Verlag, 1984.

———. *Studien zur Komposition des Pentateuch.* BZAW 189. Berlin: de Gruyter, 1990.

Bowker, J. *The Targums and Rabbinic Literature.* Cambridge: Cambridge Univ. Press, 1969.

Bowra, C. M. *Tradition and Design in the Iliad.* Oxford: Clarendon, 1930.

Braybrooke, M. *Time to Meet: Towards a Deeper Relationship between Christians and Jews.* London: SCM; Philadelphia: Trinity International, 1990.

Bright, J. *A History of Israel.* 3d ed. London: SCM, 1981.

Brooks, R., and J. J. Collins, eds. *Hebrew Bible or Old Testament?* Notre Dame: Notre Dame Univ. Press, 1991.

Brown, R. E., J. A. Fitzmyer, and R. E. Murphy, eds. *The New Jerome Biblical Commentary.* 2d ed. Chapman: London, 1990.

Brueggemann, W. "The Kerygma of the Priestly Writers." *ZAW* 84 (1972): 397–413.

Buber, M. *Moses.* Oxford and London: Phaidon, 1946.

Buren, P. van. *Theology of the Jewish-Christian Reality I: Discerning the Way.* San Francisco: Harper & Row, 1980.

———. *Theology of the Jewish-Christian Reality II: A Christian Theology of the People Israel.* San Francisco: Harper & Row, 1983.

———. *Theology of the Jewish-Christian Reality III: Christ in Context.* San Francisco: Harper & Row, 1988.

Cassuto, U. *A Commentary on the Book of Genesis.* Vol. 2. Jerusalem: Magnes, 1964. ET from Hebrew of 1949.

———. *A Commentary on the Book of Exodus.* Jerusalem: Magnes, 1967. ET from Hebrew of 1951.

Charity, A. C. *Events and Their Afterlife.* Cambridge: Cambridge Univ. Press, 1966.

Childs, B. S. *Exodus.* OTL. London: SCM, 1974.

———. *Old Testament Theology in a Canonical Context.* London: SCM, 1985.

Clifford, R. J. *The Cosmic Mountain in Canaan and the Old Testament.* Cambridge, Mass.: Harvard Univ. Press, 1972.

Clines, D. J. A. *What Does Eve Do to Help? And Other Readerly Questions to the Old Testament.* JSOTS 94. Sheffield: JSOT, 1990.

Coats, G. W. *Moses: Heroic Man, Man of God.* JSOTS 57. Sheffield: JSOT, 1988.

Cross, F. M. "Yahweh and the God of the Patriarchs." *HTR* 55 (1962): 225–59.

———. *Canaanite Myth and Hebrew Epic.* Cambridge, Mass.: Harvard Univ. Press, 1973.

Dachslager, E. L. "Getting Rid of the 'Old Testament.'" *Reconstructionist* 44 (1978): 7–10.

Driver, S. R. *Exodus.* Cambridge Bible for Schools and Colleges. Cambridge: Cambridge Univ. Press, 1911.

Driver, G. R. "Affirmation by Exclamatory Negation." *Journal of the Ancient Near Eastern Society of Columbia University (T. H. Gaster Festschrift)* 5 (1973): 107–14.

Durham, J. I. *Exodus.* WBC 3. Waco, Tex.: Word, 1987.

Dus, J. "Moses or Joshua? On the Problem of the Founder of the Israelite Religion." *Radical Religion* 2 (1975): 26–41.

Emerton, J. A. "An Examination of Some Attempts to Defend the Unity of the Flood Narrative in Genesis, Part I." *VT* 37 (1987): 401–20.

———. "An Examination of Some Attempts to Defend the Unity of the Flood Narrative in Genesis, Part II." *VT* 38 (1988): 1–21.

———. "The Priestly Writer in Genesis." *JTS* 39 (1988): 381–400.

Fischer, G. *Jahwe Unser Gott: Sprache, Aufbau und Erzähtechnik in der Berufung des Mose (Ex 3–4).* OBO 91. Freiburg Schweiz, Universitätsverlag/Göttingen: Vandenhoeck & Ruprecht, 1989.

Fishbane, M. *Text and Texture: Close Readings of Selected Biblical Texts.* New York: Schocken, 1979.

———. *Biblical Interpretation in Ancient Israel.* Oxford: Clarendon, 1985.

Flanders, H. J., Jr., R. W. Crapps, and D. A. Smith. *People of the Covenant: An Introduction to the Old Testament.* 3d ed. New York and Oxford: Oxford Univ. Press, 1988.

Fohrer, G. *History of Israelite Religion.* London: SPCK, 1973. ET of *Geschichte der Israelitischen Religion.* Berlin: de Gruyter, 1968.

Fokkelman, J. P. *Narrative Art in Genesis.* Assen/Amsterdam: Van Gorcum, 1975. Reissued Sheffield: JSOT, 1991.

Fox, R. Lane. *Pagans and Christians.* Harmondsworth: Viking, 1986.

Fuller, D. P. *Gospel and Law: Contrast or Continuum? The Hermeneutics of Dispensationalism and Covenant Theology.* Grand Rapids: Eerdmans, 1980.

Gammie, J. G. *Holiness in Israel.* Overtures to Biblical Theology. Minneapolis: Fortress, 1989.

Garbini, G. *History and Ideology in Ancient Israel.* London: SCM, 1988. ET of *Storia e Ideologia nell' Israele Antico.* Brescia: Paideia, 1986.

Glisson, S. D. "Exodus 6:3 in Pentateuchal Criticism." *Restoration Quarterly* 28 (1985–86): 135–43.

Goshen-Gottstein, M. H. "Tanakh Theology: The Religion of the Old Testament and the Place of Jewish Biblical Theology." In P. D. Miller et al., eds., *Ancient Israelite Religion,* 617–44. Philadelphia: Fortress, 1987.

Gottwald, N. *The Tribes of Yahweh: A Sociology of the Religion of Liberated Israel, 1250–1050 BCE.* London: SCM, 1980.

Gressmann, H. *Mose und seine Zeit.* FRLANT 18. Göttingen: Vandenhoeck & Ruprecht, 1913.

Gunkel, H. *Genesis.* 5th ed. Göttingen: Vandenhoeck & Ruprecht, 1922.

———. *The Legends of Genesis.* New York: Schocken, 1964. Originally the introduction to his *Genesis* of 1901.

Ha, J. *Genesis 15.* BZAW 181. Berlin and New York: de Gruyter, 1989.

Hanson, P. D. "Biblical Interpretation: Meeting Place of Jews and Christians." In G. M. Tucker, D. L. Petersen, and R. R. Wilson, eds., *Canon, Theology, and Old Testament Interpretation: Essays in Honor of Brevard S. Childs,* 32–47. Philadelphia: Fortress, 1988.

Haran, M. "The Religion of the Patriarchs." *ASTI* 4 (1965): 30–55.

Hogenhaven, J. *Problems and Prospects of Old Testament Theology.* Biblical Seminar. Sheffield: JSOT, 1988.

Houtman, C. *Exodus I (1:1—7:13).* Commentaar op het Oude Testament. Kampen: J. H. Kok, 1986.

Jacob, B. *The Second Book of the Bible: Exodus.* New Jersey: Ktav, 1991. ET from German.

Jacob, E. *Theology of the Old Testament.* London: Hodder & Stoughton, 1958. ET from French, Neuchâtel: Delachaux & Niestle, 1955.

Jenks, A. W. *The Elohist and North Israelite Traditions.* SBLMS 22. Missoula, Mont.: Scholars, 1977.

Johnstone, W. *Exodus.* OT Guides. Sheffield: JSOT, 1990.

Josipovici, G. *The Book of God.* New Haven and London: Yale Univ. Press, 1988.

Kaiser, W. C., Jr. "Exodus." In F. E. Gaebelein, ed., *The Expositor's Bible Commentary,* vol. 2, 287–497. Grand Rapids: Zondervan, 1990.

Kaufmann, Y. *The Religion of Israel From Its Beginnings to the Babylonian Exile.* New York: Schocken, 1960, 1972. An abridgement and translation by M. Greenberg of 7 vols. in Hebrew, 1937–48.

Keil, C. F., and F. Delitzsch. *Commentary on the Old Testament, I: The Pentateuch.* Reprint. Grand Rapids: Eerdmans, 1980.

Kirkpatrick, P. *The Old Testament and Folklore Study.* JSOTS 62. Sheffield: JSOT, 1988.

Klassen, W. "Anti-Judaism in Early Christianity: The State of the Question." In P. Richardson, ed., *Anti-Judaism in Early Christianity.* Vol. 1, *Paul and the Gospels,* 1–19. Waterloo, Ontario: Wilfrid Laurier Univ. Press, 1986.

Koch, K. "P—Kein Redaktor! Erinnerung an zwei Eckdaten der Quellenscheidung." *VT* 37 (1987): 446–67.

Köckert, M. *Vätergott und Väterverheissungen.* FRLANT 142. Göttingen: Vandenhoeck & Ruprecht, 1988.

Labuschagne, C. J. "The emphasizing particle *gam* and its connotations." In W. C. van Unnik and A. S. van der Woude, eds., *Studia Biblica et Semitica (T. C. Vriezen Festschrift,* 193–203. Wageningen: Veenman, 1966.

Lash, N. *Easter in Ordinary: Reflections on Human Experience and the Knowledge of God.* Virginia: Virginia Univ. Press; London: SCM, 1988.

Leibowitz, N. *Studies in Shemot: Exodus.* Vol. 1. Jerusalem: World Zionist Organization, 1976.

Lemche, N. P. *Early Israel: Anthropological and Historical Studies on the Israelite Society before the Monarchy.* Leiden: Brill, 1985.

———. *Ancient Israel: A New History of Israelite Society.* Sheffield: JSOT, 1988.

Lemke, W. E. "Is Old Testament Theology an Essentially Christian Theological Discipline?" *HBT* 11 (1989): 59–71.

Levenson, J. D. "Why Jews Are Not Interested in Biblical Theology." In J. Neusner, B. A. Levine, and E. S. Frerichs, eds., *Judaic Perspectives on Ancient Israel,* 281–307. Philadelphia: Fortress, 1987.

Long, B. O. "On Finding the Hidden Premises." *JSOT* 39 (1987): 10–14.

Magonet, J. "The Bush That Never Burnt (Narrative Techniques in Exodus 3 and 6)." *Heythrop Journal* 16 (1975), 304–11.

———. "The Rhetoric of God: Exodus 6.2-8." *JSOT* 27 (1983): 56–67.

Mann, T. W. *The Book of the Torah: The Narrative Integrity of the Pentateuch.* Atlanta: John Knox, 1988.

Martens, E. A. *Plot and Purpose in the Old Testament.* Leicester: IVP, 1981.

Martin, W. J. *Stylistic Criteria and the Analysis of the Pentateuch.* London: Tyndale, 1955.

McKane, W. *Studies in the Patriarchal Narratives.* Edinburgh: Handsel, 1979.

McNeile, A. H. *The Book of Exodus.* Westminster Commentaries. London: Methuen, 1908, 1917, 1931.

Meyers, C. L. *The Tabernacle Menorah.* Missoula, Mont.: Scholars, 1976.

Mikra'ot Gedolot: Shemot. Jerusalem: 1971.

Miller, J. M., and J. H. Hayes. *A History of Ancient Israel and Judah.* London: SCM, 1986.

Miller, P. D., Jr., P. D. Hanson, and S. D. McBride, eds. *Ancient Israelite Religion: Essays in Honor of Frank Moore Cross.* Philadelphia: Fortress, 1987.

Moberly, R. W. L. *At the Mountain of God: Story and Theology in Exodus 32–34.* JSOTS 22. Sheffield: JSOT, 1983.

———. "Did the Serpent Get It Right?" *JTS* 39 (1988): 1–27.

———. "The Earliest Commentary on the Akedah." *VT* 38 (1988): 302–23.

———. "Abraham's Righteousness (Gen. xv 6)." In J. A. Emerton, ed., *Studies in the Pentateuch* VTS, vol. 41, 103–30. Leiden and New York: Brill, 1990.

Motyer, J. A. *The Revelation of the Divine Name.* London: Tyndale Press, 1959.

Mowinckel, S. "The Name of the God of Moses." *HUCA* 32 (1961): 121–33.

Neusner, J. *Studying Classical Judaism: A Primer.* Louisville: Westminster/John Knox Press, 1991.

New International Version Study Bible. London: Hodder & Stoughton, 1985, 1987.

Noth, M. *A History of Pentateuchal Traditions.* Chico, California: Scholars, 1981. ET of *Überlieferungsgeschichte des Pentateuch.* Stuttgart: 1948.

———. *Exodus.* OTL. London: SCM, 1962. ET of *Das zweite Buch Mose, Exodus.* ATD 5. Göttingen: Vandenhoeck & Ruprecht, 1959.

Oesterley, W. O. E., and T. H. Robinson. *Hebrew Religion: Its Origin and Development.* London: SPCK, 1930.

Ohler, A. *Studying the Old Testament: From Tradition to Canon.* Edinburgh: T. & T. Clark, 1985. ET of *Gattungen im AT.* Düsseldorf: Patmos, 1972, 1973.

Otto, R. *The Idea of the Holy.* Oxford: Oxford Univ. Press, 1924. ET of 9th ed. of *Das Heilige,* 1917, 1923.

Parke-Taylor, G. H. *Yahweh: The Divine Name in the Bible.* Waterloo, Ontario: Wilfrid Laurier Univ. Press, 1975.

Pawlikowski, J. *Jesus and the Theology of Israel.* Zacchaeus Studies: Theology. Wilmington, Delaware: Michael Glazier, 1989.

Plaut, W. G., ed. *The Torah: A Modern Commentary.* New York: Union of American Hebrew Congregations, 1981.

Porteous, N. W., and R. E. Clements. "Old Testament Theology." In A. Richardson and J. Bowden, eds., *The Westminster Dictionary of Christian Theology.* Philadelphia: Westminster, 1983.

Pury, A. de, ed. *Le Pentateuque en Question.* Geneva: Labor et Fides, 1989.

Quell, G. "Kurios." In G. Kittel, ed., *Theological Dictionary of the New Testament.* Vol. 3. Grand Rapids: Eerdmans, 1965. ET of *Theologisches Wörterbuch zum Neuen Testament* III. Stuttgart: Kohlhammer.

Rad, G. von. *The Problem of the Hexateuch and Other Essays.* Edinburgh and London: Oliver & Boyd, 1966. ET of *Gesammelte Studien zum Alten Testament.* Munich: Chr. Kaiser, 1958.

———. *Old Testament Theology.* Vol. 1. London: SCM, 1965, 1975. ET of *Theologie des Alten Testaments* I. Munich: Chr. Kaiser, 1957.

———. "History and the Patriarchs." *ExpTim* 71 (1961): 213–16.

Radday, Y. T. "'Wie ist sein Name?' (Ex 3:13)." *Linguistica Biblica* 58 (1986): 87–104.

Räisänen, H. *Beyond New Testament Theology.* London: SCM; Philadelphia: Trinity International, 1990.

Rendtorff, R. *The Problem of the Process of Transmission in the Pentateuch.* JSOTS 89. Sheffield: JSOT, 1990. ET by J. J. Scullion from *Das überlieferungsgeschichtliche problem des Pentateuch.* BZAW 147. Berlin and New York: de Gruyter, 1977.

———. "The Future of Pentateuchal Criticism." *Henoch* 6 (1984): 1–15.

Reventlow, H. G. *Problems of Biblical Theology in the Twentieth Century.* London: SCM, 1986. ET of *Hauptprobleme der Biblischen Theologie im 20. Jahrhundert.* Darmstadt: Wissenschaftliche Buchgesellschaft, 1983.

Roberts, J. J. M. "In Defense of the Monarchy." In P. D. Miller et al., eds., *Ancient Israelite Religion,* 377–96. Philadelphia: Fortress, 1987.

Rose, M. "'Entmilitarizierung des Krieges'? (Erwagungen zu den Patriarchen-Erzählungen der Genesis)." *BZ* 20 (1976): 197–211.

Rosenbaum, M., and A. M. Silbermann. *The Pentateuch with the Commentary of Rashi: Genesis.* Jerusalem: Silbermann, 1972.

———. *The Pentateuch with the Commentary of Rashi: Exodus.* Jerusalem: Silbermann, 1972.

Rowley, H. H. *From Joseph to Joshua.* London: Oxford University Press, 1950.

Saebø, M. "Offenbarung oder Verhüllung? Bemerkungen zum Charakter des Gottesnamens in Ex 3,13–15." In J. Jeremias and L. Perlitt, eds., *Die Botschaft und die Boten (H. W. Wolff Festschrift),* 43–55. Neukirchen-Vluyn: Neukirchener Verlag, 1981.

Saggs, H. W. F. *The Encounter with the Divine in Mesopotamia and Israel.* London: Athlone; Atlantic Highlands, N.J.: Humanities, 1978.

Sanders, E. P. *Paul and Palestinian Judaism.* London: SCM, 1977.

Sanders, J. A. "First Testament and Second." *Biblical Theology Bulletin* 17 (1987): 47–49.

Sandmel, S. "Genesis 4:26b." *HUCA* 32 (1961): 19–29.

———. "The Haggadah within Scripture." *JBL* 80 (1961): 105–22.

Sarna, N. M. *Exploring Exodus: The Heritage of Biblical Israel.* New York: Schocken, 1987.

———. *Shemot/Exodus.* JPS Torah Commentary. Philadelphia/New York: Jewish Publication Society, 5751/1991.

Sawyer, J. F. A. "Combating Prejudices about the Bible and Judaism." *Theology* 94 (1991): 269–78.

Schmid, H. H. *Der Sogennante Jahwist.* Zurich: Theologischer Verlag, 1976.

Schmidt, W. H. *The Faith of the Old Testament.* Oxford: Blackwell, 1983. ET of *Alttestamentlicher Glaube in seiner Geschichte.* Neukirchen-Vluyn: Neukirchener Verlag, 1968, 1972.

———. *Introduction to the Old Testament.* London: SCM, 1984. ET of *Einführung in das Alte Testament.* Berlin: de Gruyter, 1979, 1982.

———. *Exodus.* Pts. 1–4. BKAT 2. Neukirchen-Vluyn: Neukirchener Verlag, 1974, 1977, 1983, 1988.

Segal, M. H. *The Pentateuch—Its Composition and Its Authorship, and Other Biblical Studies.* Jerusalem: Magnes, 1967.

Sidic (Service International de Documentation Ioudéo-Chrétienne) 21:3 (1988). Issue devoted to discussion of typology.

Ska, J.-L. "La place d'Ex 6:2-8 dans la narration de l'exode." *ZAW* 94 (1982): 530–48.

Smith, F. G. "Observations on the Use of the Names and Titles of God in Genesis." *Evangelical Quarterly* 40 (1968): 103–9.

Soggin, J. "Kultätiologische Sagen und Katechese im Hexateuch." *VT* 10 (1960): 341–47.

Spinoza, B. *A Theologico-Political Treatise.* New York: Dover, 1951. ET from Latin by R. Elwes.

Stendahl, K. "The Bible as a Classic and the Bible as Holy Scripture." *JBL* 103 (1984): 3–10.

Sternberg, M. *The Poetics of Biblical Narrative.* Bloomington: Indiana Univ. Press, 1985.

Taizé, Br. John of. *The Pilgrim God: A Biblical Journey.* Washington, D.C.: Pastoral Press, 1985.

Thompson, T. L. *The Historicity of the Patriarchal Narratives.* BZAW 133. Berlin and New York: de Gruyter, 1974.

Thompson, T. L., and D. Irvin. "The Joseph and Moses Narratives." In J. H. Hayes and J. M. Miller, eds., *Israelite and Judaean History,* 149–212. London: SCM, 1977.

———. *The Origin Tradition of Ancient Israel: I. The Literary Formation of Genesis and Exodus 1–23.* JSOTS 55. Sheffield. JSOT, 1987.

Van Seters, J. *Abraham in History and Tradition.* New Haven and London: Yale Univ. Press, 1975.

———. "The Religion of the Patriarchs in Genesis." *Biblica* 61 (1980): 220–33.

———. *In Search of History.* New Haven and London: Yale Univ. Press, 1983.

Vaux, R. de. *The Early History of Israel.* 2 vols. London: DLT, 1978. ET of *Histoire Ancienne d'Israel.* Paris: Gabalda & Cie, 1971.

Vriezen, Th. C. *The Religion of Ancient Israel.* London: Lutterworth, 1967. ET of *De godsdienst van Israel.* Arnhem: De Haan, 1963.

Weidmann, H. *Die Patriarchen und ihre Religion im Licht der Forschung seit Wellhausen.* FRLANT 94. Göttingen: Vandenhoeck & Ruprecht, 1968.

Weimar, P. *Die Berufung des Mose.* OBO 32. Göttingen: Vandenhoeck & Ruprecht, 1980.

Weinfeld, M. "The Tribal League at Sinai." In P. D. Miller et al., eds., *Ancient Israelite Religion,* 303–14. Philadelphia: Fortress, 1987.

Weiser, A. *Introduction to the Old Testament.* London: DLT, 1961. ET of *Einleitung in das Alte Testament.* 4th ed. Göttingen: Vandenhoeck & Ruprecht, 1957.

Wellhausen, J. *Prolegomena to the History of Ancient Israel.* Reprint. Gloucester, Mass.: Peter Smith, 1973. ET of German of 1878.

Wenham, G. J. "The Religion of the Patriarchs." In A. R. Millard and D. J. Wiseman, eds., *Essays on the Patriarchal Narratives,* 157–88. Leicester: IVP, 1980.

Westermann, C. *Genesis 1–11.* Minneapolis: Augsburg; London: SPCK, 1984. ET of *Genesis (Kapitel 1–11).* BKAT. Neukirchen-Vluyn: Neukirchener Verlag, 1974, 1976.

———. *Genesis 12–36.* Minneapolis: Augsburg; London: SPCK, 1985, 1986. ET from German of 1981.

———. *Genesis 37–50.* Minneapolis: Augsburg; London: SPCK, 1986, 1987. ET from German of 1982.

———. *Elements of Old Testament Theology.* Atlanta: John Knox, 1982. ET of *Theologie des Alten Testaments in Grundzugen.* Göttingen: Vandenhoeck & Ruprecht, 1978.

Whitney, G. E. "Alternative Interpretations of *lō'* in Exodus 6:3 and Jeremiah 7:22." *WTJ* 48 (1986): 151–59.

Whybray, R. N. *The Making of the Pentateuch: A Methodological Study.* JSOTS 53. Sheffield: JSOT, 1987.

Williamson, C. M., and R. J. Allen. *Interpreting Difficult Texts: Anti-Judaism and Christian Preaching.* London: SCM; Philadelphia: Trinity International, 1989.

Wilson, R. D. "Yahweh (Jehovah) and Exodus 6:3." *Princeton Theological Review* 22 (1924): 108–19. Reprinted in W. C. Kaiser, Jr., ed., *Classical Evangelical Essays in Old Testament Interpretation,* 29–39. Grand Rapids: Baker, 1972.

Wolff, H. W. "The Kerygma of the Yahwist." *Interpretation* 20 (1966): 131–58.

———. "The Elohistic Fragments in the Pentateuch." *Interpretation* 26 (1972): 158–73.

Ziesler, J. A. "New Testament Theology." In A. Richardson and

J. Bowden, eds., *The Westminster Dictionary of Christian Theology,* 398–403. Philadelphia: Westminster, 1983.

Zimmerli, W. "Sinaibund und Abrahambund." *TZ* 16 (1960): 268–80. Reprinted in his *Gottes Offenbarung,* 205–16. 2d ed. Munich: Kaiser, 1969.

———. *Old Testament Theology in Outline.* Atlanta: John Knox; Edinburgh: T. & T. Clark, 1978. ET of *Grundriss der alttestamentlichen Theologie.* Stuttgart: Kohlhammer.

———. *I Am Yahweh.* Atlanta: John Knox, 1982. Collection of articles translated from German.

Zlotowitz, M., and N. Scherman, eds., *Bereishis: Genesis/A New Translation with a Commentary Anthologized from Talmudic, Midrashic and Rabbinic Sources.* ArtScroll Tanach I. New York: Mesorah Publications, 1977, 1986.

Index of Modern Authors

Abba, R., 53 n.31
Adam, A. K. M., 171 n.29
Albertz, R., 195 n.31
Albright, W. F., 113
Alt, A., 73f, 80 n.1, 81, 86, 95f, 106, 108, 111, 113, 165, 193
Andersen, F. I., 57, 61 n.47
Auffret, P., 29 n.29

Baker, D. L., 126 n.33, 138 n.46
Bar-Efrat, S., 18 n.19
Barton, J., 174 n.33
Bigger, S., 13 n.15
Blum, E., 32, 42 nn.11,12, 180, 181 n.7
Bossman, D. M., 162 n.21
Bowker, J., 144 n.51
Bowra, C. M., 154 n.12
Braybrooke, M., 147 n.1, 159
Bright, J., 37, 82 n.3, 106 n.1
Brooks, R., 149 n.5
Brown, R. E., 40 n.7
Brueggemann, W., 186 n.10
Buber, M., 53 n.31, 59 n.43
Buren, P. van, 5 n.1, 148 n.2, 160

Cassuto, U., 53 n.30, 143 n.49
Charity, A. C., 138 n.46
Childs, B. S., xi, 7 n.5, 13 n.14, 21 n.24, 28, 32, 33, 46 nn.19,22, 60 n.45, 132f, 185
Clements, R. E., 152 n.9
Clifford, R. J., 10 n.7
Clines, D. J. A., 153 n.10
Coats, G. W., 16 n.16, 146
Cross, F. M., 32, 48 n.27, 113f

Dachslager, E. L., 159 n.16
Driver, G. R., 56f
Driver, S. R., 9 n.6, 201 n.40
Durham, J. I., 7 n.5, 21 n.24, 32 n.36, 50
Dus, J., 48 n.27

Emerton, J. A., 33 n.37, 177 n.3

Finet, A., 200
Fischer, G., 18 n.19, 46 n.21, 47 n.23
Fishbane, M., 18 n.18, 143 n.49
Flanders, H. J., 37 n.1
Fohrer, G., 82 n.3
Fokkelman, J. P., 101 n.25
Fox, R. Lane, 154 n.11
Fuller, D. P., 128 n.35

Gabler, J., 171 n.29
Gammie, J. G., 100 n.22, 103
Garbini, G., 195 n.32, 199ff
Glisson, S. D., 55 n.34, 66 n.51
Goshen-Gottstein, M. H., 150
Gottwald, N., 82 n.3, 85 n.4, 114ff, 118 n.21, 197
Gressmann, H., 64 n.49
Gunkel, H., 73, 135 n.42, 176, 180, 185

Ha, J., 137 n.45, 143 n.49, 187f
Hanson, P. D., 162 n.21
Haran, M., 80 n.1, 111ff, 124
Hogenhaven, J., 171 n.29
Houtman, C., 7 n.5, 58 n.41

Ibn Ezra, 37, 39 n.4, 54
Irwin, D., 201 n.42

Jacob, B., 33, 53 n.30
Jacob, E., 53 n.31
Jenks, A. W., 19 n.21

Johnstone, W., 200 n. 40
Josipovici, G., 153 n. 10

Kaiser, W. C., 53 n. 30
Kaufmann, Y., 82 n. 3, 186
Keil, C. F., 53 n. 30
Kirkpatrick, P., 74
Klassen, W., 149 n. 3
Koch, K., 33 n. 37
Köert, M., 74, 80 n. 1, 86, 193ff

Labuschange, C. J., 29 n. 29
Lash, N., 173 n. 32
Leibowitz, N., 53 n. 30
Lemche, N. P., 82 n. 3, 192, 201f
Lemke, W. E., 171 n. 29
Levenson, J. D., 150
Long, B. O., 192 n. 24

Magonet, J., 46 n. 21, 53 n. 31
Mann, T. W., 41
Martens, E. A., 53 n. 30
Martin, W. J., 55 n. 34, 56
McKane, W., 76
McNeile, A. H., 41 n. 10
Meyers, C. L., 11 n. 9
Miller, J. M., 40, 192
Moberly, R. W. L., 92 n. 13, 142 n. 48, 167 nn. 26,27, 188 n. 19, 198 n. 35
Motyer, J. A., 53 n. 30, 58, 59 n. 43, 65 n. 50, 66 n. 51
Mowinckel, S., 53 n. 31, 61 n. 47

Neusner, J., 149 n. 4
Noth, M., 31f, 43, 46 n. 20, 75, 85 n. 4, 124, 180

Oesterley, W. O. E., 96 n. 16
Ohler, A., 40
Otto, R., 100ff

Parke-Taylor, G. H., 6 n. 3
Pawlikowski, J., 147 n. 1
Plaut, W. G., 54
Porteous, N. W., 152 n. 9
Pury, A. de, 176 n. 1

Quell, G., 6 n. 2

Rad, G. von, 77, 119ff, 132f, 137 n. 44, 141 n. 47, 149 n. 6, 180, 185
Radday, Y. T., 53 n. 31
Räisänen, H., 153 n. 9
Rashi, 57, 66 n. 51, 89 n. 9
Rendtorff, R., 32, 42 n. 11, 176, 179f, 181 n. 7, 186 n. 10
Reventlow, H. G., 126 n. 33, 138 n. 46
Roberts, J. J. M., 9 n. 6
Rose, M., 187
Rowley, H. H., 38, 41

Saebø, M., 17 n. 17
Saggs, H. W. F., 106 n. 2, 111 n. 9, 165
Sanders, E. P., 149 n. 4
Sanders, J. A., 160, 162
Sandmel, S., 50, 67 n. 52
Sarna, N. M., 9 n. 6, 61 n. 47
Sawyer, J. F. A., 159 n. 16
Schmid, H. H., 42 n. 11
Schmidt, W. H., 6 n. 2, 7 n. 5, 19 n. 21, 29 n. 29, 32 n. 36, 39 n. 4, 44, 46 nn. 19,22, 58 n. 41, 88, 124f, 177 n. 3
Segal, M. H., 53 n. 30
Sellin, E., 103
Ska, J.-L., 32 n. 35
Smith, F. G., 38 n. 3
Soggin, J., 19 n. 22
Spinoza, B., 37 n. 3
Stendahl, K., 153 n. 10
Sternberg, M., 190 n. 23

Taizé, Br. John of, 159 n. 15
Thompson, T. L., 42 n. 11, 180, 181 n. 7, 192ff, 201 n. 42

Van Seters, J., 32, 42 n. 11, 74–75, 193ff
Vaux, R. de, 82 n. 3
Vriezen, T. C., 85 n. 5

Weidmann, H., 80 n. 1
Weimar, P., 7 n. 5, 17 n. 17
Weinfeld, M., 8, 9 n. 6
Weiser, A., 43f
Wellhausen, J., 75, 107f, 113, 176, 180, 194f
Wenham, G. J., 72, 80 n. 1, 85 n. 5, 99
Westermann, C., 43 n. 13, 67, 68 n. 56, 69, 77, 85 n. 5, 90, 104 n. 28, 149 n. 6, 178 n. 4, 188, 194, 198
Whitney, G. E., 55 n. 34, 57 n. 39
Whybray, R. N., 42 n. 12, 74, 176 n. 1
Williamson, C. M., 159 n. 17
Wilson, R. D., 55 n. 34
Wolff, H. W., 186, 188f

Ziesler, J. A., 152 n. 9
Zimmerli, W., 31 n. 30, 40, 187 n. 18
Zlotowitz, M., 88 n. 8, 91 nn. 11,12

Index of Biblical References

Old Testament

Genesis
1–11—68, 78, 141, 167
2–3—167
2:3—99 n.21
2:4ff—67
4—68
4:3-4—68
4:26—39, 40, 42 n.12, 50, 52, 53, 56, 57, 66, 67-70, 78, 122
6:5–9:17—49
6:8—67
8:21—67
9:26—67
12—9, 39, 73
12–13—137 n.45, 145
12–25—140
12–50—5, 12, 70, 71, 74, 78, 83, 86, 93, 94, 99, 105, 118, 126, 131, 132, 138, 146, 147, 167, 192, 197, 198, 202
12:1—67
12:1-3—141, 142
12:1-9—132, 135
12:6-7—92, 137 n.45
12:7—94, 96, 145
12:8—68 n.54, 77, 95, 137 n.45, 145
12:10-20—49
12:10–13:1—135, 142, 143
13—39, 73, 135
13:3—145
13:4—68 n.54, 95
13:13—90, 98
13:15-17—96
13:18—92, 95, 137 n.45, 145
14—117
14:7—100
14:11—135
14:14—77
14:14-16—97
14:18-20—72, 86 n.6, 91
14:18—95
14:21-24—135
14:22—72
15—39, 73, 101, 187, 188, 196
15:1-6—132
15:6—67, 98, 142, 188 n.19
15:7—38, 66, 143
15:16—90, 104
15:18—96
16:1-2—135
16:11-13—72
16:13—86 n.6
16:14—100
17—29, 30, 57, 86, 93
17:1—43, 44, 71, 86, 98
17:3—18 n.19
17:8—96, 97
17:9—18 n.19
17:15—18 n.19
17:17—135
17:25-26—93
18—39
18:1–19:28—73
18:16–19:29—98
18:16ff—136
18:19—98, 98, 144
18:22-33—94
20:1-18—49, 135
20:1—100
20:3ff—88
20:4-6—89
20:7—94
20:9-10—18 n.19
20:11—89, 188, 189
20:12—89
20:18—43, 44
21:1—43
21:6-7—18 n.19
21:22—98
21:23—97
21:33—68 n.54, 86 n.6, 92, 95
21:34—97
22:1-19—91, 95, 101, 123, 132, 144, 145, 185, 189
22:1—144, 189
22:2—91 n.13, 144
22:3—144
22:8—92 n.13, 135
22:11—43, 44
22:12—144, 145, 188, 190
22:13—91 n.13

22:14—9 n.7, 43, 44, 67, 91 n.13, 135, 144
22:15-18—142
22:16-18—98
23—97
24—39, 73, 90
24:1—98
24:4—97
24:5-8—90
25—136
25:23—136, 137
25:29-34—137
26:3—97
26:5—98, 136, 144
26:6-11—49
26:12-13—98
26:24—71
26:25—68 n.54, 95
26:34-35—91
27—136
27:1-45—95, 136
27:29—136, 142
27:46—91
27:46–28:9—90
28:3—86
28:8-9—91
28:10-22—101, 137
28:13—39, 56, 67, 72, 96
28:18-22—92
28:16-19—73
28:19—77
30:25-43—137
30:27-30—98
30:43—98, 137
31:13—86 n.6
31:19—88
31:34-35—88
31:45—92
32:3-5—94
32:6-12—137
32:10—72
32:22-32—101, 137
32:27—59 n.44
32:28—5
33—136
33:18-20—137 n.45
33:19—97
33:20—86 n.6, 95, 137
34—117
34:13-24—93
34:14-17—104
34:25-31—97
35:1—95
35:1-4—137
35:1-8—137 n.45
35:2-4—88, 104
35:6—77
35:7—86 n.6, 95
35:11—86
35:14—92
35:19—77
35:27—97, 137 n.45
37—73, 98, 134
37–50—178
37:3-4—137
37:5-11—134
37:23-24—134
37:35—137
38:2—90
38:7-10—179
38:21-22—100
39–45—73, 98, 134
39—179
39:2-6—134
39:2-5—179
39:9—98, 134, 179
39:20—134
39:21-23—134, 179
40:8—134
40:23—134
41—88
41:16—134
41:37-45—134
41:39—18 n.19
41:41—18 n.19
41:45—88, 95
41:50—88, 90
42:18—188, 189
42–44—134
42–46—143
42:36-38—137
43:11-14—137
43:14—86
43:32—93
44:16—98
45—134
45:5-8—13 n.13
46:1-2—95
46:1-4—84
46:10—90
46:20—88
47:3-4—18 n.19
47:10—95
47:22—95
48—136
48:3—86
48:8-22—95
48:22—97, 104
49:18—179
49:25—86
49:28—95
50:20—134

Exodus
1—26
1:7—143
1:15ff—135
1:17—188, 189
1:21—188, 189
2—26
2:15—10
2:21-22—10
2:23–7:7—6, 33
2:23-25—7
2:24—29
3—5, 9, 10, 19, 31, 32, 34, 35, 38, 39, 42, 43, 45, 48, 52-55, 60, 63-70, 74, 79, 85, 86, 94, 105, 108, 109, 112, 114, 119, 121, 122, 125, 178, 190, 198, 199
3–4—6 n.4, 13 n.15, 27, 33
3:1-6:1—49
3:1-6—7, 46
3:1-12—8-13
3:1—8, 9, 10, 45, 46, 185
3:2-4—46
3:2—11, 47 n.26
3:4—11, 46 n.21
3:5—9, 46, 100, 102, 104
3:5-6—11
3:6—11 n.11, 22, 24, 29, 46, 109, 122
3:7-8—12, 47
3:7-10—7, 14
3:8—89
3:9-10—12, 46, 47 n.23
3:9-15—19, 46, 47
3:10-15—40
3:11—19, 47
3:11–4:12—7
3:11-12—7, 13, 47
3:13-14—50, 108, 122
3:13-15—6, 8, 13, 14, 17, 18 n.19, 19, 20, 21-26, 28, 33, 36, 40, 42 n.12, 46, 47, 48, 59-67, 113
3:13-22—7, 16, 17, 20

3:13—8, 11 n. 11, 13, 16, 17, 18, 19, 20, 21, 22, 23, 24, 29, 59, 61 n. 47, 62, 109,
3:14—6, 14, 15, 16, 17, 18, 21, 22, 23, 62,
3:14-15—15, 16, 22
3:15—11 n. 11, 15, 16, 17, 18, 19, 21, 22, 23,
3:16—11 n. 11, 16
3:16-17—46
3:16-22—17, 20, 46
3:18—17, 26 n. 27
3:19—27
4:1—19, 46, 47, 63
4:1-9—7,
4:1-16—46
4:10—19, 46, 47
4:10-12—7
4:13-17—7
4:13—46
4:18-31—7
4:21—27
4:21-23—17
4:27—8, 10
4:31—34
5:1—24, 26
5:2—61 n. 47
5:3—26
5:1-21—8
5:4-21—27
5:22-23—8, 27, 34
6—5, 6 n. 4, 34, 35, 38, 39, 42, 43, 52-55, 65-70, 74, 79, 114, 119, 122, 125, 178, 190
6:1-7:13—49
6:1-8—8,
6:1—27, 32
6:2-3—6, 26-35, 36, 37 n. 3, 38, 40, 41, 42 n. 12, 48 n. 27, 54 n. 32, 55-59, 105, 107, 108, 114, 119-122, 125
6:2-5—29
6:2-8—27, 28, 34, 35, 40
6:2-7:13—33
6:2—12
6:3—29, 30, 34, 37, 40, 42, 43 n. 12, 50, 54, 55, 55 n. 34, 56, 57, 58, 66 n. 51, 70, 78, 86, 87
6:3-4—57
6:4—30, 57, 97
6:4-5—29
6:6-7—28
6:6-8—29
6:9-12—8
6:12—34
6:13-27—8
6:28-7:7—8
7-12—143
12—19
12:16—102
12:24—19
12:26—59
12:26-27—19
12:31—143
12:35-38—143
13—19
13:2—102
13:14—59
13:14-15—19
14—12
15:13—10 n. 8, 102
15:17—10 n. 8, 102
16:4—144, 189
16:8—57 n. 39
16:23—102
18:5—8, 9, 10
18:6—21 n. 24
18:12—9
18:21—188, 189
19—10 19ff—102
19:5-6—98
19:6—100, 102
19:9—21 n. 24
19:10ff—102
19:18—10
20—12, 188, 189
20:1-21—15
20:2—67, 143
20:3—87
20:18-21—102
20:20—144, 188, 189, 190
20:24—144
23:23-24—89
23:20-33—102
23:23-33—96
23:24—92
24:1-2—102
24:3-8—102
24:1-11—84
24:1-18—102
24:9-11—92 n. 13
24:13—10
25:8—102
25:10-22—50
29:38-46—102
32-34—167
33:11-34:35—92 n. 13
33:19—15
34:5-7—15
34:11-16—90
34:13—92
34:14—15
40:34-38—102

Leviticus
18:9-11—89
18:24-30—89
20:17—89
26:1—92

Numbers
6:22-27—95
10:33—9 n. 7, 92 n. 13
16—49
22-24—63, 142
22:6—142
24:9—142
24:16—87

Deuteronomy
4:11—10
4:12—10, 11
4:15—10
4:33—10
4:36—10
5:4—10
5:22-26—10
5:22-33—15, 25
5:29—144
6—19
6:20—59
6:20-25—19
7—96
8:2—144, 189
10:8—95
10:12-13—144
11:8-17—89
12:5—144
13:1-5—63
13:3—189
16:21-22—92
18:9-22—25
28:1-14—98
30:15-20—98

Joshua
4—19
4:6—59
4:6-7—19

4:7—19
4:21—59
4:21-33—19
7—145
8—145
8:30-35—145
10—145
11:1-15—145
24:23—89

Judges
2:22—189
3:4—189
3:6—90
6—14
6:11-16—98
13:15-20—84
13:17—59, 60
14:3—93
18:29—77

Ruth
1:20—5
2:20—18 n. 19

1 Samuel
3:10-14—98
8:7—57 n. 39
12:19-23—94
14:6—93
17:8-10—18 n. 19
17:26—93
17:34-37—18 n. 19
24:21-22—47 n. 23
25:25—5
25:26-27—47 n. 23
26:9-10—18 n. 19
26:17-18—18 n. 19
26:19-20—47 n. 23

2 Samuel
24:15-17—92 n. 13

1 Kings
8:1-13—103
11:1-10—90
14:21—144
19:8—10
18:24—68 n. 54
18:30-40—84
19:9-18—92 n. 13
22:19-23—63

2 Kings
19:1-7—94

Ezra
6:20-21—89
9-10—90

Job
1:5—101
5:1—101
6:10—101
15:15—101
36:14—101

Psalms
2:6—9 n. 7
3:5—9 n. 7
15—145
15:1—9 n. 7
24—145
24:3—9 n. 7, 92 n. 13
43:3—9 n. 7
46:4—72
47:2—72
48:1—9 n. 7
76:2—72
84:5-8—92 n. 13
91:1-2—87
99:9—9 n. 7
105:1—68 n. 54
110:4—72
116:4—68 n. 54
116:13—68 n. 54
116:17—68:n. 54
132:13—145
135:13—22 n. 25

Proverbs
9:10—101
20:25—101
30:3—101

Ecclesiastes
8:10—101

Isaiah
2:3—9 n. 7, 92 n. 13
6—14
6:1—92 n. 13
6:8—24
11:9—9 n. 7
26:8—22 n. 25
27:13—9 n. 7
57:13—9 n. 7
65:11—9 n. 7
65:25—9 n. 7
66:20—9 n. 7

Jeremiah
1—14
1:7—24
7:1-15—145
7:16—94
14:14-15—24
23:16-32—63
31:23—9 n. 7
31:31-34—125, 168
31:31—156

Ezekiel
2:3—24
13:2-3—63
13:17—63
14:9—63
20:5—34 n. 40
20:40—9 n. 7
28:13—10 n. 7
28:14—10 n. 7
28:16—10 n. 7

Daniel
9:16—9 n. 7
9:20—9 n. 7
11:45—9 n. 7

Hosea
2:5ff—89
4:1-3—98
12:2-6—136
12:5—22 n. 25

Joel
2:1—9 n. 7
3:17—9 n. 7

Amos
1:3-9—24

Obadiah
16—9 n. 7

Micah
4:2—9 n. 7

Zephaniah
3:9—68 n. 54
3:11—9 n. 7

Zechariah
8:3—9 n. 7

New Testament

Acts
10—164

Romans
4—203

2 Corinthians
3—168

Galatians
3—203
3:24—111

Hebrews
8—168